Headquarters
Departments of the Army, Air Force
Washington, DC
28 February 1989

Army Regulation 633–30
AFR 125–30

Effective 28 March 1989

Apprehensions and Confinement

Military Sentences to Confinement

By Order of the Secretaries of the Army
and the Air Force:

CARL E. VUONO
General, United States Army
Chief of Staff

Official:

LARRY D. WELCH
General, United States Air Force
Chief of Staff

Official:

MILTON H. HAMILTON
Administrative Assistant to the
Secretary of the Army

WILLIAM O. NATIONS
Colonel, United States Air Force
Director of Information Management
and Administration

I0502446

History. This publication has been reorganized to make it compatible with the Army electronic publishing database. No content has been changed.

Summary. This is a change to AR 633–30, 6 November 1964. This change implements policies and procedures required by DOD Directive 1325.4, the decision of the U.S. Court of Military Appeals in the case of U.S. v. Allen, 17 MJ 126 (CMA 1984) and the Manual for Courts–Martial, United States, 1984.

Applicability. Not applicable

Proponent and exception authority. The proponent agency of this regulation is the office of the Deputy Chief of Staff for Operations and Plans.

Army management control process. Not applicable.

Supplementation. Not applicable

Interim changes. Not applicable

Suggested Improvements. Users are invited to send comments and suggested improvements on DA Form 2028 (Recommended Changes to Publications and Blank Forms) directly to HQDA (DAMO–ODL), WASH DC 20310

Distribution. Army:*Active Army,* ARNG, USAR: To be distributed in accordance with DA Form 12–9A requirements for AR, Military Police—D.

Air Force: F:

Active Army: To be distributed in accordance with DA Form 12–09–E. requirements for AR 633–30, (D) ARNG and USAR: None.

Contents (Listed by paragraph and page number)

UNCLASSIFIED

Contents—Continued

Figure List

Contents—Continued

Contents—Continued

Contents—Continued

RESERVED

Section I
GENERAL

1. Purpose.

a. This regulation prescribes procedures for the computation of sentences to confinement of persons subject to the Uniform Code of Military Justice serving sentences in the custody of the Department of the Army or Air Force. Such persons are hereinafter referred to as prisoners.

b. The premature or tardy release of prisoners from confinement results in poor prisoner morale and reflects unfavorably upon the administration of confinement by the Departments of the Army and the Air Force. Further, it is imperative that the essential legal rights of the individual be protected by insuring that he is not held beyond the proper release date. Accordingly, commanding officers of confinement facilities will exercise close and continuing command supervision over the computation of sentence expiration dates.

c. Questions regarding clarification of computation of expiration date for Army prisoners will be forwarded to the Office of the Deputy Chief of Staff for Operations and Plans (DAMO–ODL), Washington, DC 20310–0440. Questions regarding clarification of computation for Air Force prisoners will be forwarded to HQ AFOSP/SPOL, Kirkland AFB NM 87117–6001.

2. Definitions.

For the purpose of this regulation, the following definitions, in addition to those contained in AR 190–47 and AFR 125–18, are applicable:

a. Abatements.

(1) *Good conduct time.* Any deductions from the term of a sentence for good conduct.

(2) *Extra good time.* Any deductions from the term of a sentence which may be earned for actual employment in assignments for which extra good time has been approved.

b. Inoperative time. Any period of time during which a prisoner is not credited with serving his sentence to confinement (para. 5b).

c. Full term of sentence. The entire sentence to confinement without deductions for abatements.

d. Short term of sentence. The full term of sentence as reduced by credit for abatements.

e. Maximum release date. (Applicable to sentences adjudged on or after 31 May 1951.) The day preceding the date determined by adding the full term of the sentence to the beginning date of the sentence.

f. Minimum release date. (Applicable to sentences adjudged on or after 31 May 1951.) The maximum release date reduced by the actual number of days of abatement credited on the sentence and further adjusted by forfeitures of abatement, where applicable.

g. Short term release date. (Applicable to sentences adjudged prior to 31 May 1951.) The day preceding the date determined by adding the term of the sentence as reduced by abatements to the beginning date of the sentence.

h. Parole violator term. The unexpired term of the sentence to be served by a prisoner who has violated parole determined as follows:

(1) For a prisoner whose sentence was adjudged prior to 31 May 1951, such term will be determined by extending the short term release date of the sentence prior to his going on parole, by the time difference (number of calendar months and days) between the date of release on parole and the date of return to confinement and further extending that date on an actual day basis by the number of days good conduct time to the prisoner's credit on the date of parole. Such term may later be reduced by the restoration of the good conduct time forfeited.

(2) For a prisoner whose sentence is adjudged on or after 31 May 1951, such term will be the actual number of days difference between the date of release on parole and the maximum expiration date of his sentence. This term may be reduced by the good conduct time which may be earned on the parole violator term at the rate applicable to the full term of the sentence. The day of release on parole is credited as a day in confinement. Parole violators will not be credited with good conduct time or extra good time which was earned prior to the date of their release on parole.

3. Abbreviations.

For the purpose of this regulation only, the following abbreviations are applicable to the "examples" shown in sections II and III:

Adjd	Adjudged
Alw	Allowance
Conf	Confined, confinement
Dy	Duty
Dt	Date, dated
EGT	Extra good time
Expr	Expires, expiration
Forf	Forfeit, forfeited, forfeiture
Inop	Inoperative
Max	Maximum
M/C	Military control
MGCT	Military good conduct time
Min	Minimum
P	Parole
PV	Parole violator
Rel	Release, released
Restr	Restored, restoration
Rtn	Return, returned
Sent	Sentence, sentenced
SGT	Statutory good time
Subq	Subsequent
Susp	Suspended, suspension
Sv	Serve, served
Vac	Vacated, vacation

Figure 1-1.

4. Operation of sentences.

a. Beginning date. The date the sentence of a court–martial is adjudged will mark the beginning date of the sentence to confinement. If a prisoner served pretrial confinement for the offense(s) or act(s) for which the sentence was imposed, the beginning date will be administratively adjusted to reflect the time spent in pretrial confinement and any additional pretrial confinement credit ordered by the military judge, convening authority, or appellate court. Any days not spent in confinement will be counted as inoperative time.

b. Multiple sentences. A sentence to confinement adjudged by a court–martial will not be served concurrently with any other sentence to confinement adjudged by a court–martial or a civil court.

(1) When a prisoner serving a court–martial sentence to confinement adjudged on or after 31 May 1951 is subsequently convicted by a court–martial for another offense and sentenced to a term of confinement, the subsequent sentence, upon being ordered into execution, will begin to run as of the date adjudged and will interrupt the running of the prior sentence. After the subsequent sentence has been executed fully the prisoner will resume the service of any unremitted interrupted sentence to confinement. When the suspension of a sentence is vacated, the unexecuted portion of the sentence to confinement will begin to run on the date the vacation of the suspension becomes effective, and the execution thereof will interrupt the running of any other sentence to confinement which the prisoner may be serving at the time.

(2) A sentence adjudged prior to 31 May 1951 which includes confinement without discharge, followed by a sentence including both confinement and discharge, whether or not the discharge is suspended, will be regarded as having terminated upon the date the sentence including discharge takes effect, leaving to be executed only the discharge and confinement adjudged by the second sentence.

(3) A prisoner in confinement under sentence including discharge, whether or not the discharge is suspended, who receives a subsequent sentence or sentences to confinement adjudged prior to 31 May 1951, either with or without discharge, will serve all of the sentences consecutively.

(4) A prisoner in confinement under a sentence including discharge, whether or not the discharge is suspended, adjudged prior to 31 May 1951, who receives a subsequent sentence or sentences to confinement, adjudged on or after 31 May 1951, will, subject to any limitation as to the designation of the place of confinement, serve all of the sentences in the manner prescribed in (1) above.

(5) The vacation of the suspension of a prior sentence which includes a discharge and confinement operates to remit the unexecuted portion of any sentence adjudged prior to 31 May 1951 which does not include discharge and is ordered executed during the period of suspension.

c. Aggregation of sentences.

(1) Two or more sentences which were adjudged prior to 31 May 1951 standing against a prisoner will be considered in the aggregate for the purpose of computing the date of eligibility for parole, restoration to duty, and the short term expiration date of the sentences.

(2) Except as provided in (4) below, two or more sentences adjudged on or after 31 May 1951, standing against a prisoner will be considered in the aggregate to determine the rate of earning abatement for good conduct time and the dates of eligibility for parole and restoration to duty.

(3) Sentences adjudged prior to 31 May 1951, will be considered in the aggregate with sentences adjudged on or after 31 May 1951, for the purpose of determining dates of eligibility for parole and restoration to duty, but not for the purpose of determining expiration dates or rates of earning good conduct time.

(4) A parole violator term on a sentence adjudged on or after 31 May 1951, will not be considered in the aggregate with any subsequent sentence to determine the rate of earning abatement for good conduct, but will be considered in the aggregate to determine the date of eligibility for reparole and restoration to duty.

(5) A parole violator term on a sentence adjudged prior to 31 May 1951, will be considered in the aggregate with any other sentence adjudged prior to 31 May 1951, for the purpose of computing the date of eligibility for reparole, restoration to duty, and the short term expiration date of the sentence.

(6) A parole violator term on a sentence adjudged prior to 31 May 1951, will be considered in the aggregate with any sentence adjudged on or after 31 May 1951, for the purpose of determining dates of eligibility for reparole and restoration to duty, but not for the purpose of determining expiration dates or rates of earning abatement.

d. Sentences adjudged on rehearing and new trials. In computing the term of confinement actually to be served under a sentence adjudged upon a rehearing, or upon a new trial ordered under Uniform Code of Military Justice Article 73, the prisoner will be credited with any confinement, served or executed under the original sentence prior to the date upon which the new sentence was adjudged. Unless the confinement adjudged at the original trial was suspended or deferred, any confinement served between the date the original sentence was set aside and the date new sentence was adjudged is also to be credited. Appropriate credit under this subparagraph will be given all prisoners in confinement on or after the date of the promulgation of this change.

e. Sentences adjudged at "another trial" (para 92b, MCM, 1969 (Revised edition)). When court–martial proceedings have been declared invalid because of lack of jurisdiction or failure of the charges to allege any offense cognizable by courts–martial and another trial has been ordered, credit for confinement served or executed under the prior sentence will be granted in the same fashion as set, forth in paragraph 4d, above.

f. Remission, vacation, or suspension of sentences. See Uniform Code of Military Justice, Articles 71, 72, and 74.

g. Release of prisoners. A prisoner shall be released at the expiration of his sentence to confinement, less the time deducted for good conduct (and, if applicable, extra good time). If release date falls upon a Saturday, Sunday, or holiday the prisoner will be released on the preceding duty day.

5. Operative and inoperative time.

a. Operative. A sentence to confinement, hard labor without confinement, restriction to limits, or deprivation of privileges is continuous until the term expires and is interrupted only by inoperative time.

b. Inoperative. Inoperative time consists of any period during which a prisoner is not credited with serving his sentence. Inoperative time will include the period while absent without authority; while absent from confinement on a parole which proper authority has suspended and later revoked, only as provided in paragraphs (1) and (2) below; while erroneously released from confinement through misrepresentation or fraud on the part of the prisoner; while absent after delivery to civil authorities, if subsequently convicted by a civil tribunal; while in a restored to duty status under a suspended sentence, the suspension of which is later vacated; the time between release from pretrial confinement and the date of re–entry into pretrial confinement (if convicted of the offense(s)for which the soldier was placed in pretrial confinement)or the date the sentence of a court martial is adjudged (if the prisoner was not convicted of any of the offense(s) for which the soldier was placed in pretrial confinement) or while the sentence is interrupted as prescribed in paragraph 4b(1). An escaped prisoner who is returned to military authority, but whose status, as a prisoner is not known to such authority, and who conceals their status as a prisoner, continues to be "absent without authority" within the meaning of this regulation.

(1) If the parolee has been convicted of a new offense committed subsequent to release on parole, which is punishable by a term of imprisonment, the time from the date of release to the date of suspension or revocation of that parole as a result of that new offense may be declared inoperative by the Service Clemency and Parole Board. An actual term of confinement need not have been imposed for such conviction if the statute under which the parolee was convicted permits the trial court to impose any term of confinement. If such conviction occurs subsequent to a parole violation hearing, the Clemency and Parole Board may reopen the hearing for the purpose of reconsidering whether time served on parole should be declared inoperative.

(2) If the Clemency and Parole Board finds that a parolee intentionally refused or failed to respond to any reasonable request, order, or summons of the Clemency and Parole Board or any agent thereof, including the assigned Probation Officer, or if the Clemency and Parole Board finds that the parolee was materially not in compliance with the conditions of parole, the Clemency and Parole Board may declare inoperative the time during which the parolee so refused or failed to respond or comply.

c. Rehearings and new trials. Operative and inoperative time on sentences adjudged upon rein hearings or new trials will be governed by the operation of sentences as set forth in paragraph 4d.

6. Abatements.

a. Good conduct time.

(1) Abatement of sentence for good conduct will be credited according to the rates authorized in paragraphs 10 and 13.

(2) For the purpose of computing good conduct time which can be earned on a sentence, all months of the sentence will be considered as calendar months and all fractions of months will be considered as fractions of 30 days.

(3) In order to secure uniformity in computing abatement of terms of confinement, a prisoner will be credited at the beginning of his confinement under sentence with all good conduct time which can be carried during the entire period of his sentence.

(4) In crediting abatements earnable under a sentence, fractions of days will be disregarded.

(5) An action that results in the remission, mitigation, or disapproval of a portion of the sentence to confinement may result in the application of a lesser rate of earning good conduct abatement, and thereby increase the sentence to confinement by extending the minimum release date. To prevent this increase, it is necessary in such cases to determine the minimum release date which would have resulted if such action had not been taken to reduce the sentence, and the minimum release date of the sentence as reduced, and to select the date which will permit the earlier release of the prisoner. However, in all cases, the maximum release date will be the date established for the sentence as finally approved or as subsequently modified.

b. Extra good time.

(1) A prisoner in confinement in a disciplinary barracks serving a sentence or sentences for a definite term or terms of confinement, other than for life, may earn extra good time for employment in industries, work projects, or other activities or assignments at the rates and under the conditions prescribed in AR 190–47.

(2) A military prisoner in confinement in a Federal penal or correctional institution may earn extra good time at the rates and under the conditions prescribed by the United States Department of Justice.

(3) All extra good time earned while serving a sentence to confinement will reduce the period of time to be spent in confinement under that sentence on an actual day basis, regardless of the date the sentence was adjudged.

c. Abatement earned and credited while in Federal custody.

(1) Sentences adjudged prior to 31 May 1951.

(a) Good conduct abatement, earned on sentences which provided for confinement in Federal penal or correctional institutions will be credited at the statutory rate prescribed for such institutions for that period of the sentence served in a Federal penal or correctional institution and at the rate prescribed for Army and Air Force confinement facilities for that period of time actually served in such facilities. If a prisoner having served a period of time in a Federal penal or correctional institution is transferred to an Army or Air Force confinement facility, the good conduct abatement credited at statutory rates prescribed for Federal institutions will be recomputed, whenever the sentence is reduced, on the basis of the current length of sentence. For the effect a reduction in length of sentence will have on forfeitures, see paragraph 7a(3).

(b) Good conduct abatement earned on sentences in which military custody was originally designated, even though the prisoner is subsequently transferred to a Federal penal or correctional institution and returned, will be credited at the rate prescribed for an Army or Air Force confinement facility for the entire period of the sentence.

(2) Sentences adjudged on or after 31 May 1951.

(a) Good time abatement for Army or Air Force prisoners confined in Federal penal or correctional institutions is computed according to the rates established by 18 USC 4161. Good time abatement for Army or Air Force prisoners confined in institutions over which the Departments of the Army or Air Force have control, is computed according to paragraph 13a through g of this regulation.

(b) The good conduct time credited on the sentence of a prisoner who served in a Federal penal or correctional institution any portion of a sentence and who is returned to an Army or Air Force confinement facility, will be recomputed whenever the length of the sentence or sentence is changed so as to change the rate of earning good conduct abatement.(For the effect a change in length of sentence will have on forfeitures, see paragraph 7a(4).)

d. Abatement for prisoners whose sentences include fines. The period of confinement imposed solely for nonpayment of a fine will not be reduced by credit for good conduct time or extra good time.

e. Abatements while awaiting rehearing. The period between the date on which a trial is disapproved and a rehearing is conducted is inoperative time. Sentence abatement of any type, or forfeiture thereof, is not, contemplated during this period.

7. Forfeiture of abatements.

a. Good conduct abatement.

(1) Forfeiture of good conduct time will be computed according to the rates authorized in paragraphs 10 and 13. The

provisions of this paragraph apply also to those prisoners in confinement who have forfeited good conduct time still outstanding computed at rates of forfeiture set aside by this regulation. Such forfeitures will be recomputed.

(2) If, during the term of imprisonment, a prisoner violates the rules of the institution or commits any offense, all or any part of the good conduct time which has been earned on any unexpired sentence, regardless of where earned, may be forfeited upon approval by the commanding officer of the installation where the prisoner is confined.

(3) When forfeitures of good conduct time are imposed, the minimum release date of the sentence will be extended by the actual number of days forfeited. Forfeiture will not be imposed in excess of the amount of good conduct time that has actually been earned at the date of the forfeiture.

(4) If a reduction in the length of a sentence adjudged on or after 31 May 1951, requires the recomputation of the good conduct time earnable on the sentence at a rate lower than that applicable at the time of imposition of a forfeiture of all good conduct time earned to the date of the forfeiture, the amount of good conduct time forfeited will be recomputed at the rate applicable to the length of the sentence, as reduced. An increase in the rate of earning good conduct time on a sentence will have no effect upon the amount of good conduct time previously forfeited.

(5) On sentences adjudged prior to 31 May 1951, all good conduct time earned prior to the date of release on parole will be forfeited for violation of the terms of parole. Note. For instructions covering a parole violator term on a sentence adjudged on or after 31 May 1951, see paragraph 2h(2).

(6) If a prisoner absents himself from a place of confinement through escape, violation of local parole, failure to return from a temporary home parole, or any other unauthorized absence, all of his good conduct time earned prior to and including the day such unauthorized absence begins, will be forfeited.

(7) Good conduct time may be forfeited administratively for the following reasons:

(a) A sentenced military person whose sentence includes confinement and discharge or dismissal may be temporarily retained in the status of a prisoner for a brief period of time following the date on which he is due for release with credits for abatement, provided he agrees in writing to remain voluntarily in confinement for the period desired. Such action will be taken only in exceptional cases, such as those in which temporary hospitalization or medical treatment is required or where brief periods of time are required for completion of restoration proceedings or other arrangements for the benefit of the prisoner.

(b) Pending disposition of a psychotic or suspected psychotic sentenced military person whose sentence includes confinement and discharge or dismissal, credit for abatement may be administratively forfeited without prejudice to the record of the prisoner and without his consent.

(8) Sentences which have expired with allowance for abatement may not be revived for the purpose of forfeiting abatements earned thereon.

(9) If the computation of the total amount of good conduct time forfeited to the date of the last forfeiture results in a fraction of a day, the fraction will be disregarded.

(10) To determine the amount of good conduct time which may be forfeited, the rates prescribed in sections II and III will be used.

b. Extra good time.

(1) Extra good time earned on a sentence adjudged prior to 31 May 1951, may not be forfeited.

(2) Extra good time earned on a sentence adjudged on or after 31 May 1951, is subject to forfeiture in the same manner as good conduct time.

8. Restoration of forfeited abatement.

a. Forfeited abatements, regardless of where forfeited, may be restored by the commanding officer of the installation where the prisoner is presently confined.

b. Good conduct time forfeited for parole violation on a sentence adjudged prior to 31 May 1951, may be restored. *Note.* For instructions concerning a parole violator term on a sentence adjudged on or after 31 May 1951, see paragraph 2h(2).

9. Remission of sentence.

The remission of a sentence operates to cancel all credits for good conduct time and extra good time earned under the sentence and all inoperative time applicable to that sentence.

Section II
SENTENCES ADJUDGED PRIOR TO 31 MAY 1951

10. Rate of abatement for good conduct.

All prisoners with a sentence adjudged prior to 31 May 1951, will be credited with good time at the applicable rates as shown in a through d below for that portion of sentences served in military installations. These rates will be used for determination of tentative minimum release dates (deducting from the maximum release date the total good time allowance for the sentence, the allowance determined by multiplying the number of months in the sentence by the applicable monthly rate) and for forfeiture and withholding of good time. Forfeiture of good time will be limited to an amount, computed by multiplying the number of months served at the time of the offense for which forfeiture action is taken times the applicable rate specified below (less any previous forfeiture and withholding still outstanding). Good time will continue to accrue, for purpose of forfeiture computation, beyond the minimum release date. Similarly, good time may be withheld from prisoners serving past the minimum release date.

a. Five days for each month of the sentence for a sentence of 1 year or less.

b. Five days for each month for the first 12 months of the sentence and 10 days for each succeeding month of the sentence if the sentence, other than life, exceeds 1 year.

c. Upon each succeeding sentence adjudged prior to 31 May 1951, abatement will be credited at the rate of 10 days for each month of the sentence, provided the prisoner has served 1 year of an immediately preceding sentence which included discharge and the prisoner has not been on a duty status subsequent to the date the immediately preceding sentence either was remitted or expired with credit for abatement.

d. Good conduct time will be credited on a portion of a month of a sentence in accordance with the following chart:

Rate of Earning

Days in confinement	Minimum, or 1 day for each 6 days in confinement	Maximum, or 1 day for each 3 days in confinement	Days in confinement	Minimum, or 1 day for each 6 days in confinement	Maximum, or 1 day for each 3 days in confinement
1	0	0	16	2	5
2	0	0	17	2	5
3	0	1	18	3	6
4	0	1	19	3	6
5	0	1	20	3	6
6	1	2	21	3	7
7	1	2	22	3	7
8	1	2	23	3	7
9	1	3	24	4	8
10	1	3	25	4	8
11	1	3	26	4	8
12	2	4	27	4	9
13	2	4	28	4	9
14	2	4	29	4	9
15	2	5	30	5	10

Figure 2-1. Rate of Earning

---

11. Inoperative time.

For sentences adjudged prior to 31 May 1951, inoperative time will extend the expiration date of a sentence on an actual day basis for any period of time spent in escape, and on a calendar month and days basis for all other periods of inoperative time. The beginning date of such period of inoperative time will be considered as a day out of confinement, but the portion of a day spent in confinement which terminated the period will be credited as a full day in confinement. Periods of less than 24 hours spent in an escape status will not extend the expiration date of a sentence.

12. Method of computation.

a. In converting to years, months, and days the amount of good conduct time which a military prisoner can earn on a sentence, years are assumed to consist of 360 days and months of 30 days; thus, on a sentence of 5 years, a prisoner can earn 540 days of good conduct time at the rates prescribed in paragraph 10, which, converted to months and days, equals 1 year and 6 months. To arrive at the amount of time to be served in confinement on the sentence, convert the good conduct earnings to months and days (if more than 30 days), and subtract this amount from the total sentence.

b. Examples.

(1) An individual was sentenced to dishonorable discharge and confinement for 5 years. The sentence was adjudged 31 August 1948 and was uninterrupted.

```
Computation:
Sent adjd_____  1948- 8-31
Full term_____  5- 0- 0
MGCT earnable_____  1- 6- 0
                                           _____
To sv in conf_____        3- 6- 0
                                                         _____
Sent expr_____  1952- 2-29
```

Figure 2-2.

(2) An individual was sentenced to dishonorable discharge and confinement for 5 years. The sentence was adjudged 30 August 1946. He was restored to duty under a suspension of the sentence 25 July 1948. The suspension was vacated on 20 April 1949, and prisoner returned to confinement under same sentence.

```
Computation:
Sent adjd_____  1946- 8-30
Full term_____  5- 0- 0
MGCT earnable_____  1- 6- 0
                                           _____
To sv in conf_____        3- 6- 0
                                                         _____
                                                    1950- 2-28
Susp vac_____  1949- 4-20
Sent susp_____  1948- 7-25
Inop time_____        8-25
                                                         _____
Sent expr_____  1950-11-23
```

Figure 2-3.

(3) An individual was sentenced to dishonorable discharge and confinement for 5 years. The sentence was adjudged 25 November 1946. He was restored to duty under a suspension of this sentence on 25 July 1948. While in a restored status, he received another 5–year sentence to confinement, together with dishonorable discharge suspended, adjudged 23 January 1949. On 11 February 1949, the suspension of the first sentence was vacated.

```
Computation:
1st sent adjd_____  1946-11-25
Full term_____  10- 0- 0
MGCT earnable_____  3- 2- 0
                                           _____
To sv in conf_____        6-10- 0
                                                         _____
                                                    1953- 9-24
2d sent adjd_____  1949- 1-23
1st sent susp_____  1948- 7-25
                                           _____
Inop time_____        0- 5-28
                                                         _____
Sent expr_____  1954- 3-22
```

Figure 2-4.

(4) An individual was sentenced to dishonorable discharge and confinement for 20 years, adjudged 16 January 1945. He was restored to duty 3 December 1945 under a suspension of the sentence. The suspension of the sentence was vacated 20 April 1949 and, by the same order, so much of the unexecuted portion of the sentence to confinement as was in excess of 5 years was remitted, and the prisoner was returned to confinement to complete his sentence.

Computation:

Sent adjd..		1945- 1-16
Restr to dy	1945-12- 3	
Sent adjd	1945- 1-16	
	————	
Time in conf at date of restr	10-17	
MGCT earned	1-22	
	————	
Amt of sent sv at date restr	1- 0- 9	
Sent remaining to sv	5- 0- 0	
	————	
Full term	6- 0- 9	
MGCT earnable	1-10- 3	
	————	
To sv in conf		4- 2- 6
		————
		1949- 3-21
Susp of sent vac	1949- 4-20	
Restr to dy	1945-12- 3	
	————	
Inop time		3- 4-17
		————
Sent expr		1952- 8- 8

Figure 2-5.

(5) An individual was sentenced to discharge and confinement for 5 years for an offense committed 16 February 1950. The sentence was adjudged 22 March 1950. Upon application of the accused, and upon good cause shown, The Judge Advocate General granted a new trial. As a result of the new trial, a similar sentence was adjudged on 16 January 1951 and promulgated 29 March 1951.

Computation:

Sent adjd		1951- 1-16
Full term	5- 0- 0	
MGCT earnable	1- 6- 0	
	————	
To sv in conf		3- 6- 0
		————
Sent expr		1954- 7-15

Figure 2-6.

Section III
SENTENCES ADJUDGED ON OR AFTER 31 MAY 1951

13. Rate of abatement for good conduct.

All prisoners with a sentence adjudged on or after 31 May 1931, who are confined in institutions over which the Departments of the Army or Air Force have control, will be credited with good time at the applicable rates as shown in a through g below. These rates will be used for determination of tentative minimum release dates (deducting from the maximum release date the total good time allowance for the sentence, the allowance determined by multiplying the number of months in the sentence by the applicable monthly rate) and for forfeiture and withholding of good time. Forfeiture of good time will be limited to an amount computed by multiplying the number of months served at the time of the offense for which forfeiture action is taken times the applicable rate specified below (less any previous forfeiture and withholding still outstanding). Good time will continue to accrue, for purposes of forfeiture computation, beyond the minimum release date. Similarly, good time may be withheld from prisoners serving past the minimum release date.

  a. Five days for each month of the sentence for a sentence of less than 1 year.

  b. Six days for each month of the sentence for a sentence of not less than 1 year and less than 3 years.

  c. Seven days for each month of the sentence for a sentence of not less than 3 years and less than 5 years.

  d. Eight days for each month of the sentence for a sentence of not less than 5 years and less than 10 years.

  e. Ten days for each month of the sentence for a sentence of 10 years or more, excluding life.

  f. If the term of confinement is reduced, or if an additional sentence increases the term of confinement to be served, the good conduct time will be recomputed at the rate of abatement appropriate to the new term of confinement, provided consideration of the sentences in the aggregate is not prohibited.

  g. Good conduct time will be credited on a portion of a month of a sentence in accordance with the following chart:

Rate of Earnings

Portion of month of sent	Less than 1 year	Not less than 1 year and less than 3 years	Not less than 3 years and less than 5 years	Not less than 5 years and less than 10 years	10 years and over, excluding life	Portion of month of sent
1	0	0	0	0	0	1
2	0	0	0	0	0	2
3	0	0	0	0	1	3
4	0	0	0	1	1	4
5	0	1	1	1	1	5
6	1	1	1	1	2	6
7	1	1	1	1	2	7
8	1	1	1	2	2	8
9	1	1	2	2	3	9
10	1	2	2	2	3	10
11	1	2	2	2	3	11
12	2	2	2	3	4	12
13	2	2	3	3	4	13
14	2	2	3	3	4	14
15	2	3	3	4	5	15
16	2	3	3	4	5	16
17	2	3	3	4	5	17
18	3	3	4	4	6	18
19	3	3	4	5	6	19
20	3	4	4	5	6	20
21	3	4	4	5	7	21
22	3	4	5	5	7	22
23	3	4	5	6	7	23
24	4	4	5	6	8	24
25	4	5	5	6	8	25
26	4	5	6	6	8	26
27	4	5	6	7	9	27
28	4	5	6	7	9	28
29	4	5	6	7	9	29
30	5	6	7	8	10	30

Figure 3-1. Rate of Earning

h. Good conduct time will be credited for periods of pretrial confinement to prisoners who have served pretrial confinement for the offenses for which they are later convicted.

14. Method of Computation.

a. All abatement time reduces the maximum release date on an actual day basis and all inoperative time extends the maximum release date on an actual day basis. Portions of days served in confinement on the dates beginning and terminating any inoperative period, including a period of escapes, will be considered as full days in confinement.

b. Examples.

(1) An individual was sentenced to confinement for 6 months, without discharge, adjudged 8 June 1955, and promulgated 24 June 1955. The sentence was uninterrupted.

```
Computation:
Sent adjd_____  1955- 6- 8
Full term_____   0- 6- 0
                                    _____
Max rel dt_____  1955-12- 7...*4724
MGCT earnable_____             30
                                    _____
Min rel dt_____  1955-11- 7...*4694
```

Figure 3-2.

(2) An individual was sentenced to confinement for 8 1/2 months, without discharge, adjudged 8 June 1955, and promulgated 24 June 1955. He was restored to duty under a suspension of the sentence 13 October 1955. The suspension was vacated on 21 November 1955, and prisoner was returned to confinement under same sentence.

```
Computation:
Sent adjd_____  1955- 6- 8
Full term_____     8-15
                                    _____
                                   1956- 2-22....4801
Susp vac_____  1955-11-21..4708
Day subq to susp.  1955-10-14..4670
Inop time in restr status_____           38
                                    _____
Max rel dt_____  1956- 3-31....4839
MGCT earnable_____             42
                                    _____
Min rel dt_____  1956- 2-18....4797
```

Figure 3-3.

(3) An individual was sentenced to confinement for 6 months, without discharge, adjudged 8 June 1955, and promulgated 24 June 1955. He received an additional sentence to confinement for 6 months, without discharge, adjudged 15 July 1955, and promulgated 30 July 1955.

```
Computation:
1st sent adjd_____  1955- 6- 8
Full term_____   1- 0- 0
                                    _____
Max rel dt_____  1956- 6- 7....4907
MGCT earnable_____             72
                                    _____
Min rel dt_____  1956- 3-27....4835
```

Figure 3-4.

AR 633–30/AFR 125–30 • 28 February 1989

(4) An individual was sentenced to confinement for 6 months, without discharge, adjudged 8 June 1955, and promulgated 24 June 1955. He received an additional sentence to confinement for 1 year which included discharge, adjudged 15 July 1955, and promulgated 20 August 1955.

Computation:

1st sent adjd	1955- 6- 8	
Full term	1- 6- 0	
Max rel dt	1956-12- 7	5090
MGCT earnable		108
Min rel dt	1956- 8-21	4982

Figure 3-5.

(5) An individual was sentenced to confinement for 5 years, with discharge, adjudged 8 June 1955, and promulgated 24 June 1955. He received an additional sentence to confinement for 5 years, with or without discharge, adjudged 15 July 1955, and promulgated 20 August 1955.

Computation:

1st sent adjd	1955- 6- 8	
Full term	10- 0- 0	
Max rel dt	1965- 6- 7	8194
MGCT earnable		1200
Min rel dt	1962- 2-23	6994

Figure 3-6.

(6) An individual was sentenced to discharge and confinement for 3 years, adjudged 8 June 1955, and promulgated 24 June 1955. He escaped from confinement on 3 July 1955, and was returned to confinement 2 August 1955. He received an additional sentence to confinement, with discharge, for 8 years, adjudged 15 August 1955, and promulgated 25 September 1955. The unexecuted portion of the confinement adjudged by the first sentence was remitted 5 June 1956.

Computation:

Current sent adjd	1955- 8-15	
Full term	8- 0- 0	
Max rel dt	1963- 8-14	7531
MGCT earnable		768
Min rel dt	1961- 7- 7	6763

Figure 3-7.

(7) An individual was sentenced to discharge and confinement for 5 years, adjudged 8 June 1955, and promulgated 24 June 1955. He was released on parole 7 February 1957, and returned to confinement as a parole violator 29 August 1957.

```
Computation:
Sent adjd............. ............    1955- 6- 8
Full term.....................         5- 0- 0
                                      _____
Max rel dt....................        1960- 6- 7....6368
Rel on P.....................         1957- 2- 7....5152
PV term...................... ......               1216

Day prior to rtn as PV............    1957- 8-28....5354
New max rel dt...............         1960-12-26....6570
MGCT to be earned on PV term
29 Aug 57—28 Aug 60....   3 yrs
29 Aug 60—28 Nov 60... .......    3 mos
29 Nov 60—26 Dec 60  ...                    28 days
                                      _____
Time to sv as PV......... 3 yrs  3 mos  28 days
MGCT at rate of 8 days per mo.....                  319
                                      _____
Min rel dt......................      1960- 2-11....6251
```

Figure 3-8.

(8) An individual was sentenced to discharge and confinement for 5 years, adjudged 8 June 1955, and promulgated 24 June 1955. He was released on parole 7 February 1957 returned to confinement as a parole violator 29 August 1957; and subsequently given an additional sentence to confinement for 5 years, adjudged 25 November 1957, and promulgated 1 January 1958. The prisoner had 18 days extra good time to his credit at the date of release on parole.

```
Computation:
Current sent adjd...................    1957-11-25
Full term..........................      5- 0- 0
                                        _____
Max rel dt.........................     1962-11-24....7268
MGCT earnable.....................                   480
                                        _____
Min rel dt on current sent...........   1961- 8- 1....6788
Prior sent adjd....................     1955- 6- 8
Full term..........................      5- 0- 0
                                        _____
Max rel dt.........................     1960- 6- 7....6368
Rel on P...........................     1957- 2- 7....5152
                                        _____
PV term............................                 1216
Day prior to rtn as PV.............     1957- 8-28....5354
                                        _____
New Max rel dt.....................     1960-12-26....6570
MGCT to be earned on PV term
29 Aug 57—28 Aug 60....   3 yrs
29 Aug 60—28 Nov 60...........    3 mos
29 Nov 60—26 Dec 60....                     28 days
                                        _____
Time to sv as PV......... 3 yrs  3 mos  28 days
MGCT at rate of 8 days per mo......                 319
                                        _____
Min rel dt on PV term.............      1960- 2-11....6251
Day subq to mil rel dt PV term.......   1960- 2-12....6252
Current sent adjd..................     1957-11-25....5443
                                        _____
Inop time on PV term.............                   809
Min rel dt aggregate sent............   1963-10-19....7597
```

Figure 3-9.

(9) An individual was sentenced to discharge and confinement for 5 years, adjudged 8 June 1955, and promulgated 24 June 1955. He escaped from confinement 15 March 1957, and was returned to military control 12 January 1958. He had earned 36 days extra good time prior to the date of escape. He forfeited all good conduct time and extra good time earned at the date of escape.

Computation:

Sent adjd	1955- 6- 8	
Full term	5- 0- 0	
Max rel dt	1960- 6- 7	6368
MGCT earnable		480
		5888
EGT credited		36
		5852
Rtn to M/C	1958- 1-12	5491
Day subq to escape	1957- 3-16	5189
Inop time in escape		302
		6154

MGCT forf
8 Jun 55—7 Jun 56 .... 1 yr
8 Jun 56—7 Mar 57 .... 9 mos
8 Mar 57—15 Mar 57 .... 8 days

Time sv at date of escape	1 yr	9 mos	8 days
MGCT forf			170
			6324
EGT forf			36
Min rel dt	1960- 6-30		6360

Figure 3-10.

(10) An individual was sentenced to discharge and confinement for 2 years which was adjudged 2 February 1963. On 1 August 1963 the sentence was set aside because of lack of jurisdiction and "another trial" was directed after prisoner had served 6 months in confinement and had earned 6 days extra good time. On 1 October 1963 he was sentenced to discharge and 3 months' confinement as a result of "another trial".

Computation:

Sent adjd	1963-10- 1	
Full term	3- 0	
Max rel dt	1963-12-31	7670
MGCT earnable *		51
		7619
Extra good time earned prior to date original sentence was set aside		6
Min rel dt	1963-11- 4	7613

Figure 3-11.

(11) An individual was sentenced to discharge and confinement for 5 years, adjudged 5 January 1950. He escaped from confinement at a disciplinary barracks 12 May 1950, and was returned to military control 16 April 1951. He received an additional sentence to 5 years confinement, adjudged 8 June 1951. He escaped from confinement 14 August 1954, and was returned to military control 25 August 1954.

Computation:

Current sent adjd	1951- 6- 8	
Full term	5- 0- 0	
Max rel dt	1956- 6- 7	4907
MGCT earnable		480
		————
		4427
Ret to M/C	1954- 8-25	4255
Day subq to dt of escape	1954- 8-15	4245
Inop time in escape		10
		————
		4437

Time sv at date of escape
8 Jun 51—7 Jun 54	3 yrs		
8 Jun 54—7 Aug 54		2 mos	
8 Aug 54—14 Aug 54			7 days
			————
Time sv at dt of escape	3 yrs	2 mos	7 days

MGCT forf (8 days/mo)		305
		————
Min rel dt current sent	1955-12-25	4742
Prior sent adjd	1950- 1- 5	
Full term	5- 0- 0	
MGCT earnable	1- 6- 0	
	————	
To sv in conf	3- 6- 0	
	————	
	1953- 7- 4	3838
Rtn to M/C	1951- 4-16	3028
Escape	1950- 5-12	2689
Time lost in escape		339
		————
		4177
Escaped	1950- 5-12	
Sent adjd	1950- 1- 5	
In conf at dt of escape and MGCT forf	4-7	21
		————
Prior sent exp	1954- 6-29	4198
Day subq to min rel dt		
prior sent	1954- 6-30	4199
Current sent adjd	1951- 6- 8	3081
		————
Inop time on prior sent		1118
Min rel current sent		4742
		————
Min rel dt aggregate sent	1959- 1-16	5860

Figure 3-12.

(12) An individual was sentenced to discharge and confinement for 5 years, adjudged 8 June 1955, and promulgated 24 June 1955. He was restored to duty under a suspended sentence 7 February 1957. While in a restored to duty status, he was sentenced to confinement for 6 months, without discharge, adjudged 5 June 1957. The suspension of the sentence restoring him to duty was vacated 18 August 1957.

```
Computation:
Sent adjd.............................  1955- 6- 8
Full term.............................        5- 6
Max rel dt............................  1960-12- 7.....6551
MGCT earnable.....................              528

                                        1959- 6-28.....6023

Subq sent adjd........  1957- 6- 5.........5270
Day subq to restr......  1957- 2- 8.........5153

Inop time in restr status.............                117
                                        _____
Min rel dt aggregate sent............  1959-10-23.....6140
```

Figure 3-13.

(13) An individual was sentenced to discharge and confinement for 6 months for an offense committed 4 June 1955, adjudged 24 July 1955. Upon the publication of the initial court–martial order, the following sentence was included in the action of the convening authority, "The accused will be credited with confinement from 18 July 1955 to 19 July 1955 and any other portion of the punishment served or executed from 13 July 1955 to 19 July 1955 under the sentence adjudged at the former trial of this case," which indicated that the sentence was originally adjudged on 13 July 1955, and set aside for a rehearing on 19 July 1955.

```
Computation:
Sent adjd on rehearing...............  1955- 7-24
Full term............................        6
                                        _____
                                        1956- 1-23.....4771
Dt subq to dt orig sent set
   aside................  1955- 7-20.........4584
Dt sent originally adjd.  1955- 7-13.........4577
                                              ____
Amt of sent completed at dt orig sent set aside....          7
                                                     ____
Max rel dt...........................  1956- 1-16.....4764
MGCT earnable........................              30
                                        _____
Min rel dt...........................  1955-12-17.....4734
```

Figure 3-14.

(14) An individual was sentenced to discharge and confinement for 5 years, adjudged 8 June 1955, and promulgated 24 June 1955. Under the provisions of Article 14, Uniform Code of Military Justice, the prisoner was delivered, upon request, to civil authorities for trial, on 29 October 1955. The trial by civil authorities resulted in a conviction for which the prisoner served a sentence and was subsequently returned to military custody on 15 November 1956 to complete his military sentence.

```
Computation:
Sent adjd....................... 1955- 6- 8
Full term....................... 5- 0- 0
                               ------------
                               1960- 6- 7....6368
Rtn to M.C. .......... 1956-11-15.......5068
Day subq to delivery
  under Art 14.......  1955-10-30.......4686
                               ------
Inop time. .................................... 382
                                             ------
Max rel dt........ ........... 1961- 6-24....6750
MGCT earnable ................ ....         480
                               ------------
Min rel dt.. ...................... 1960- 3- 1....6270
```

Figure 3-15.

(15) An individual was sentenced to discharge and confinement for 5 years, adjudged 15 April 1951, and promulgated 29 June 1951. He subsequently received an additional sentence of 5 years, with discharge, adjudged 8 June 1951, and promulgated 7 July 1951.

```
Computation:
Current sent adjd................. 1951- 6- 8
Full term......................... 5- 0- 0
                               -----------
Max rel dt........................ 1956- 6- 7....4907
MGCT earnable.....................           480
                               -----------
Min rel dt current sent........... 1955- 2-13....4427
Prior sent adjd................... 1951- 4-15
Full term......................... 5- 0- 0
MGCT earnable..................... 1- 6- 0
                               -----------
To sv in conf..................... 3- 6- 0
                               -----------
Sent exp.......................... 1954-10-14
Day subq to exp dt
  prior sent........... 1954-10-15.......4306
Current sent adjd...... 1951- 6- 8.......3081
Inop time on prior sent...................... 1225
                                           -----------
Min rel dt aggregate sent........... 1958- 6-22....5652
```

Figure 3-16.

(16) An individual was sentenced to discharge and confinement for 11 months and 29 days, adjudged 22 June 1955, and promulgated 9 July 1955.

Computation:

```
Sent adjd _____  1955- 6-22
Full term _____      11
                                   _____
                                    1956- 5-21 ___ 4890
     (plus 29 days) _____    29
                                                _____
Max rel dt _____   1956- 6-19 ___ 4919

Computation of MGCT earnable
22 Jun 55—21 May 56 __  11 mos at 5 days
                        per mo _____ 55 days
22 May 56—19 Jun 56 __  29 days at 5 days
                        per mo _____  4 days
                                        ____
MGCT earnable _____    59
                                            _____
Min rel dt _____   1956- 4-21 ___ 4860
```

Figure 3-17.

(17) An individual was sentenced to discharge and confinement for 364 days, adjudged 19 July 1955, and promulgated 25 August 1955.

Computation:

```
Dt prior to dt sent adjd _____  1955- 7-18 ___ 4582
Full term _____               364
                                   _____
Max rel dt _____   1956- 7-16 ___ 4946
Computation of MGCT earnable
19 Jul 55—18 Jun 56 ___  11 mos at 5 days
                         per mo _____ 55 days
19 Jun 56—16 Jul 56 ___  28 days at 5 days
                         per mo _____  4 days
                                         ____
MGCT earnable _____    59
                                            _____
Min rel dt _____   1956- 5-18 ___ 4887
```

Figure 3-18.

(18) An individual was sentenced to discharge and confinement for 2 years and 75 days, adjudged 26 June 1955 and promulgated 17 July 1955.

Computation:
```
Sent adjd ............................ 1955- 6-26
Full term ...........................     2
                                      _____
                                      1957- 6-25 .... 5290
    (plus 75 days) ..................              75
                                      _____
Max rel dt .......................... 1957- 9- 8 .... 5365
```
Computation of MGCT earnable

```
26 Jun 55—25 Jun 57 ...  24 mos at 6 days
                         per mo ........ 144 days
26 Jun 57—25 Aug 57 ...  2 mos at 6 days
                         per mo .........  12 days
26 Aug 57—8 Sep 57 ....  14 days at 6 days
                         per mo .........   2 days
                                         _____
MGCT earnable ..............................  158
                                         _____
Min rel dt ........................... 1957- 4- 3 .... 5207
```

Figure 3-19.

(19) An individual was sentenced to discharge and confinement for 1 year, adjudged 1 October 1955. The convening authority approved the sentence but remitted 1 day of the sentence to confinement in his promulgating action 18 October 1955.

Computation:
```
Sent adjd ............................ 1955-10- 1
Full term ...........................     1
                                      _____
                                      1956- 9-30 .... 5022
    (less 1 day) ....................              1
                                      _____
Max rel dt [1] ....................... 1956- 9-29 .... 5021
```
Computation of MGCT earnable

```
1 Oct 55—31 Aug 56 ....  11 mos at 5 days
                         per mo ......... 55 days
1 Sep 56—29 Sep 56 ....  29 days at 5 days
                         per mo .........  4 days
                                         _____
MGCT earnable ..............................   59
                                         _____
Min rel dt [2] ....................... 1956- 8- 1 .... 4962
```

Alternate computation:
```
Sent adjd ............................ 1955-10- 1
Full term ...........................     1
                                      _____
                                      1956- 9-30 .... 5022
MGCT earnable .......................              72
                                      _____
Min rel dt [3] ....................... 1956- 7-20 .... 4950
```

[1] Proper maximum release date.

[2] Improper minimum release date in view of an increase in the portion of the sentence to be served over that indicated in the alternate computation.

[3] Proper minimum release date as it reflects the earlier date on which the prisoner could be released by computing the sentence both prior to and after approval by the convening authority.

Figure 3-20.

AR 633–30/AFR 125–30 • 28 February 1989

(20) An individual was sentenced to confinement for 6 months, without discharge, adjudged 28 June 1955. The execution of the sentence was suspended by the reviewing authority upon the promulgation of the order on 7 July 1955, at which time the prisoner was restored to duty and served in a duty status until the suspension of the sentence was vacated on 7 September 1955. While serving this sentence, he was sentenced to 11 years confinement, including discharge, adjudged 2 November 1955 and promulgated 12 December 1955.

```
Computation:
1st sent adjd_____  1955- 6-28
Full term_____   11- 6- 0
                                   ───────────
                                   1966-12-27____8762
Susp vac_____  1955- 9- 7_____4633

Day subq to susp of 1st
    sent_____  1955- 7- 8_____4572
                                          ────
Inop time in restr status_____   61
                                               ────
Max rel dt aggregate sent_____  1967- 2-26____8823
MGCT earnable_____               1380
                                   ───────────────
Min rel dt aggregate sent_____  1963- 5-18____7443
```

Figure 3-21.

(21) An individual was sentenced to confinement for 6 months without discharge, adjudged 14 August 1955, and promulgated 16 August 1955. The sentence was approved but the execution thereof was suspended on 16 August 1955. He received an additional sentence to confinement for 3 months, without discharge, adjudged 6 September 1955, and promulgated 7 September 1955. The suspension of the first sentence was vacated 7 September 1955.

```
Computation:
1st sent adjd_____  1955- 8-14
Full term_____    0- 9- 0
                                   ───────────
                                   1956- 5-13____4882
2d sent adjd_____  1955- 9- 6_____4632
Day subq to susp of 1st
    sent_____  1955- 8-17_____4612
                                          ────
Inop time on prior sent_____   20
                                               ────
Max rel dt aggregate sent_____  1956- 6- 2____4902
MGCT earnable_____                45
                                   ───────────────
Min rel dt aggregate sent_____  1956- 4-18____4857
```

Figure 3-22.

(22) An individual was sentenced to discharge and 6 months confinement, adjudged 8 March 1951, and promulgated 25 April 1951. He forfeited 24 days good time on 7 August 1951 and received an additional sentence to confinement for 1 year, adjudged 21 August 1951, and promulgated 4 September 1951.

```
Computation:
Current sent adjd................     1951- 8-21
Full term.......................        1- 0- 0
                                      _____
                                      1952- 8-20....3520

Prior sent adj..........  1951- 3- 8
Full term....    0- 6- 0
MGCT earn-
  able.......    0- 1- 0
                 _____
To sv in conf...........     0- 5- 0

                          _____
                          1951- 8- 7........3141
GCT for..............                   24
                          _____
Prior sent exp..........  1951- 8-31........3165
Day subq to exp dt of
  prior sent............  1951- 9- 1........3166
Current sent adjd......   1951- 8-21........3155
                          _____
Inop time prior sent....................    11
                                          _____
Max rel dt aggregate sent...........  1952- 8-31....3531
MGCT earnable on current sent.....              72
                                      _____
Min rel dt aggregate sent...........  1952- 6-20....3459
```

Figure 3-23.

23. An individual was sentenced to discharge and six months confinement, adjudged 4 Feb 83, and promulgated 4 Mar 83. An individual was placed in continuous pretrial confinement on 16 Jan 83 for the offense for which they were later convicted.

```
Computation:
Pretrial confinement .......... 1983  -  1  -  16
Full term ....................    0   -  6  -   0
                                _____
Maximum release date........  1983  -  7  -  15   14806
MGCT earnable ...................                    30
                                _____
Minimum release date ....... 1983  -  6  -  15   14776
```

Figure 3-24.

24. An individual was sentenced to confinement for eight months, with discharge; adjudged 16 Jul 83 and promulgated 20 Sep 83. An individual was placed in pretrial confinement on 4 Jun 83 and released by the magistrate on 25 Jun 83. An individual was convicted for the offense for which they were placed in pretrial confinement.

```
Computation:
Pretrial confinement .......... 1983  -  6  -   4
Full term ....................    0   -  8  -   0
                                _____
                                1984  -  2  -   3   15009
Sentence adjudged........... 1983  -  7  -  16   14807
Day subj to pretrial rel........ 1983  -  6  -  26   14787
        Inoperative time.........                    20
Maximum release date...... 1984  -  2  -  23   15029
MGCT earnable ...........                           40
                                _____
Minimum release date ...... 1984  -  1  -  14   14989
```

Figure 3-25.

25. An individual was sentenced to discharge and 6 months confinement adjudged 4 Feb 87, and promulgated 4 Mar 87. An individual was placed in continuous pretrial confinement on 16 Jan 87 for the offense for which they were later convicted. After announcing the sentence, the military judge ordered that 15 days additional pretrial confinement credit be given to the individual because of the Government's noncompliance with a timely pretrial magistrate's review.

```
Computation:
Pretrial confinement .......... 1987  –  1  –  16
Full term .................... 0  –  6  –   0
                              1987  –  7  –  15    16267
Additional pretrial confinement credit....................   15
Maximum release date........ 1987  –  6  –   0    16252
MGCT earnable ..............                        30
Minimum release date ........ 1987  –  5  –  31    16222
```

Figure 3-26.

Section IV
TABLE OF CONSECUTIVE DAYS

15. Use of table.

Use of table. In the table, paragraph 16, each day from 1 January 1950 through 31 December 1994 has been numbered in sequence, taking into consideration the varying number of days in each month, including leap years. The table may be used to compute the exact number of days between any two dates and may be used in adding or subtracting any actual number of days to or from a given date. The following are examples of use of table:

a. It is desired to determine the exact number of days between 7 February 1962 and 31 December 1966. The exact number of days between these two dates is 1788.

```
Computation:
31 Dec 1966.................................... *8766
7 Feb 1962.................................... **6978
                                              ——
No. of days difference.......................... 1788
```

    *On page headed "1966" and opposite "31" under column headed "Dec" will be found "8766".
    **On page headed "1962" and opposite "7" under column headed "Feb" will be found "6978".

Figure 4-1.

---

b. It is desired to arrive at a new expiration of a sentence by extending the former date, 17 May 1964, by 384 actual days due to a forfeiture of good conduct time. The new expiration date of the sentence is 5 June 1965.

```
Computation:
17 May 1964................................... *7808
Forfeiture.................................... 384
                                              ——
5 June 1965................................... **8192
```

    *On page headed "1964" and opposite "17" under column headed "May" will be found "7808".
    **It will be found that "8192" is on the page headed "1965" and under the column headed "Jun" opposite "5".

Figure 4-2.

---

c. It is desired to compute the minimum release date of a prisoner's sentence which, when added the adjudged date, extends beyond the last date included in the table.

Computation:

```
Sent adjd........................   1981-11-28
Full term........................     30- 0- 0
                                    ─────────────
Max rel dt.......................   2011-11-27
                                     *20- 0- 0
                                    ─────────────
                                    1991-11-27...17863
MGCT earnable....................            3600
                                    ─────────────
                                    1982- 1-18...14263
                                    **20- 0- 0
                                    ─────────────
Min rel dt.......................   2002- 1-18
```

*Subtract any number of years which is a multiple of 4 (e.g. 4, 8, 12, 16, 20, 24, etc.) which will result in a date appearing in the latter portion of the table.

**The same number of years as was subtracted must be added into the computation again in order to arrive at the minimum release date.

Figure 4-3.

---

16. Table

1950—EXPIRATION TABLE—1950

Day	Jan	Feb	Mar	Apr	May	Jun	Jul	Aug	Sep	Oct	Nov	Dec	Day
1	2558	2589	2617	2648	2678	2709	2739	2770	2801	2831	2862	2892	1
2	2559	2590	2618	2649	2679	2710	2740	2771	2802	2832	2863	2893	2
3	2560	2591	2619	2650	2680	2711	2741	2772	2803	2833	2864	2894	3
4	2561	2592	2620	2651	2681	2712	2742	2773	2804	2834	2865	2895	4
5	2562	2593	2621	2652	2682	2713	2743	2774	2805	2835	2866	2896	5
6	2563	2594	2622	2653	2683	2714	2744	2775	2806	2836	2867	2897	6
7	2564	2595	2623	2654	2684	2715	2745	2776	2807	2837	2868	2898	7
8	2565	2596	2624	2655	2685	2716	2746	2777	2808	2838	2869	2899	8
9	2566	2597	2625	2656	2686	2717	2747	2778	2809	2839	2870	2900	9
10	2567	2598	2626	2657	2687	2718	2748	2779	2810	2840	2871	2901	10
11	2568	2599	2627	2658	2688	2719	2749	2780	2811	2841	2872	2902	11
12	2569	2600	2628	2659	2689	2720	2750	2781	2812	2842	2873	2903	12
13	2570	2601	2629	2660	2690	2721	2751	2782	2813	2843	2874	2904	13
14	2571	2602	2630	2661	2691	2722	2752	2783	2814	2844	2875	2905	14
15	2572	2603	2631	2662	2692	2723	2753	2784	2815	2845	2876	2906	15
16	2573	2604	2632	2663	2693	2724	2754	2785	2816	2846	2877	2907	16
17	2574	2605	2633	2664	2694	2725	2755	2786	2817	2847	2878	2908	17
18	2575	2606	2634	2665	2695	2726	2756	2787	2818	2848	2879	2909	18
19	2576	2607	2635	2666	2696	2727	2757	2788	2819	2849	2880	2910	19
20	2577	2608	2636	2667	2697	2728	2758	2789	2820	2850	2881	2911	20
21	2578	2609	2637	2668	2698	2729	2759	2790	2821	2851	2882	2912	21
22	2579	2610	2638	2669	2699	2730	2760	2791	2822	2852	2883	2913	22
23	2580	2611	2639	2670	2700	2731	2761	2792	2823	2853	2884	2914	23
24	2581	2612	2640	2671	2701	2732	2762	2793	2824	2854	2885	2915	24
25	2582	2613	2641	2672	2702	2733	2763	2794	2825	2855	2886	2916	25
26	2583	2614	2642	2673	2703	2734	2764	2795	2826	2856	2887	2917	26
27	2584	2615	2643	2674	2704	2735	2765	2796	2827	2857	2888	2918	27
28	2585	2616	2644	2675	2705	2736	2766	2797	2828	2858	2889	2919	28
29	2586	xxxx	2645	2676	2706	2737	2767	2798	2829	2859	2890	2920	29
30	2587	xxxx	2646	2677	2707	2738	2768	2799	2830	2860	2891	2921	30
31	2588	xxxx	2647	xxxx	2708	xxxx	2769	2800	xxxx	2861	xxxx	2922	31

Figure T-1. 1950 Expiration Table

1951—EXPIRATION TABLE—1951

Day	Jan	Feb	Mar	Apr	May	Jun	Jul	Aug	Sep	Oct	Nov	Dec	Day
1	2923	2954	2982	3013	3043	3074	3104	3135	3166	3196	3227	3257	1
2	2924	2955	2983	3014	3044	3075	3105	3136	3167	3197	3228	3258	2
3	2925	2956	2984	3015	3045	3076	3106	3137	3168	3198	3229	3259	3
4	2926	2957	2985	3016	3046	3077	3107	3138	3169	3199	3230	3260	4
5	2927	2958	2986	3017	3047	3078	3108	3139	3170	3200	3231	3261	5
6	2928	2959	2987	3018	3048	3079	3109	3140	3171	3201	3232	3262	6
7	2929	2960	2988	3019	3049	3080	3110	3141	3172	3202	3233	3263	7
8	2930	2961	2989	3020	3050	3081	3111	3142	3173	3203	3234	3264	8
9	2931	2962	2990	3021	3051	3082	3112	3143	3174	3204	3235	3265	9
10	2932	2963	2991	3022	3052	3083	3113	3144	3175	3205	3236	3266	10
11	2933	2964	2992	3023	3053	3084	3114	3145	3176	3206	3237	3267	11
12	2934	2965	2993	3024	3054	3085	3115	3146	3177	3207	3238	3268	12
13	2935	2966	2994	3025	3055	3086	3116	3147	3178	3208	3239	3269	13
14	2936	2967	2995	3026	3056	3087	3117	3148	3179	3209	3240	3270	14
15	2937	2968	2996	3027	3057	3088	3118	3149	3180	3210	3241	3271	15
16	2938	2969	2997	3028	3058	3089	3119	3150	3181	3211	3242	3272	16
17	2939	2970	2998	3029	3059	3090	3120	3151	3182	3212	3243	3273	17
18	2940	2971	2999	3030	3060	3091	3121	3152	3183	3213	3244	3274	18
19	2941	2972	3000	3031	3061	3092	3122	3153	3184	3214	3245	3275	19
20	2942	2973	3001	3032	3062	3093	3123	3154	3185	3215	3246	3276	20
21	2943	2974	3002	3033	3063	3094	3124	3155	3186	3216	3247	3277	21
22	2944	2975	3003	3034	3064	3095	3125	3156	3187	3217	3248	3278	22
23	2945	2976	3004	3035	3065	3096	3126	3157	3188	3218	3249	3279	23
24	2946	2977	3005	3036	3066	3097	3127	3158	3189	3219	3250	3280	24
25	2947	2978	3006	3037	3067	3098	3128	3159	3190	3220	3251	3281	25
26	2948	2979	3007	3038	3068	3099	3129	3160	3191	3221	3252	3282	26
27	2949	2980	3008	3039	3069	3100	3130	3161	3192	3222	3253	3283	27
28	2950	2981	3009	3040	3070	3101	3131	3162	3193	3223	3254	3284	28
29	2951	xxxx	3010	3041	3071	3102	3132	3163	3194	3224	3255	3285	29
30	2952	xxxx	3011	3042	3072	3103	3133	3164	3195	3225	3256	3286	30
31	2953	xxxx	3012	xxxx	3073	xxxx	3134	3165	xxxx	3226	xxxx	3287	31

Figure T-2. 1951 Expiration Table

Day	Jan	Feb	Mar	Apr	May	Jun	Jul	Aug	Sep	Oct	Nov	Dec	Day
1	3288	3319	3348	3379	3409	3440	3470	3501	3532	3562	3593	3623	1
2	3289	3320	3349	3380	3410	3441	3471	3502	3533	3563	3594	3624	2
3	3290	3321	3350	3381	3411	3442	3472	3503	3534	3564	3595	3625	3
4	3291	3322	3351	3382	3412	3443	3473	3504	3535	3565	3596	3626	4
5	3292	3323	3352	3383	3413	3444	3474	3505	3536	3566	3597	3627	5
6	3293	3324	3353	3384	3414	3445	3475	3506	3537	3567	3598	3628	6
7	3294	3325	3354	3385	3415	3446	3476	3507	3538	3568	3599	3629	7
8	3295	3326	3355	3386	3416	3447	3477	3508	3539	3569	3600	3630	8
9	3296	3327	3356	3387	3417	3448	3478	3509	3540	3570	3601	3631	9
10	3297	3328	3357	3388	3418	3449	3479	3510	3541	3571	3602	3632	10
11	3298	3329	3358	3389	3419	3450	3480	3511	3542	3572	3603	3633	11
12	3299	3330	3359	3390	3420	3451	3481	3512	3543	3573	3604	3634	12
13	3300	3331	3360	3391	3421	3452	3482	3513	3544	3574	3605	3635	13
14	3301	3332	3361	3392	3422	3453	3483	3514	3545	3575	3606	3636	14
15	3302	3333	3362	3393	3423	3454	3484	3515	3546	3576	3607	3637	15
16	3303	3334	3363	3394	3424	3455	3485	3516	3547	3577	3608	3638	16
17	3304	3335	3364	3395	3425	3456	3486	3517	3548	3578	3609	3639	17
18	3305	3336	3365	3396	3426	3457	3487	3518	3549	3579	3610	3640	18
19	3306	3337	3366	3397	3427	3458	3488	3519	3550	3580	3611	3641	19
20	3307	3338	3367	3398	3428	3459	3489	3520	3551	3581	3612	3642	20
21	3308	3339	3368	3399	3429	3460	3490	3521	3552	3582	3613	3643	21
22	3309	3340	3369	3400	3430	3461	3491	3522	3553	3583	3614	3644	22
23	3310	3341	3370	3401	3431	3462	3492	3523	3554	3584	3615	3645	23
24	3311	3342	3371	3402	3432	3463	3493	3524	3555	3585	3616	3646	24
25	3312	3343	3372	3403	3433	3464	3494	3525	3556	3586	3617	3647	25
26	3313	3344	3373	3404	3434	3465	3495	3526	3557	3587	3618	3648	26
27	3314	3345	3374	3405	3435	3466	3496	3527	3558	3588	3619	3649	27
28	3315	3346	3375	3406	3436	3467	3497	3528	3559	3589	3620	3650	28
29	3316	3347	3376	3407	3437	3468	3498	3529	3560	3590	3621	3651	29
30	3317	xxxx	3377	3408	3438	3469	3499	3530	3561	3591	3622	3652	30
31	3318	xxxx	3378	xxxx	3439	xxxx	3500	3531	xxxx	3592	xxxx	3653	31

Figure T-3. 1952 Expiration Table

1953—EXPIRATION TABLE—1953

Day	Jan	Feb	Mar	Apr	May	Jun	Jul	Aug	Sep	Oct	Nov	Dec	Day
1	3654	3685	3713	3744	3774	3805	3835	3866	3897	3927	3958	3988	1
2	3655	3686	3714	3745	3775	3806	3836	3867	3898	3928	3959	3989	2
3	3656	3687	3715	3746	3776	3807	3837	3868	3899	3929	3960	3990	3
4	3657	3688	3716	3747	3777	3808	3838	3869	3900	3980	3961	3991	4
5	3658	3689	3717	3748	3778	3809	3839	3870	3901	3931	3962	3992	5
6	3659	3690	3718	3749	3779	3810	3840	3871	3902	3932	3963	3993	6
7	3660	3691	3719	3750	3780	3811	3841	3872	3903	3933	3964	3994	7
8	3661	3692	3720	3751	3781	3812	3842	3873	3904	3934	3965	3995	8
9	3662	3693	3721	3752	3782	3813	3843	3874	3905	3935	3966	3996	9
10	3663	3694	3722	3753	3783	3814	3844	3875	3906	3936	3967	3997	10
11	3664	3695	3723	3754	3784	3815	3845	3876	3907	3937	3968	3998	11
12	3665	3696	3724	3755	3785	3816	3846	3877	3908	3938	3969	3999	12
13	3666	3697	3725	3756	3786	3817	3847	3878	3909	3939	3970	4000	13
14	3667	3698	3726	3757	3787	3818	3848	3879	3910	3940	3971	4001	14
15	3668	3699	3727	3758	3788	3819	3849	3880	3911	3941	3972	4002	15
16	3669	3700	3728	3759	3789	3820	3850	3881	3912	3942	3973	4003	16
17	3670	3701	3729	3760	3790	3821	3851	3882	3913	3943	3974	4004	17
18	3671	3702	3730	3761	3791	3822	3852	3883	3914	3944	3975	4005	18
19	3672	3703	3731	3762	3792	3823	3853	3884	3915	3945	3976	4006	19
20	3673	3704	3732	3763	3793	3824	3854	3885	3916	3946	3977	4007	20
21	3674	3705	3733	3764	3794	3825	3855	3886	3917	3947	3978	4008	21
22	3675	3706	3734	3765	3795	3826	3856	3887	3918	3948	3979	4009	22
23	3676	3707	3735	3766	3796	3827	3857	3888	3919	3949	3980	4010	23
24	3677	3708	3736	3767	3797	3828	3858	3889	3920	3950	3981	4011	24
25	3678	3709	3737	3768	3798	3829	3859	3890	3921	3951	3982	4012	25
26	3679	3710	3738	3769	3799	3830	3860	3891	3922	3952	3983	4013	26
27	3680	3711	3739	3770	3800	3831	3861	3892	3923	3953	3984	4014	27
28	3681	3712	3740	3771	3801	3832	3862	3893	3924	3954	3985	4015	28
29	3682	xxxx	3741	3772	3802	3833	3863	3894	3925	3955	3986	4016	29
30	3683	xxxx	3742	3773	3803	3834	3864	3895	3926	3956	3987	4017	30
31	3684	xxxx	3743	xxxx	3804	xxxx	3865	3896	xxxx	3957	xxxx	4018	31

Figure T-4. 1953 Expiration Table

AR 633–30/AFR 125–30 • 28 February 1989

Day	Jan	Feb	Mar	Apr	May	Jun	Jul	Aug	Sep	Oct	Nov	Dec	Day
1	4019	4050	4078	4109	4139	4170	4200	4231	4262	4292	4323	4353	1
2	4020	4051	4079	4110	4140	4171	4201	4232	4263	4293	4324	4354	2
3	4021	4052	4080	4111	4141	4172	4202	4233	4264	4294	4325	4355	3
4	4022	4053	4081	4112	4142	4173	4203	4234	4265	4295	4326	4356	4
5	4023	4054	4082	4113	4143	4174	4204	4235	4266	4296	4327	4357	5
6	4024	4055	4083	4114	4144	4175	4205	4236	4267	4297	4328	4358	6
7	4025	4056	4084	4115	4145	4176	4206	4237	4268	4298	4329	4359	7
8	4026	4057	4085	4116	4146	4177	4207	4238	4269	4299	4330	4360	8
9	4027	4058	4086	4117	4147	4178	4208	4239	4270	4300	4331	4361	9
10	4028	4059	4087	4118	4148	4179	4209	4240	4271	4301	4332	4362	10
11	4029	4060	4088	4119	4149	4180	4210	4241	4272	4302	4333	4363	11
12	4030	4061	4089	4120	4150	4181	4211	4242	4273	4303	4334	4364	12
13	4031	4062	4090	4121	4151	4182	4212	4243	4274	4304	4335	4365	13
14	4032	4063	4091	4122	4152	4183	4213	4244	4275	4305	4336	4366	14
15	4033	4064	4092	4123	4153	4184	4214	4245	4276	4306	4337	4367	15
16	4034	4065	4093	4124	4154	4185	4215	4246	4277	4307	4338	4368	16
17	4035	4066	4094	4125	4155	4186	4216	4247	4278	4308	4339	4369	17
18	4036	4067	4095	4126	4156	4187	4217	4248	4279	4309	4340	4370	18
19	4037	4068	4096	4127	4157	4188	4218	4249	4280	4310	4341	4371	19
20	4038	4069	4097	4128	4158	4189	4219	4250	4281	4311	4342	4372	20
21	4039	4070	4098	4129	4159	4190	4220	4251	4282	4312	4343	4373	21
22	4040	4071	4099	4130	4160	4191	4221	4252	4283	4313	4344	4374	22
23	4041	4072	4100	4131	4161	4192	4222	4253	4284	4314	4345	4375	23
24	4042	4073	4101	4132	4162	4193	4223	4254	4285	4315	4346	4376	24
25	4043	4074	4102	4133	4163	4194	4224	4255	4286	4316	4347	4377	25
26	4044	4075	4103	4134	4164	4195	4225	4256	4287	4317	4348	4378	26
27	4045	4076	4104	4135	4165	4196	4226	4257	4288	4318	4349	4379	27
28	4046	4077	4105	4136	4166	4197	4227	4258	4289	4319	4350	4380	28
29	4047	xxxx	4106	4137	4167	4198	4228	4259	4290	4320	4351	4381	29
30	4048	xxxx	4107	4138	4168	4199	4229	4260	4291	4321	4352	4382	30
31	4049	xxxx	4108	xxxx	4169	xxxx	4230	4261	xxxx	4322	xxxx	4383	31

Figure T-5. 1954 Expiration Table

1955—EXPIRATION TABLE—1955

Day	Jan	Feb	Mar	Apr	May	Jun	Jul	Aug	Sep	Oct	Nov	Dec	Day
1	4384	4415	4443	4474	4504	4535	4565	4596	4627	4657	4688	4718	1
2	4385	4416	4444	4475	4505	4536	4566	4597	4628	4658	4689	4719	2
3	4386	4417	4445	4476	4506	4537	4567	4598	4629	4659	4690	4720	3
4	4387	4418	4446	4477	4507	4538	4568	4599	4630	4660	4691	4721	4
5	4388	4419	4447	4478	4508	4539	4569	4600	4631	4661	4692	4722	5
6	4389	4420	4448	4479	4509	4540	4570	4601	4632	4662	4693	4723	6
7	4390	4421	4449	4480	4510	4541	4571	4602	4633	4663	4694	4724	7
8	4391	4422	4450	4481	4511	4542	4572	4603	4634	4664	4695	4725	8
9	4392	4423	4451	4482	4512	4543	4573	4604	4635	4665	4696	4726	9
10	4393	4424	4452	4483	4513	4544	4574	4605	4636	4666	4697	4727	10
11	4394	4425	4453	4484	4514	4545	4575	4606	4637	4667	4698	4728	11
12	4395	4426	4454	4485	4515	4546	4576	4607	4638	4668	4699	4729	12
13	4396	4427	4455	4486	4516	4547	4577	4608	4639	4669	4700	4730	13
14	4397	4428	4456	4487	4517	4548	4578	4609	4640	4670	4701	4731	14
15	4398	4429	4457	4488	4518	4549	4579	4610	4641	4671	4702	4732	15
16	4399	4430	4458	4489	4519	4550	4580	4611	4642	4672	4703	4733	16
17	4400	4431	4459	4490	4520	4551	4581	4612	4643	4673	4704	4734	17
18	4401	4432	4460	4491	4521	4552	4582	4613	4644	4674	4705	4735	18
19	4402	4433	4461	4492	4522	4553	4583	4614	4645	4675	4706	4736	19
20	4403	4434	4462	4493	4523	4554	4584	4615	4646	4676	4707	4737	20
21	4404	4435	4463	4494	4524	4555	4585	4616	4647	4677	4708	4738	21
22	4405	4436	4464	4495	4525	4556	4586	4617	4648	4678	4709	4739	22
23	4406	4437	4465	4496	4526	4557	4587	4618	4649	4679	4710	4740	23
24	4407	4438	4466	4497	4527	4558	4588	4619	4650	4680	4711	4741	24
25	4408	4439	4467	4498	4528	4559	4589	4620	4651	4681	4712	4742	25
26	4409	4440	4468	4499	4529	4560	4590	4621	4652	4682	4713	4743	26
27	4410	4441	4469	4500	4530	4561	4591	4622	4653	4683	4714	4744	27
28	4411	4442	4470	4501	4531	4562	4592	4623	4654	4684	4715	4745	28
29	4412	xxxx	4471	4502	4532	4563	4593	4624	4655	4685	4716	4746	29
30	4413	xxxx	4472	4503	4533	4564	4594	4625	4656	4686	4717	4747	30
31	4414	xxxx	4473	xxxx	4534	xxxx	4595	4626	xxxx	4687	xxxx	4748	31

Figure T-6. 1955 Expiration Table

1956—EXPIRATION TABLE—1956

Day	Jan	Feb	Mar	Apr	May	Jun	Jul	Aug	Sep	Oct	Nov	Dec	Day
1	4749	4780	4809	4840	4870	4901	4931	4962	4993	5023	5054	5084	1
2	4750	4781	4810	4841	4871	4902	4932	4963	4994	5024	5055	5085	2
3	4751	4782	4811	4842	4872	4903	4933	4964	4995	5025	5056	5086	3
4	4752	4783	4812	4843	4873	4904	4934	4965	4996	5026	5057	5087	4
5	4753	4784	4813	4844	4874	4905	4935	4966	4997	5027	5058	5088	5
6	4754	4785	4814	4845	4875	4906	4936	4967	4998	5028	5059	5089	6
7	4755	4786	4815	4846	4876	4907	4937	4968	4999	5029	5060	5090	7
8	4756	4787	4816	4847	4877	4908	4938	4969	5000	5030	5061	5091	8
9	4757	4788	4817	4848	4878	4909	4939	4970	5001	5031	5062	5092	9
10	4758	4789	4818	4849	4879	4910	4940	4971	5002	5032	5063	5093	10
11	4759	4790	4819	4850	4880	4911	4941	4972	5003	5033	5064	5094	11
12	4760	4791	4820	4851	4881	4912	4942	4973	5004	5034	4065	5095	12
13	4761	4792	4821	4852	4882	4913	4943	4974	5005	5035	5066	5096	13
14	4762	4793	4822	4853	4883	4914	4944	4975	5006	5036	5067	5097	14
15	4763	4794	4823	4854	4884	4915	4945	4976	5007	5037	5068	5098	15
16	4764	4795	4824	4855	4885	4916	4946	4977	5008	5038	5069	5099	16
17	4765	4796	4825	4856	4886	4917	4947	4978	5009	5039	5070	5100	17
18	4766	4797	4826	4857	4887	4918	4948	4979	5010	5040	5071	5101	18
19	4767	4798	4827	4858	4888	4919	4949	4980	5011	5041	5072	5102	19
20	4768	4799	4828	4859	4889	4920	4950	4981	5012	5042	5073	5103	20
21	4769	4800	4829	4860	4890	4921	4951	4982	5013	5043	5074	5104	21
22	4770	4801	4830	4861	4891	4922	4952	4983	5014	5044	5075	5105	22
23	4771	4802	4831	4862	4892	4923	4953	4984	5015	5045	5076	5106	23
24	4772	4803	4832	4863	4893	4924	4954	4985	5016	5046	5077	5107	24
25	4773	4804	4833	4864	4894	4925	4955	4986	5017	5047	5078	5108	25
26	4774	4805	4834	4865	4895	4926	4956	4987	5018	5048	5079	5109	26
27	4775	4806	4835	4866	4896	4927	4957	4988	5019	5049	5080	5110	27
28	4776	4807	4836	4867	4897	4928	4958	4989	5020	5050	5081	5111	28
29	4777	4808	4837	4868	4898	4929	4959	4990	5021	5051	5082	5112	29
30	4778	xxxx	4838	4869	4899	4930	4960	4991	5022	5052	5083	5113	30
31	4779	xxxx	4839	xxxx	4900	xxxx	4961	4992	xxxx	5053	xxxx	5114	31

Figure T-7. 1956 Expiration Table

1957—EXPIRATION TABLE—1957

Day	Jan	Feb	Mar	Apr	May	Jun	Jul	Aug	Sep	Oct	Nov	Dec	Day
1	5115	5146	5174	5205	5235	5266	5296	5327	5358	5388	5419	5449	1
2	5116	5147	5175	5206	5236	5267	5297	5328	5359	5389	5420	5450	2
3	5117	5148	5176	5207	5237	5268	5298	5329	5360	5390	5421	5451	3
4	5118	5149	5177	5208	5238	5269	5299	5330	5361	5391	5422	5452	4
5	5119	5150	5178	5209	5239	5270	5300	5331	5362	5392	5423	5453	5
6	5120	5151	5179	5210	5240	5271	5301	5332	5363	5393	5424	5454	6
7	5121	5152	5180	5211	5241	5272	5302	5333	5364	5394	5425	5455	7
8	5122	5153	5181	5212	5242	5273	5303	5334	5365	5395	5426	5456	8
9	5123	5154	5182	5213	5243	5274	5304	5335	5366	5396	5427	5157	9
10	5124	5155	5183	5214	5244	5275	5305	5336	5367	5397	5428	5458	10
11	5125	5156	5184	5215	5245	5276	5306	5337	5368	5398	5429	5459	11
12	5126	5157	5185	5216	5246	5277	5307	5338	5369	5399	5430	5460	12
13	5127	5158	5186	5217	5247	5278	5308	5339	5370	5400	5431	5461	13
14	5128	5159	5187	5218	5248	5279	5309	5340	5371	5401	5432	5462	14
15	5129	5160	5188	5219	5249	5280	5310	5341	5372	5402	5433	5463	15
16	5130	5161	5189	5220	5250	5281	5311	5342	5373	5403	5434	5464	16
17	5131	5162	5190	5221	5251	5282	5312	5343	5374	5404	5435	5465	17
18	5132	5163	5191	5222	5252	5283	5313	5344	5375	5405	5436	5466	18
19	5133	5164	5192	5223	5253	5284	5314	5345	5376	5406	5437	5467	19
20	5134	5165	5193	5224	5254	5285	5315	5346	5377	5407	5438	5468	20
21	5135	5166	5194	5225	5255	5286	5316	5347	5378	5408	5439	5469	21
22	5136	5167	5195	5226	5256	5287	5317	5348	5379	5409	5440	5470	22
23	5137	5168	5196	5227	5257	5288	5318	5349	5380	5410	5441	5471	23
24	5138	5169	5197	5228	5258	5289	5319	5350	5381	5411	5442	5472	24
25	5139	5170	5198	5229	5259	5290	5320	5351	5382	5412	5443	5473	25
26	5140	5171	5199	5230	5260	5291	5321	5352	5383	5413	5444	5474	26
27	5141	5172	5200	5231	5261	5292	5322	5353	5384	5414	5445	5475	27
28	5142	5173	5201	5232	5262	5293	5323	5354	5385	5415	5446	5476	28
29	5143	xxxx	5202	5233	5263	5294	5324	5355	5386	5416	5447	5477	29
30	5144	xxxx	5203	5234	5264	5295	5325	5356	5387	5417	5448	5478	30
31	5145	xxxx	5204	xxxx	5265	xxxx	5226	5357	xxxx	5418	xxxx	5479	31

Figure T-8. 1957 Expiration Table

Day	Jan	Feb	Mar	Apr	May	Jun	Jul	Aug	Sep	Oct	Nov	Dec	Day
1	5480	5511	5539	5570	5600	5631	5661	5692	5723	5753	5784	5814	1
2	5481	5512	5540	5571	5601	5632	5662	5693	5724	5754	5785	5815	2
3	5482	5513	5541	5572	5602	5633	5663	5694	5725	5755	5786	5816	3
4	5483	5514	5542	5573	5603	5634	5664	5695	5726	5756	5787	5817	4
5	5484	5515	5543	5574	5604	5635	5665	5696	5727	5757	5788	5818	5
6	5485	5516	5544	5575	5605	5636	5666	5697	5728	5758	5789	5819	6
7	5486	5517	5545	5576	5606	5637	5667	5698	5729	5759	5790	5820	7
8	5487	5518	5546	5577	5607	5638	5668	5699	5730	5760	5791	5821	8
9	5488	5519	5547	5578	5608	5639	5669	5700	5731	5761	5792	5822	9
10	5489	5520	5548	5579	5609	5640	5670	5701	5732	5762	5793	5823	10
11	5490	5521	5549	5580	5610	5641	5671	5702	5733	5763	5794	5824	11
12	5491	5522	5550	5581	5611	5642	5672	5703	5734	5764	5795	5825	12
13	5492	5523	5551	5582	5612	5643	5673	5704	5735	5765	5796	5826	13
14	5493	5524	5552	5583	5613	5644	5674	5705	5736	5766	5797	5827	14
15	5494	5525	5553	5584	5614	5645	5675	5706	5737	5767	5798	5828	15
16	5495	5526	5554	5585	5615	5646	5676	5707	5738	5768	5799	5829	16
17	5496	5527	5555	5586	5616	5647	5677	5708	5739	5769	5800	5830	17
18	5497	5528	5556	5587	5617	5648	5678	5709	5740	5770	5801	5831	18
19	5498	5529	5557	5588	5618	5649	5679	5710	5741	5771	5802	5832	19
20	5499	5530	5558	5589	5619	5650	5680	5711	5742	5772	5803	5833	20
21	5500	5531	5559	5590	5620	5651	5681	5712	5743	5773	5804	5834	21
22	5501	5532	5560	5591	5621	5652	5682	5713	5744	5774	5805	5835	22
23	5502	5533	5561	5592	5622	5653	5683	5714	5745	5775	5806	5836	23
24	5503	5534	5562	5593	5623	5654	5684	5715	5746	5776	5807	5837	24
25	5504	5535	5563	5594	5624	5655	5685	5716	5747	5777	5808	5838	25
26	5505	5536	5564	5595	5625	5656	5686	5717	5748	5778	5809	5839	26
27	5506	5537	5565	5596	5626	5657	5687	5718	5749	5779	5810	5840	27
28	5507	5538	5566	5597	5627	5658	5688	5719	5750	5780	5811	5841	28
29	5508	xxxx	5567	5598	5628	5659	5689	5720	5751	5781	5812	5842	29
30	5509	xxxx	5568	5599	5629	5660	5690	5721	5752	5782	5813	5843	30
31	5510	xxxx	5569	xxxx	5630	xxxx	5691	5722	xxxx	5783	xxxx	5844	31

Figure T-9. 1958 Expiration Table

1959—EXPIRATION TABLE—1959

Day	Jan	Feb	Mar	Apr	May	Jun	Jul	Aug	Sep	Oct	Nov	Dec	Day
1	5845	5876	5904	5935	5965	5996	6026	6057	6088	6118	6149	6179	1
2	5846	5877	5905	5936	5966	5997	6027	6058	6089	6119	6150	6180	2
3	5847	5878	5906	5937	5967	5998	6028	6059	6090	6120	6151	6181	3
4	5848	5879	5907	5938	5968	5999	6029	6060	6091	6121	6152	6182	4
5	5849	5880	5908	5939	5969	6000	6030	6061	6092	6122	6153	6183	5
6	5850	5881	5909	5940	5970	6001	6031	6062	6093	6123	6154	6184	6
7	5851	5882	5910	5941	5971	6002	6032	6063	6094	6124	6155	6185	7
8	5852	5883	5911	5942	5972	6003	6033	6064	6095	6125	6156	6186	8
9	5853	5884	5912	5943	5973	6004	6034	6065	6096	6126	6157	6187	9
10	5854	5885	5913	5944	5974	6005	6035	6066	6097	6127	6158	6188	10
11	5855	5886	5914	5945	5975	6006	6036	6067	6098	6128	6159	6189	11
12	5856	5887	5915	5946	5976	6007	6037	6068	6099	6129	6160	6190	12
13	5857	5888	5916	5947	5977	6008	6038	6069	6100	6130	6161	6191	13
14	5858	5889	5917	5948	5978	6009	6039	6070	6101	6131	6162	6192	14
15	5859	5890	5918	5949	5979	6010	6040	6071	6102	6132	6163	6193	15
16	5860	5891	5919	5950	5080	6011	6041	6072	6103	6133	6164	6194	16
17	5861	5892	5920	5951	5981	6012	6042	6073	6104	6134	6165	6195	17
18	5862	5893	5921	5952	5982	6013	6043	6074	61C5	6135	6166	6196	18
19	5863	5894	5922	5953	5983	6014	6044	6075	6106	6136	6167	6197	19
20	5864	5895	5923	5954	5984	6015	6045	6076	6107	6137	6168	6198	20
21	5865	5896	5924	5955	5985	6016	6046	6077	6108	6138	6169	6199	21
22	5866	5897	5925	5956	5986	6017	6047	6078	6109	6139	6170	6200	22
23	5867	5898	5926	5957	5987	6018	6048	6079	6110	6140	6171	6201	23
24	5668	5899	5927	5958	5988	6019	6049	6080	6111	6141	6172	6202	24
25	5869	5900	5928	5959	5989	6020	6050	6081	6112	6142	6173	6203	25
26	5870	5901	5929	5960	5990	6021	6051	6082	6113	6143	6174	6204	26
27	5871	5902	5930	5961	5991	6022	6052	6083	6114	6144	6175	6205	27
28	5872	5903	5931	5962	5992	6023	6053	6084	6115	6145	6176	6206	28
29	5873	xxxx	5932	5963	5993	6024	6054	6085	6116	6146	6177	6207	29
30	5874	xxxx	5933	5964	5994	6025	6055	6086	6117	6147	6178	6208	30
31	5875	xxxx	5934	xxxx	5995	xxxx	6056	6087	xxxx	6148	xxxx	6209	31

Figure T-10. 1959 Expiration Table

Day	Jan	Feb	Mar	Apr	May	Jun	Jul	Aug	Sep	Oct	Nov	Dec	Day
1	6210	6241	6270	6301	6331	6362	6392	6423	6454	6484	6515	6545	1
2	6211	6242	6271	630C	6332	6363	6393	6424	6455	6485	6516	6546	2
3	6212	6243	6272	6303	6333	6364	6394	6425	6456	6486	6517	6547	3
4	6213	6244	6273	6304	6334	6365	6395	6426	6457	6487	6518	6548	4
5	6214	6245	6274	6305	6335	6366	6396	6427	6458	6488	6519	6549	5
6	6215	6246	6275	6306	6336	6367	6397	6428	6459	6489	6520	6550	6
7	6216	6247	6276	6307	6337	6368	6398	6429	6460	6490	6521	6551	7
8	6217	6248	6277	6308	6338	6369	6399	6430	6461	6491	6522	6552	8
9	6218	6249	6278	6309	6339	6370	6400	6431	6462	6492	6523	6553	9
10	6219	6250	6279	6310	6340	6371	6401	6432	6463	6493	6524	6554	10
11	6220	6251	6280	6311	6341	6372	6402	6433	6464	6494	6525	6555	11
12	6221	6252	6281	6312	6342	6373	6403	6434	6465	6495	6526	6556	12
13	6222	6253	6282	6313	6343	6374	6404	6435	6466	6496	6527	6557	13
14	6223	6254	6283	6314	6344	6375	6405	6436	6467	6497	6528	6558	14
15	6224	6255	6284	6315	6345	6376	6406	6437	6468	6498	6559	6559	15
16	6225	6256	6285	6316	6346	6377	6407	6438	6469	6499	6530	6560	16
17	6226	6257	6286	6317	6347	6378	6408	6439	6470	6500	6531	6561	17
18	6227	6258	6287	6318	6348	6379	6409	6410	6471	6501	6532	6562	18
19	6228	6259	6288	6319	6349	6380	6410	6441	6472	6502	6533	6563	19
20	6229	6260	6289	6320	6350	6381	6411	6442	6473	6503	6534	6564	20
21	6230	6261	6290	6321	6351	6382	6412	6443	6474	6504	6535	6565	21
22	6231	6262	6291	6322	6352	6383	6413	6444	6475	6505	6536	6566	22
23	6232	6263	6292	6323	6353	6384	6414	6445	6476	6506	6537	6567	23
24	6233	6264	6293	6324	6354	6385	6415	6446	6477	6507	6538	6568	24
25	6234	6265	6294	6325	6355	6386	6416	6447	6478	6508	6539	6569	25
26	6235	6266	6295	6326	6356	6387	6417	6448	6479	6509	6540	6570	26
27	6236	6267	6296	6327	6357	6388	6418	6449	6480	6510	6541	6571	27
28	6237	6268	6297	6328	6358	6389	6419	6450	6481	6511	6542	6572	28
29	6238	6269	6298	6329	6359	6390	6420	6451	6482	6512	6543	6573	29
30	6239	xxxx	6299	6330	6360	6391	6421	6452	6483	6513	6544	6574	30
31	6240	xxxx	6300	xxxx	6361	xxxx	6422	6453	xxxx	6514	xxxx	6575	31

Figure T-11. 1960 Expiration Table

1961—EXPIRATION TABLE—1961

Day	Jan	Feb	Mar	Apr	May	Jun	Jul	Aug	Sep	Oct	Nov	Dec	Day
1	6576	6607	6635	6666	6696	6727	6757	6788	6819	6849	6880	6910	1
2	6577	6608	6636	6667	6697	6728	6758	6789	6820	6850	6881	6911	2
3	6578	6609	6637	6668	6698	6729	6759	6790	6821	6851	6882	6912	3
4	6579	6610	6638	6669	6699	6730	6760	6791	6822	6852	6883	6913	4
5	6580	6611	6639	6670	6700	6731	6761	6792	6823	6853	6884	6914	5
6	6581	6612	6640	6671	6701	6732	6762	6793	6824	6854	6885	6915	6
7	6582	6613	6641	6672	6702	6733	6763	6794	6825	6855	6886	6916	7
8	6583	6614	6642	6673	6703	6734	6764	6795	6826	6856	6887	6917	8
9	6584	6615	6643	6674	6704	6735	6765	6796	6827	6857	6888	6918	9
10	6585	6616	6644	6675	6705	6736	6766	6797	6828	6858	6889	6919	10
11	6586	6617	6645	6676	6706	6737	6767	6798	6829	6859	6890	6920	11
12	6587	6618	6646	6677	6707	6738	6768	6799	6830	6860	6891	6921	12
13	6588	6619	6647	6678	6708	6739	6769	6800	6831	6861	6892	6922	13
14	6589	6620	6648	6679	6709	6740	6770	6801	6832	6862	6893	6923	14
15	6590	6621	6649	6680	6710	6741	6771	6802	6833	6863	6894	6924	15
16	6591	6622	6650	6681	6711	6742	6772	6803	6834	6864	6895	6925	16
17	6592	6623	6651	6682	6712	6743	6773	6804	6835	6865	6896	6926	17
18	6593	6624	6652	6683	6713	6744	6774	6805	6836	6866	6897	6927	18
19	6594	6625	6653	6684	6714	6745	6775	6806	6837	6867	6898	6928	19
20	6595	6626	6654	6685	6715	6746	6776	6807	6838	6868	6899	6929	20
21	6596	6627	6655	6686	6716	6747	6777	6808	6839	6869	6900	6930	21
22	6597	6628	6656	6687	6717	6748	6778	6809	6840	6870	6901	6931	22
23	6598	6629	6657	6688	6718	6749	6779	6810	6841	6871	6902	6932	23
24	6599	6630	6658	6689	6719	6750	6780	6811	6842	6872	6903	6933	24
25	6600	6631	6659	6690	6720	6751	6781	6812	6843	6873	6904	6934	25
26	6601	6632	6660	6691	6721	6752	6782	6813	6844	6874	6905	6935	26
27	6602	6633	6661	6692	6722	6753	6783	6814	6845	6875	6906	6936	27
28	6603	6634	6662	6693	6723	6754	6784	6815	6846	6876	6907	6937	28
29	6604	xxxx	6663	6694	6724	6755	6785	6816	6847	6877	6908	6938	29
30	6605	xxxx	6664	6695	6725	6756	6786	6817	6848	6878	6909	6939	30
31	6606	xxxx	6665	xxxx	6726	xxxx	6787	6818	xxxx	6879	xxxx	6940	31

Figure T-12. 1961 Expiration Table

1962—EXPIRATION TABLE—1962

Day	Jan	Feb	Mar	Apr	May	Jun	Jul	Aug	Sep	Oct	Nov	Dec	Day
1	6941	6972	7000	7031	7061	7092	7122	7153	7184	7214	7245	7275	1
2	6942	6973	7001	7032	7062	7093	7123	7154	7185	7215	7246	7276	2
3	6943	6974	7002	7033	7063	7094	7124	7155	7186	7216	7247	7277	3
4	6944	6975	7003	7034	7064	7095	7125	7156	7187	7217	7248	7278	4
5	6945	6976	7004	7035	7065	7096	7126	7157	7188	7218	7249	7279	5
6	6946	6977	7005	7036	7066	7097	7127	7158	7189	7219	7250	7280	6
7	6947	6978	7006	7037	7067	7098	7128	7159	7190	7220	7251	7281	7
8	6948	6979	7007	7038	7068	7099	7139	7160	7191	7221	7252	7282	8
9	6949	6980	7008	7039	7069	7100'	7130	7161	7192	7222	7253	7283	9
10	6950	6981	7009	7040	7070	7101	7131	7162	7193	7223	7254	7284	10
11	6951	6982	7010	7041	7071	7102	7132	7163	7194	7224	7255	7285	11
12	6952	6983	7011	7042	7072	7103	7133	7164	7195	7225	7256	7286	12
13	6953	6984	7012	7043	7073	7104	7134	7165	7196	7226	7257	7287	13
14	6954	6985	7013	7044	7074	7105	7135	7166	7197	7227	7258	7288	14
15	6955	6986	7014	7045	7075	7106	7136	7167	7198	7228	7259	7289	15
16	6956	6987	7015	7046	7076	7107	7137	7168	7199	7229	7260	7290	16
17	6957	6988	7016	7047	7077	7108	7138	7169	7200	7230	7261	7291	17
18	6958	6989	7017	7048	7078	7109	7139	7170	7201	7231	7262	7292	18
19	6959	6990	7018	7049	7079	7110	7140	7171	7202	7232	7263	7293	19
20	6960	6991	7019	7050	7080	7111	7141	7172	7203	7233	7264	7294	20
21	6961	6992	7020	7051	7081	7112	7142	7173	7204	7234	7265	7295	21
22	6962	6993	7021	7052	7082	7113	7143	7174	7205	7235	7266	7296	22
23	6963	6994	7022	7053	7083	7114	7144	7175	7206	7236	7267	7297	23
24	6964	6995	7023	7054	7084	7115	7145	7176	7207	7237	7268	7298	24
25	6965	6996	7024	7055	7085	7116	7146	7177	7208	7238	7269	7299	25
26	6966	6997	7025	7056	7086	7117	7147	7178	7209	7239	7270	7300	26
27	6967	6998	7026	7057	7087	7118	7148	7179	7210	7240	7271	7301	27
28	6968	6999	7027	7058	7088	7119	7149	7180	7211	7241	7272	7302	28
29	6969	xxxx	7028	7059	7089	7120	7150	7181	7212	7242	7273	7303	29
30	6970	xxxx	7029	7060	7090	7121	7151	7182	7213	7243	7274	7304	30
31	6971	xxxx	7030	xxxx	7091	xxxx	7152	7183	xxxx	7244	xxxx	7305	31

Figure T-13. 1962 Expiration Table

Day	Jan	Feb	Mar	Apr	May	Jun	Jul	Aug	Sep	Oct	Nov	Dec	Day
1	7306	7337	7365	7396	7426	7457	7487	7518	7549	7579	7610	7640	1
2	7307	7338	7366	7397	7427	7458	7488	7519	7550	7580	7611	7641	2
3	7308	7339	7367	7398	7428	7459	7489	7520	7551	7581	7612	7642	3
4	7309	7340	7368	7399	7429	7460	7490	7521	7552	7582	7613	7643	4
5	7310	7341	7369	7400	7430	7461	7491	7522	7553	7583	7614	7644	5
6	7311	7342	7370	7401	7431	7462	7492	7523	7554	7584	7615	7645	6
7	7312	7343	7371	7402	7432	7463	7493	7524	7555	7585	7616	7646	7
8	7313	7344	7372	7403	7433	7464	7494	7525	7556	7586	7617	7647	8
9	7314	7345	7373	7404	7434	7465	7495	7526	7557	7587	7618	7648	9
10	7315	7346	7374	7405	7435	7466	7496	7527	7558	7588	7619	7649	10
11	7316	7347	7375	7406	7436	7467	7497	7528	7559	7589	7620	7650	11
12	7317	7348	7376	7407	7437	7468	7498	7529	7560	7590	7621	7651	12
13	7318	7349	7377	7408	7438	7469	7499	7530	7561	7591	7622	7652	13
14	7319	7350	7378	7409	7439	7470	7500	7531	7562	7592	7623	7653	14
15	7320	7351	7379	7410	7440	7471	7501	7532	7563	7593	7624	7654	15
16	7321	7352	7380	7411	7441	7472	7502	7533	7564	7594	7625	7655	16
17	7322	7353	7381	7412	7442	7473	7503	7534	7565	7595	7626	7656	17
18	7323	7354	7382	7413	7443	7474	7504	7535	7566	7596	7627	7657	18
19	7324	7355	7383	7414	7444	7475	7505	7536	7567	7597	7628	7658	19
20	7325	7356	7384	7415	7445	7476	7506	7537	7568	7598	7629	7659	20
21	7326	7357	7385	7416	7446	7477	7507	7538	7569	7599	7630	7660	21
22	7327	7358	7386	7417	7447	7478	7508	7539	7570	7600	7631	7661	22
23	7328	7359	7387	7418	7448	7479	7509	7540	7571	7601	7632	7662	23
24	7329	7360	7388	7419	7449	7480	7510	7541	7572	7602	7633	7663	24
25	7330	7361	7389	7420	7450	7481	7511	7542	7573	7603	7634	7664	25
26	7331	7362	7390	7421	7451	7482	7512	7543	7574	7604	7635	7665	26
27	7332	7363	7391	7422	7452	7483	7513	7544	7575	7605	7636	7666	27
28	7333	7364	7392	7423	7453	7484	7514	7545	7576	7606	7637	7667	28
29	7334	xxxx	7393	7424	7454	7485	7515	7546	7577	7607	7638	7668	29
30	7335	xxxx	7394	7425	7455	7486	7516	7547	7578	7608	7639	7669	30
31	7336	xxxx	7395	xxxx	7456	xxxx	7517	7548	xxxx	7609	xxxx	7670	31

Figure T-14. 1963 Expiration Table

Day	Jan	Feb	Mar	Apr	May	Jun	Jul	Aug	Sep	Oct	Nov	Dec	Day
1	7671	7702	7731	7762	7792	7823	7853	7884	7915	7945	7976	8006	1
2	7672	7703	7732	7763	7793	7824	7854	7885	7916	7946	7977	8007	2
3	7673	7704	7733	7764	7794	7825	7855	7886	7917	7947	7978	8008	3
4	7674	7705	7734	7765	7795	7826	7856	7887	7918	7948	7979	8009	4
5	7675	7706	7735	7766	7796	7827	7857	7888	7919	7949	7980	8010	5
6	7676	7707	7736	7767	7797	7828	7858	7889	7920	7950	7981	8011	6
7	7677	7708	7737	7768	7798	7829	7859	7890	7921	7951	7982	8012	7
8	7678	7709	7738	7769	7799	7830	7860	7891	7922	7952	7983	8013	8
9	7679	7710	7739	7770	7800	7831	7861	7892	7923	7953	7984	8014	9
10	7680	7711	7740	7771	7801	7832	7862	7893	7924	7954	7985	8015	10
11	7681	7712	7741	7772	7802	7833	7863	7894	7925	7955	7986	8016	11
12	7682	7713	7742	7773	7803	7834	7864	7895	7926	7956	7987	8017	12
13	7683	7714	7743	7774	7804	7835	7865	7896	7927	7957	7988	8018	13
14	7684	7715	7744	7775	7805	7836	7866	7897	7928	7958	7989	8019	14
15	7685	7716	7745	7776	7806	7837	7867	7898	7929	7959	7990	8020	15
16	7686	7717	7746	7777	7807	7838	7868	7899	7930	7960	7991	8021	16
17	7687	7718	7747	7778	7808	7839	7869	7900	7931	7961	7992	8022	17
18	7688	7719	7748	7779	7809	7840	7870	7901	7932	7962	7993	8023	18
19	7689	7720	7749	7780	7810	7841	7871	7902	7933	7963	7994	8024	19
20	7690	7721	7750	7781	7811	7842	7872	7903	7934	7964	7995	8025	20
21	7691	7722	7751	7782	7812	7843	7873	7904	7935	7965	7996	8026	21
22	7692	7723	7752	7783	7813	7844	7874	7905	7936	7966	7997	8027	22
23	7693	7724	7753	7784	7814	7845	7875	7906	7937	7967	7998	8028	23
24	7694	7725	7754	7785	7815	7846	7876	7907	7938	7968	7999	8029	24
25	7695	7726	7755	7786	7816	7847	7877	7908	7939	7969	8000	8030	25
26	7696	7727	7756	7787	7817	7848	7878	7909	7940	7970	8001	8031	26
27	7697	7728	7757	7788	7818	7849	7879	7910	7941	7971	8002	8032	27
28	7698	7729	7758	7789	7819	7850	7880	7911	7942	7972	8003	8033	28
29	7699	7730	7759	7790	7820	7851	7881	7912	7943	7973	8004	8034	29
30	7700	xxxx	7760	7791	7821	7852	7882	7913	7944	7974	8005	8035	30
31	7701	xxxx	7761	xxxx	7822	xxxx	7883	7914	xxxx	7975	xxxx	8036	31

Figure T-15. 1964 Expiration Table

Day	Jan	Feb	Mar	Apr	May	Jun	Jul	Aug	Sep	Oct	Nov	Dec	Day
1	8037	8068	8096	8127	8157	8188	8218	8249	8280	8310	8341	8371	1
2	8038	8069	8097	8128	8158	8189	8219	8250	8281	8311	8342	8372	2
3	8039	8070	8098	8129	8159	8190	8220	8251	8282	8312	8343	8373	3
4	8040	8071	8099	8130	8160	8191	8221	8252	8283	8313	8344	8374	4
5	8041	8072	8100	8131	8161	8192	8222	8253	8284	8314	8345	8375	5
6	8042	8073	8101	8132	8162	8193	8223	8254	8285	8315	8346	8376	6
7	8043	8074	8102	8133	8163	8194	8224	8255	8286	8316	8347	8377	7
8	8044	8075	8103	8134	8164	8195	8225	8256	8287	8317	8348	8378	8
9	8045	8076	8104	8135	8165	8196	8226	8257	8288	8318	8349	8379	9
10	8046	8077	8105	8136	8166	8197	8227	8258	8289	8319	8350	8380	10
11	8047	8078	8106	8137	8167	8198	8228	8259	8290	8320	8351	8381	11
12	8048	8079	8107	8138	8168	8199	8229	8260	8291	8321	8352	8382	12
13	8049	8080	8108	8139	8169	8200	8230	8261	8292	8322	8353	8383	13
14	8050	8081	8109	8140	8170	8201	8231	8262	8293	8323	8354	8384	14
15	8051	8082	8110	8141	8171	8202	8232	8263	8294	8324	8355	8385	15
16	8052	8083	8111	8142	8172	8203	8233	8264	8295	8325	8356	8386	16
17	8053	8084	8112	8143	8173	8204	8234	8265	8296	8326	8357	8387	17
18	8054	8085	8113	8144	8174	8205	8235	8266	8297	8327	8358	8388	18
19	8055	8086	8114	8145	8175	8206	8236	8267	8298	8328	8359	8389	19
20	8056	8087	8115	8146	8176	8207	8237	8268	8299	8329	8360	8390	20
21	8057	8088	8116	8147	8177	8208	8238	8269	8300	8330	8361	8391	21
22	8058	8089	8117	8148	8178	8209	8239	8270	8301	8331	8362	8392	22
23	8059	8090	8118	8149	8179	8210	8240	8271	8302	8332	8363	8393	23
24	8060	8091	8119	8150	8180	8211	8241	8272	8303	8333	8364	8394	24
25	8061	8092	8120	8151	8181	8212	8242	8273	8304	8334	8365	8395	25
26	8062	8093	8121	8152	8182	8213	8243	8274	8305	8335	8366	8396	26
27	8063	8094	8122	8153	8183	8214	8244	8275	8306	8336	8367	8397	27
28	8064	8095	8123	8154	8184	8215	8245	8276	8307	8337	8368	8398	28
29	8065	xxxx	8124	8155	8185	8216	8246	8277	8308	8338	8369	8399	29
30	8066	xxxx	8125	8156	8186	8217	8247	8278	8309	8339	8370	8400	30
31	8067	xxxx	8126	xxxx	8187	xxxx	8248	8279	xxxx	8340	xxxx	8401	31

Figure T-16. 1965 Expiration Table

1966—EXPIRATION TABLE—1966

Day	Jan	Feb	Mar	Apr	May	Jun	Jul	Aug	Sep	Oct	Nov	Dec	Day
1	8402	8433	8461	8492	8522	8553	8583	8614	8645	8675	8706	8736	1
2	8403	8434	8462	8493	8523	8554	8584	8615	8646	8676	8707	8737	2
3	8404	8435	8463	8494	8524	8555	8585	8616	8647	8677	8708	8738	3
4	8405	8436	8464	8495	8525	8556	8586	8617	8648	8678	8709	8739	4
5	8406	8437	8465	8496	8526	8557	8587	8618	8649	8679	8710	8740	5
6	8407	8438	8466	8497	8527	8558	8588	8619	8650	8680	8711	8741	6
7	8408	8439	8467	8498	8528	8559	8589	8620	8651	8681	8712	8742	7
8	8409	8440	8468	8499	8529	8560	8590	8621	8652	8682	8713	8743	8
9	8410	8441	8469	8500	8530	8561	8591	8622	8653	8683	8714	8744	9
10	8411	8442	8470	8501	8531	8562	8592	8623	8654	8684	8715	8745	10
11	8412	8443	8471	8502	8532	8563	8593	8624	8655	8685	8716	8746	11
12	8413	8444	8472	8503	8533	8564	8594	8625	8656	8686	8717	8747	12
13	8414	8445	8473	8504	8534	8565	8595	8626	8657	8687	8718	8748	13
14	8415	8446	8474	8505	8535	8566	8596	8627	8658	8688	8719	8749	14
15	8416	8447	8475	8506	8536	8567	8597	8628	8659	8689	8720	8750	15
16	8417	8448	8476	8507	8537	8568	8598	8629	8660	8690	8721	8751	16
17	8418	8449	8477	8508	8538	8569	8599	8630	8661	8691	8722	8752	17
18	8419	8450	8478	8509	8539	8570	8600	8631	8662	8692	8723	8753	18
19	8420	8451	8479	8510	8540	8571	8601	8632	8663	8693	8724	8754	19
20	8421	8452	8480	8511	8541	8572	8602	8633	8664	8694	8725	8755	20
21	8422	8453	8481	8512	8542	8573	8603	8634	8665	8695	8726	8756	21
22	8423	8454	8482	8513	8543	8574	8604	8635	8666	8696	8727	8757	22
23	8424	8455	8483	8514	8544	8575	8605	8636	8667	8697	8728	8758	23
24	8425	8456	8484	8515	8545	8576	8606	8637	8668	8698	8729	8759	24
25	8426	8457	8485	8516	8546	8577	8607	8638	8669	8699	8730	8760	25
26	8427	8458	8486	8517	8547	8578	8608	8639	8670	8700	8731	8761	26
27	8428	8459	8487	8518	8548	8579	8609	8640	8671	8701	8732	8762	27
28	8429	8460	8488	8519	8549	8580	8610	8641	8672	8702	8733	8763	28
29	8430	xxxx	8489	8520	8550	8581	8611	8642	8673	8703	8734	8764	29
30	8431	xxxx	8490	8521	8551	8582	8612	8643	8674	8704	8735	8765	30
31	8432	xxxx	8491	xxxx	8552	xxxx	8613	8644	xxxx	8705	xxxx	8766	31

Figure T-17. 1966 Expiration Table

Day	Jan	Feb	Mar	Apr	May	Jun	Jul	Aug	Sep	Oct	Nov	Dec	Day
1	8767	8798	8826	8857	8887	8918	8948	8979	9010	9040	9071	9101	1
2	8768	8799	8827	8858	8888	8919	8949	8980	9011	9041	9072	9102	2
3	8769	8800	8828	8859	8889	8920	8950	8981	9012	9042	9073	9103	3
4	8770	8801	8829	8860	8890	8921	8951	8982	9013	9043	9074	9104	4
5	8771	8802	8830	8861	8891	8922	8952	8983	9014	9044	9075	9105	5
6	8772	8803	8831	8862	8892	8923	8953	8984	9015	9045	9076	9106	6
7	8773	8804	8832	8863	8893	8924	8954	8985	9016	9046	9077	9107	7
8	8774	8805	8833	8864	8894	8925	8955	8986	9017	9047	9078	9108	8
9	8775	8806	8834	8865	8895	8926	8956	8987	9018	9048	9079	9109	9
10	8776	8807	8835	8866	8896	8927	8957	8988	9019	9049	9080	9110	10
11	8777	8808	8836	8867	8897	8928	8958	8989	9020	9050	9081	9111	11
12	8778	8809	8837	8868	8898	8929	8959	8990	9021	9051	9082	9112	12
13	8779	8810	8838	8869	8899	8930	8960	8991	9022	9052	9083	9113	13
14	8780	8811	8839	8870	8900	8931	8961	8992	9023	9053	9084	9114	14
15	8781	8812	8840	8871	8901	8932	8962	8993	9024	9054	9085	9115	15
16	8782	8813	8841	8872	8902	8933	8963	8994	9025	9055	9086	9116	16
17	8783	8814	8842	8873	8903	8934	8964	8995	9026	9056	9087	9117	17
18	8784	8815	8843	8874	8904	8935	8965	8996	9027	9057	9088	9118	18
19	8785	8816	8844	8875	8905	8936	8966	8997	9028	9058	9089	9119	19
20	8786	8817	8845	8876	8906	8937	8967	8998	9029	9059	9090	9120	20
21	8787	8818	8846	8877	8907	8938	8968	8999	9030	9060	9091	9121	21
22	8788	8819	8847	8878	8908	8939	8969	9000	9031	9061	9092	9122	22
23	8789	8820	8848	8879	8909	8940	8970	9001	9032	9062	9093	9123	23
24	8790	8821	8849	8880	8910	8941	8971	9002	9033	9063	9094	9124	24
25	8791	8822	8850	8881	8911	8942	8972	9003	9034	9064	9095	9125	25
26	8792	8823	8851	8882	8912	8943	8973	9004	9035	9065	9096	9126	26
27	8793	8824	8852	8883	8913	8944	8974	9005	9036	9066	9097	9127	27
28	8794	8825	8853	8884	8914	8945	8975	9006	9037	9067	9098	9128	28
29	8795	xxxx	8854	8885	8915	8946	8976	9007	9038	9068	9099	9129	29
30	8796	xxxx	8855	8886	8916	8947	8977	9008	9039	9069	9100	9130	30
31	8797	xxxx	8856	xxxx	8917	xxxx	8978	9009	xxxx	9070	xxxx	9131	31

Figure T-18. 1967 Expiration Table

1968—EXPIRATION TABLE—1968

Day	Jan	Feb	Mar	Apr	May	Jun	Jul	Aug	Sep	Oct	Nov	Dec	Day
1	9132	9163	9192	9223	9253	9284	9314	9345	9376	9406	9437	9467	1
2	9133	9164	9193	9224	9254	9285	9315	9346	9377	9407	9438	9468	2
3	9134	9165	9194	9225	9255	9286	9316	9347	9378	9408	9439	9469	3
4	9135	9166	9195	9226	9256	9287	9317	9348	9379	9409	9440	9470	4
5	9136	9167	9196	9227	9257	9288	9318	9349	9380	9410	9441	9471	5
6	9137	9168	9197	9228	9258	9289	9319	9350	9381	9411	9442	9472	6
7	9138	9169	9198	9229	9259	9290	9320	9351	9382	9412	9443	9473	7
8	9139	9170	9199	9230	9260	9291	9321	9352	9383	9413	9444	9474	8
9	9140	9171	9200	9231	9261	9292	9322	9353	9384	9414	9445	9475	9
10	9141	9172	9201	9232	9262	9293	9323	9354	9385	9415	9446	9476	10
11	9142	9173	9202	9233	9263	9294	9324	9355	9386	9416	9447	9477	11
12	9143	9174	9203	9234	9264	9295	9325	9356	9387	9418	9448	9478	12
13	9144	9175	9204	9235	9265	9296	9326	9357	9388	9418	9449	9479	13
14	9145	9176	9205	9236	9266	9297	9327	9358	9389	9419	9450	9480	14
15	9146	9177	9206	9237	9267	9298	9328	9359	9390	9420	9451	9481	15
16	9147	9178	9207	9238	9268	9299	9329	9360	9391	9421	9452	9482	16
17	9148	9179	9208	9239	9269	9300	9330	9361	9392	9422	9453	9483	17
18	9149	9180	9209	9240	9270	9301	9331	9362	9393	9424	9454	9484	18
19	9150	9181	9210	9241	9271	9302	9332	9363	9394	9424	9455	9485	19
20	9151	9182	9211	9242	9272	9303	9333	9364	9395	9425	9456	9486	20
21	9152	9183	9212	9243	9273	9304	9334	9365	9396	9426	9457	9487	21
22	9153	9184	9213	9244	9274	9305	9335	9366	9397	9427	9458	9488	22
23	9154	9185	9214	9245	9275	9306	9336	9367	9398	9428	9459	9489	23
24	9155	9186	9215	9246	9276	9307	9337	9368	9399	9429	9460	9490	24
25	9156	9187	9216	9247	9277	9308	9338	9369	9400	9430	9461	9491	25
26	9157	9188	9217	9248	9278	9309	9339	9370	9401	9431	9462	9492	26
27	9158	9189	9218	9249	9279	9310	9340	9371	9402	9432	9463	9493	27
28	9159	9190	9219	9250	9280	9311	9341	9372	9403	9433	9464	9494	28
29	9160	9191	9220	9251	9281	9312	9342	9373	9404	9434	9465	9495	29
30	9161	xxxx	9221	9252	9282	9313	9343	9374	9405	9435	9466	9496	30
31	9162	xxxx	9222	xxxx	9283	xxxx	9344	9375	xxxx	9436	xxxx	9497	31

Figure T-19. 1968 Expiration Table

Day	Jan	Feb	Mar	Apr	May	Jun	Jul	Aug	Sep	Oct	Nov	Dec	Day
1	9498	9529	9557	9588	9618	9649	9679	9710	9741	9771	9802	9832	1
2	9499	9530	9558	9589	9619	9650	9680	9711	9742	9772	9803	9833	2
3	9500	9531	9559	9590	9620	9651	9681	9712	9743	9773	9804	9834	3
4	9501	9532	9560	9591	9621	9652	9682	9713	9744	9774	9805	9835	4
5	9502	9533	9561	9592	9622	9653	9683	9714	9745	9775	9806	9836	5
6	9503	9534	9562	9593	9623	9654	9684	9715	9746	9776	9807	9837	6
7	9504	9535	9563	9594	9624	9655	9685	9716	9747	9777	9808	9838	7
8	9505	9536	9564	9595	9625	9656	9686	9717	9748	9778	9809	9839	8
9	9506	9537	9565	9596	9626	9657	9687	9718	9749	9779	9810	9840	9
10	9507	9538	9566	9597	9627	9658	9688	9719	9750	9780	9811	9841	10
11	9508	9539	9567	9598	9628	9659	9689	9720	9751	9781	9812	9842	11
12	9509	9540	9568	9599	9629	9660	9690	9721	9752	9782	9813	9843	12
13	9510	9541	9569	9600	9630	9661	9691	9722	9753	9783	9814	9844	13
14	9511	9542	9570	9601	9631	9662	9692	9723	9754	9784	9815	9845	14
15	9512	9543	9571	9602	9632	9663	9693	9724	9755	9785	9816	9846	15
16	9513	9544	9572	9603	9633	9664	9694	9725	9756	9786	9817	9847	16
17	9514	9545	9573	9604	9634	9665	9695	9726	9757	9787	9818	9848	17
18	9515	9546	9574	9605	9635	9666	9696	9727	9758	9788	9819	9849	18
19	9516	9547	9575	9606	9636	9667	9697	9728	9759	9789	9820	9850	19
20	9517	9548	9576	9607	9637	9668	9698	9729	9760	9790	9821	9851	20
21	9518	9549	9577	9608	9638	9669	9699	9730	9761	9791	9822	9852	21
22	9519	9550	9578	9609	9639	9670	9700	9731	9762	9792	9823	9853	22
23	9520	9551	9579	9610	9640	9671	9701	9732	9763	9793	9824	9854	23
24	9521	9552	9580	9611	9641	9672	9702	9733	9764	9794	9825	9855	24
25	9522	9553	9581	9612	9642	9673	9703	9734	9765	9795	9826	9856	25
26	9523	9554	9582	9613	9643	9674	9704	9735	9766	9796	9827	9857	26
27	9524	9555	9583	9614	9644	9675	9705	9736	9767	9797	9828	9858	27
28	9525	9556	9584	9615	9645	9676	9706	9737	9768	9798	9829	9859	28
29	9526	xxxx	9585	9616	9646	9677	9707	9738	9769	9799	9830	9860	29
30	9527	xxxx	9586	9617	9647	9678	9708	9739	9770	9800	9831	9861	30
31	9528	xxxx	9587	xxxx	9648	xxxx	9709	9740	xxxx	9801	xxxx	9862	31

Figure T-20. 1969 Expiration Table

Day	Jan	Feb	Mar	Apr	May	Jun	Jul	Aug	Sep	Oct	Nov	Dec	Day
1	9863	9894	9922	9953	9983	10014	10044	10075	10106	10136	10167	10197	1
2	9864	9895	9923	9954	9984	10015	10045	10076	10107	10137	10168	10198	2
3	9865	9896	9924	9955	9985	10016	10046	10077	10108	10138	10169	10199	3
4	9866	9897	9925	9956	9986	10017	10047	10078	10109	10139	10170	10200	4
5	9867	9898	9926	9957	9987	10018	10048	10079	10110	10140	10171	10201	5
6	9868	9899	9927	9958	9988	10019	10049	10080	10111	10141	10172	10202	6
7	9869	9900	9928	9959	9989	10020	10050	10081	10112	10142	10173	10203	7
8	9870	9901	9929	9960	9990	10021	10051	10082	10113	10143	10174	10204	8
9	9871	9902	9930	9961	9991	10022	10052	10083	10114	10144	10175	10205	9
10	9872	9903	9931	9962	9992	10023	10053	10084	10115	10145	10176	10206	10
11	9873	9904	9932	9963	9993	10024	10054	10085	10116	10146	10177	10207	11
12	9874	9905	9933	9964	9994	10025	10055	10086	10117	10147	10178	10208	12
13	9875	9906	9934	9965	9995	10026	10056	10087	10118	10148	10179	10209	13
14	9876	9907	9935	9966	9996	10027	10057	10088	10119	10149	10180	10210	14
15	9877	9908	9936	9967	9997	10028	10058	10089	10120	10150	10181	10211	15
16	9878	9909	9937	9968	9998	10029	10059	10090	10121	10151	10182	10212	16
17	9879	9910	9938	9969	9999	10030	10060	10091	10122	10152	10183	10213	17
18	9880	9911	9939	9970	10000	10031	10061	10092	10123	10153	10184	10214	18
19	9881	9912	9940	9971	10001	10032	10062	10093	10124	10154	10185	10215	19
20	9882	9913	9941	9972	10002	10033	10063	10094	10125	10155	10186	10216	20
21	9883	9914	9942	9973	10003	10034	10064	10095	10126	10156	10187	10217	21
22	9884	9915	9943	9974	10004	10035	10065	10096	10127	10157	10188	10218	22
23	9885	9916	9944	9975	10005	10036	10066	10097	10128	10158	10189	10219	23
24	9886	9917	9945	9976	10006	10037	10067	10098	10129	10159	10190	10220	24
25	9887	9918	9946	9977	10007	10038	10068	10099	10130	10160	10191	10221	25
26	9888	9919	9947	9978	10008	10039	10069	10100	10131	10161	10192	10222	26
27	9889	9920	9948	9979	10009	10040	10070	10101	10132	10162	10193	10223	27
28	9890	9921	9949	9980	10010	10041	10071	10102	10133	10163	10194	10224	28
29	9891	xxxx	9950	9981	10011	10042	10072	10103	10134	10164	10195	10225	29
30	9892	xxxx	9951	9982	10012	10043	10073	10104	10135	10165	10196	10226	30
31	9893	xxxx	9952	xxxx	10013	xxxxx	10074	10105	xxxxx	10166	xxxxx	10227	31

Figure T-21. 1970 Expiration Table

1971—EXPIRATION TABLE—1971

Day	Jan	Feb	Mar	Apr	May	Jun	Jul	Aug	Sep	Oct	Nov	Dec	Day
1	10228	10259	10287	10318	10348	10379	10409	10440	10471	10501	10532	10562	1
2	10229	10260	10288	10319	10349	10380	10410	10441	10472	10502	10533	10563	2
3	10230	10261	10289	10320	10350	10381	10411	10442	10473	10503	10534	10564	3
4	10231	10262	10290	10321	10352	10382	10412	10443	10474	10504	10535	10565	4
5	10232	10263	10291	10322	10352	10383	10413	10444	10475	10505	10536	10566	5
6	10233	10264	10292	10323	10353	10384	10414	10445	10476	10506	10537	10567	6
7	10234	10265	10293	10324	10354	10385	10415	10446	10477	10507	10538	10568	7
8	10235	10266	10294	10325	10355	10386	10416	10447	10478	10508	10539	10569	8
9	10236	10267	10295	10326	10356	10387	10417	10448	10479	10509	10540	10570	9
10	10237	10268	10296	10327	10357	10388	10418	10449	10480	10510	10541	10571	10
11	10238	10269	10297	10328	10358	10389	10419	10450	10481	10511	10542	10572	11
12	10239	10270	10298	10329	10359	10390	10420	10451	10482	10512	10543	10573	12
13	10240	10271	10299	10330	10360	10391	10421	10452	10483	10513	10544	10574	13
14	10241	10272	10300	10331	10361	10392	10422	10453	10484	10514	10545	10575	14
15	10242	10273	10301	10332	10362	10393	10423	10454	10485	10515	10546	10576	15
16	10243	10274	10302	10333	10363	10394	10424	10455	10486	10516	10547	10577	16
17	10244	10275	10303	10334	10364	10395	10425	10456	10487	10517	10548	10578	17
18	10245	10276	10304	10335	10365	10396	10426	10457	10488	10518	10549	10579	18
19	10246	10277	10305	10336	10366	10397	10427	10458	10489	10519	10550	10580	19
20	10247	10278	10306	10337	10367	10398	10428	10459	10490	10520	10551	10581	20
21	10248	10279	10307	10338	10368	10399	10429	10460	10491	10521	10552	10582	21
22	10249	10280	10308	10339	10369	10400	10430	10461	10492	10522	10553	10583	22
23	10250	10281	10309	10340	10370	10401	10431	10462	10493	10523	10554	10584	23
24	10251	10282	10310	10341	10371	10402	10432	10463	10494	10524	10555	10585	24
25	10252	10283	10311	10342	10372	10403	10433	10464	10495	10525	10556	10586	25
26	10253	10284	10312	10343	10373	10404	10434	10465	10496	10526	10557	10587	26
27	10254	10285	10313	10344	10374	10405	10435	10466	10497	10527	10558	10588	27
28	10255	10286	10314	10345	10375	10406	10436	10467	10498	10528	10559	10589	28
29	10256	xxxxx	10315	10346	10376	10407	10437	10468	10499	10529	10560	10590	29
30	10257	xxxxx	10316	10347	10377	10408	10438	10469	10500	10530	10561	10591	30
31	10258	xxxxx	10317	xxxxx	10378	xxxxx	10439	10470	xxxxx	10531	xxxxx	10592	31

Figure T-22. 1971 Expiration Table

1972—EXPIRATION TABLE—1972

Day	Jan	Feb	Mar	Apr	May	Jun	Jul	Aug	Sep	Oct	Nov	Dec	Day
1	10593	10624	10653	10684	10714	10745	10775	10806	10837	10867	10898	10928	1
2	10594	10625	10654	10685	10715	10746	10776	10807	10838	10868	10899	10929	2
3	10595	10626	10655	10686	10716	10747	10777	10808	10839	10869	10900	10930	3
4	10596	10627	10656	10687	10717	10748	10778	10809	10840	10870	10901	10931	4
5	10597	10628	10657	10688	10718	10749	10779	10810	10841	10871	10902	10932	5
6	10598	10629	10658	10689	10719	10750	10780	10811	10842	10872	10903	10933	6
7	10599	10630	10659	10690	10720	10751	10781	10812	10843	10873	10904	10934	7
8	10600	10631	10660	10691	10721	10752	10782	10813	10844	10874	10905	10935	8
9	10601	10632	10661	10692	10722	10753	10783	10814	10845	10875	10906	10936	9
10	10602	10633	10662	10693	10723	10754	10784	10815	10846	10876	10907	10937	10
11	10603	10634	10663	10694	10724	10755	10785	10816	10847	10877	10908	10938	11
12	10604	10635	10664	10695	10725	10756	10786	10817	10848	10878	10909	10939	12
13	10605	10636	10665	10696	10726	10757	10787	10818	10849	10879	10910	10940	13
14	10606	10637	10666	10697	10727	10758	10788	10819	10850	10880	10911	10941	14
15	10607	10638	10667	10698	10728	10759	10789	10820	10851	10881	10912	10942	15
16	10608	10639	10668	10699	10729	10760	10790	10821	10852	10882	10913	10943	16
17	10609	10640	10669	10700	10730	10761	10791	10822	10853	10883	10914	10944	17
18	10610	10641	10670	10701	10731	10762	10792	10823	10854	10884	10915	10945	18
19	10611	10642	10671	10702	10732	10763	10793	10824	10855	10885	10916	10946	19
20	10612	10643	10672	10703	10733	10764	10794	10825	10856	10886	10917	10947	20
21	10613	10644	10673	10704	10734	10765	10795	10826	10857	10887	10918	10948	21
22	10614	10645	10674	10705	10735	10766	10796	10827	10858	10888	10919	10949	22
23	10615	10646	10675	10706	10736	10767	10797	10828	10859	10889	10920	10950	23
24	10616	10647	10676	10707	10737	10768	10798	10829	10860	10890	10921	10951	24
25	10617	10648	10677	10708	10738	10769	10799	10830	10861	10891	10922	10952	25
26	10618	10649	10678	10709	10739	10770	10800	10831	10862	10892	10923	10953	26
27	10619	10650	10679	10710	10740	10771	10801	10832	10863	10893	10924	10954	27
28	10620	10651	10680	10711	10741	10772	10802	10833	10864	10894	10925	10955	28
29	10621	10652	10681	10712	10742	10773	10803	10834	10865	10895	10926	10956	29
30	10622	xxxxx	10682	10713	10743	10774	10804	10835	10866	10896	10927	10957	30
31	10623	xxxxx	10683	xxxxx	10744	xxxxx	10805	10836	xxxxx	10897	xxxxx	10958	31

Figure T-23. 1972 Expiration Table

Day	Jan	Feb	Mar	Apr	May	Jun	Jul	Aug	Sep	Oct	Nov	Dec	Day
1	10959	10990	11018	11049	11079	11110	11140	11171	11202	11232	11263	11293	1
2	10960	10991	11019	11050	11080	11111	11141	11172	11203	11233	11264	11294	2
3	10961	10992	11020	11051	11081	11112	11142	11173	11204	11234	11265	11295	3
4	10962	10993	11021	11052	11082	11113	11143	11174	11205	11235	11266	11296	4
5	10963	10994	11022	11053	11083	11114	11144	11175	11206	11236	11267	11297	5
6	10964	10995	11023	11054	11084	11115	11145	11176	11207	11237	11268	11298	6
7	10965	10996	11024	11055	11085	11116	11146	11177	11208	11238	11269	11299	7
8	10966	10997	11025	11056	11086	11117	11147	11178	11209	11239	11270	11300	8
9	10967	10998	11026	11057	11087	11118	11148	11179	11210	11240	11271	11301	9
10	10968	10999	11027	11058	11088	11119	11149	11180	11211	11241	11272	11302	10
11	10969	11000	11028	11059	11089	11120	11150	11181	11212	11242	11273	11303	11
12	10970	11001	11029	11060	11090	11121	11151	11182	11213	11243	11274	11304	12
13	10971	11002	11030	11061	11091	11122	11152	11183	11214	11244	11275	11305	13
14	10972	11003	11031	11062	11092	11123	11153	11184	11215	11245	11276	11306	14
15	10973	11004	11032	11063	11093	11124	11154	11185	11216	11246	11277	11307	15
16	10974	11005	11033	11064	11094	11125	11155	11186	11217	11247	11278	11308	16
17	10975	11006	11034	11065	11095	11126	11156	11187	11218	11248	11279	11309	17
18	10976	11007	11035	11066	11096	11127	11157	11188	11219	11249	11280	11310	18
19	10977	11008	11036	11067	11097	11128	11158	11189	11220	11250	11281	11311	19
20	10978	11009	11037	11068	11098	11129	11159	11190	11221	11251	11282	11312	20
21	10979	11010	11038	11069	11099	11130	11160	11191	11222	11252	11283	11313	21
22	10980	11011	11039	11070	11100	11131	11161	11192	11223	11253	11284	11314	22
23	10981	11012	11040	11071	11101	11132	11162	11193	11224	11254	11285	11315	23
24	10982	11013	11041	11072	11102	11133	11163	11194	11225	11255	11286	11316	24
25	10983	11014	11042	11073	11103	11134	11164	11195	11226	11256	11287	11317	25
26	10984	11015	11043	11074	11104	11135	11165	11196	11227	11257	11288	11318	26
27	10985	11016	11044	11075	11105	11136	11166	11197	11228	11258	11289	11319	27
28	10986	11017	11045	11076	11106	11137	11167	11198	11229	11259	11290	11320	28
29	10987	xxxxx	11046	11077	11107	11138	11168	11199	11230	11260	11291	11321	29
30	10988	xxxxx	11047·	11078	11108	11139	11169	11200	11231	11261	11292	11322	30
31	10989	xxxxx	11048	xxxxx	11109	xxxxx	11170	11201	xxxxx	11262	xxxxx	11323	31

Figure T-24. 1973 Expiration Table

1974—EXPIRATION TABLE—1974

Day	Jan	Feb	Mar	Apr	May	Jun	Jul	Aug	Sep	Oct	Nov	Dec	Day
1	11324	11355	11383	11414	11444	11475	11505	11536	11567	11597	11628	11658	1
2	11325	11356	11384	11415	11445	11476	11506	11537	11568	11598	11629	11659	2
3	11326	11357	11385	11416	11446	11477	11507	11538	11569	11599	11630	11660	3
4	11327	11358	11386	11417	11447	11478	11508	11539	11570	11600	11631	11661	4
5	11328	11359	11387	11418	11448	11479	11509	11540	11571	11601	11632	11662	5
6	11329	11360	11388	11419	11449	11480	11510	11541	11572	11602	11633	11663	6
7	11330	11361	11389	11420	11450	11481	11511	11542	11573	11603	11634	11664	7
8	11331	11362	11390	11421	11451	11482	11512	11543	11574	11604	11635	11665	8
9	11332	11363	11391	11422	11452	11483	11513	11544	11575	11605	11636	11666	9
10	11333	11364	11392	11423	11453	11484	11514	11545	11576	11606	11637	11667	10
11	11334	11365	11393	11424	11454	11485	11515	11546	11577	11607	11638	11668	11
12	11335	11366	11394	11425	11455	11486	11516	11547	11578	11608	11639	11669	12
13	11336	11367	11395	11426	11456	11487	11517	11548	11579	11609	11640	11670	13
14	11337	11368	11396	11427	11457	11488	11518	11549	11580	11610	11641	11671	14
15	11338	11369	11397	11428	11458	11489	11519	11550	11581	11611	11642	11672	15
16	11339	11370	11398	11429	11459	11490	11520	11551	11582	11612	11643	11673	16
17	11340	11371	11399	11430	11460	11491	11521	11552	11583	11613	11644	11674	17
18	11341	11372	11400	11431	11461	11492	11522	11553	11584	11614	11645	11675	18
19	11342	11373	11401	11432	11462	11493	11523	11554	11585	11615	11646	11676	19
20	11343	11374	11402	11433	11463	11494	11524	11555	11586	11616	11647	11677	20
21	11344	11375	11403	11434	11464	11495	11525	11556	11587	11617	11648	11678	21
22	11345	11376	11404	11435	11465	11496	11526	11557	11588	11618	11649	11679	22
23	11346	11377	11405	11436	11466	11497	11527	11558	11589	11619	11650	11680	23
24	11347	11378	11406	11437	11467	11498	11528	11559	11590	11620	11651	11681	24
25	11348	11379	11407	11438	11468	11499	11529	11560	11591	11621	11652	11682	25
26	11349	11380	11408	11439	11469	11500	11530	11561	11592	11622	11653	11683	26
27	11350	11381	11409	11440	11470	11501	11531	11562	11593	11623	11654	11684	27
28	11351	11382	11410	11441	11471	11502	11532	11563	11594	11624	11655	11685	28
29	11352	xxxxx	11411	11442	11472	11503	11533	11564	11595	11625	11656	11686	29
30	11353	xxxxx	11412	11443	11473	11504	11534	11565	11596	11626	11657	11687	30
31	11354	xxxxx	11413	xxxxx	11474	xxxxx	11535	11566	xxxxx	11627	xxxxx	11688	31

Figure T-25. 1974 Expiration Table

Day	Jan	Feb	Mar	Apr	May	Jun	Jul	Aug	Sep	Oct	Nov	Dec	Day
1	11689	11720	11748	11779	11809	11840	11870	11901	11932	11962	11993	12023	1
2	11690	11721	11749	11780	11810	11841	11871	11902	11933	11963	11994	12024	2
3	11691	11722	11750	11781	11811	11842	11872	11903	11934	11964	11995	12025	3
4	11692	11723	11751	11782	11812	11843	11873	11904	11935	11965	11996	12026	4
5	11693	11724	11752	11783	11813	11844	11874	11905	11936	11966	11997	12027	5
6	11694	11725	11753	11784	11814	11845	11875	11906	11937	11967	11998	12028	6
7	11695	11726	11754	11785	11815	11846	11876	11907	11938	11968	11999	12029	7
8	11696	11727	11755	11786	11816	11847	11877	11908	11939	11969	12000	12030	8
9	11697	11728	11756	11787	11817	11848	11878	11909	11940	11970	12001	12031	9
10	11698	11729	11757	11788	11818	11849	11879	11910	11941	11971	12002	12032	10
11	11699	11730	11758	11789	11819	11850	11880	11911	11942	11972	12003	12033	11
12	11700	11731	11759	11790	11820	11851	11881	11912	11943	11973	12004	12034	12
13	11701	11732	11760	11791	11821	11852	11882	11913	11944	11974	12005	12035	13
14	11702	11733	11761	11792	11822	11853	11883	11914	11945	11975	12006	12036	14
15	11703	11734	11762	11793	11823	11854	11884	11915	11946	11976	12007	12037	15
16	11704	11735	11763	11794	11824	11855	11885	11916	11947	11977	12008	12038	16
17	11705	11736	11764	11795	11825	11856	11886	11917	11948	11978	12009	12039	17
18	11706	11737	11765	11796	11826	11857	11887	11918	11949	11979	12010	12040	18
19	11707	11738	11766	11797	11827	11858	11888	11919	11950	11980	12011	12041	19
20	11708	11739	11767	11798	11828	11859	11889	11920	11951	11981	12012	12042	20
21	11709	11740	11768	11799	11829	11860	11890	11921	11952	11982	12013	12043	21
22	11710	11741	11769	11800	11830	11861	11891	11922	11953	11983	12014	12044	22
23	11711	11742	11770	11801	11831	11862	11892	11923	11954	11984	12015	12045	23
24	11712	11743	11771	11802	11832	11863	11893	11924	11955	11985	12016	11046	24
25	11713	11744	11772	11803	11833	11864	11894	11925	11956	11986	12017	12047	25
26	11714	11745	11773	11804	11834	11865	11895	11926	11957	11987	12018	12048	26
27	11715	11746	11774	11805	11835	11866	11896	11927	11958	11988	12019	12049	27
28	11716	11747	11775	11806	11836	11867	11897	11928	11959	11989	12020	12050	28
29	11717	xxxxx	11776	11807	11837	11868	11898	11929	11960	11990	12021	12051	29
30	11718	xxxxx	11777	11808	11838	11869	11899	11930	11961	11991	12022	12052	30
31	11719	xxxxx	11778	xxxxx	11839	xxxxx	11900	11931	xxxxx	11992	xxxxx	12053	31

Figure T-26. 1975 Expiration Table

Day	Jan	Feb	Mar	Apr	May	Jun	Jul	Aug	Sep	Oct	Nov	Dec	Day
1	12054	12085	12114	12145	12175	12206	12236	12267	12298	12328	12359	12389	1
2	12055	12086	12115	12146	12176	12207	12237	12268	12299	12329	12360	12390	2
3	12056	12087	12116	12147	12177	12208	12238	12269	12300	12330	12361	12391	3
4	12057	12088	12117	12148	12178	12209	12239	12270	12301	12331	12362	12392	4
5	12058	12089	12118	12149	12179	12210	12240	12271	12302	12332	12363	12393	5
6	12059	12090	12119	12150	12180	12211	12241	12272	12303	12333	12364	12394	6
7	12060	12091	12120	12151	12181	12212	12242	12273	12304	12334	12365	12395	7
8	12061	12092	12121	12152	12182	12213	12243	12274	12305	12335	12366	12396	8
9	12062	12093	12122	12153	12183	12214	12244	12275	12306	12336	12367	12397	9
10	12063	12094	12123	12154	12184	12215	12245	12276	12307	12337	12368	12398	10
11	12064	12095	12124	12155	12185	12216	12246	12277	12308	12338	12369	12399	11
12	12065	12096	12125	12156	12186	12217	12247	12278	12309	12339	12370	12400	12
13	12066	12097	12126	12157	12187	12218	12248	12279	12310	12340	12371	12401	13
14	12067	12098	12127	12158	12188	12219	12249	12280	12311	12341	12372	12402	14
15	12068	12099	12128	12159	12189	12220	12250	12281	12312	12342	12373	12403	15
16	12069	12100	12129	12160	12190	12221	12251	12282	12313	12343	12374	12404	16
17	12070	12101	12130	12161	12191	12222	12252	12283	12314	12344	12375	12405	17
18	12071	12102	12131	12162	12192	12223	12253	12284	12315	12345	12376	12406	18
19	12072	12103	12132	12163	12193	12224	12254	12285	12316	12346	12377	12407	19
20	12073	12104	12133	12164	12194	12225	12255	12286	12317	12347	12378	12408	20
21	12074	12105	12134	12165	12195	12226	12256	12287	12318	12348	12379	12409	21
22	12075	12106	12135	12166	12196	12227	12257	12288	12319	12349	12380	12410	22
23	12076	12107	12136	12167	12197	12228	12258	12289	12320	12350	12381	12411	23
24	12077	12108	12137	12168	12198	12229	12259	12290	12321	12351	12382	12412	24
25	12078	12109	12138	12169	12199	12230	12260	12291	12322	12352	12383	12413	25
26	12079	12110	12139	12170	12200	12231	12261	12292	12323	12353	12384	12414	26
27	12080	12111	12140	12171	12201	12232	12262	12293	12324	12354	12385	12415	27
28	12081	12112	12141	12172	12202	12233	12263	12294	12325	12355	12386	12416	28
29	12082	12113	12142	12173	12203	12234	12264	12295	12326	12356	12387	12417	29
30	12083	xxxxx	12143	12174	12204	12235	12265	12296	12327	12357	12388	12418	30
31	12084	xxxxx	12144	xxxxx	12205	xxxxx	12266	12297	xxxxx	12358	xxxxx	12419	31

Figure T-27. 1976 Expiration Table

1977—EXPIRATION TABLE—1977

Day	Jan	Feb	Mar	Apr	May	Jun	Jul	Aug	Sep	Oct	Nov	Dec	Day
1	12420	12451	12479	12510	12540	12571	12601	12632	12663	12693	12724	12754	1
2	12421	12452	12480	12511	12541	12572	12602	12633	12664	12694	12725	12755	2
3	12422	12453	12481	12512	12542	12573	12603	12634	12665	12695	12726	12756	3
4	12423	12454	12482	12513	12543	12574	12604	12635	12666	12696	12727	12757	4
5	12424	12455	12483	12514	12544	12575	12605	12636	12667	12697	12728	12758	5
6	12425	12456	12484	12515	12545	12576	12606	12637	12668	12698	12729	12759	6
7	12426	12457	12485	12516	12546	12577	12607	12638	12669	12699	12730	12760	7
8	12427	12458	12486	12517	12547	12578	12608	12639	12670	12700	12731	12761	8
9	12428	12459	12487	12518	12548	12579	12609	12640	12671	12701	12732	12762	9
10	12429	12460	12488	12519	12549	12580	12610	12641	12672	12702	12733	12763	10
11	12430	12461	12489	12520	12550	12581	12611	12642	12673	12703	12734	12764	11
12	12431	12462	12490	12521	12551	12582	12612	12643	12674	12704	12735	12765	12
13	12432	12463	12491	12522	12552	12583	12613	12644	12675	12705	12736	12766	13
14	12433	12464	12492	12523	12553	12584	12614	12645	12676	12706	12737	12767	14
15	12434	12465	12493	12524	12554	12585	12615	12646	12677	12707	12738	12768	15
16	12435	12466	12494	12525	12555	12586	12616	12647	12678	12708	12739	12769	16
17	12436	12467	12495	12526	12556	12587	12617	12648	12679	12709	12740	12770	17
18	12437	12468	12496	12527	12557	12588	12618	12649	12680	12710	12741	12771	18
19	12438	12469	12497	12528	12558	12589	12619	12650	12681	12711	12742	12772	19
20	12439	12470	12498	12529	12559	12590	12620	12651	12682	12712	12743	12773	20
21	12440	12471	12499	12530	12560	12591	12621	12652	12683	12713	12744	12774	21
22	12441	12472	12500	12531	12561	12592	12622	12653	12684	12714	12745	12775	22
23	12442	12473	12501	12532	12562	12593	12623	12654	12685	12715	12746	12776	23
24	12443	12474	12502	12533	12563	12594	12624	12655	12686	12716	12747	12777	24
25	12444	12475	12503	12534	12564	12595	12625	12656	12687	12717	12748	12778	25
26	12445	12476	12504	12535	12565	12596	12626	12657	12688	12718	12749	12779	26
27	12446	12477	12505	12536	12566	12597	12627	12658	12689	12719	12750	12780	27
28	12447	12478	12506	12537	12567	12598	12628	12659	12690	12720	12751	12781	28
29	12448	xxxxx	12507	12538	12568	12599	12629	12660	12691	12721	12752	12782	29
30	12449	xxxxx	12508	12539	12569	12600	12630	12661	12692	12722	12753	12783	30
31	12450	xxxxx	12509	xxxxx	12570	xxxxx	12631	12662	xxxxx	12723	xxxxx	12784	31

Figure T-28. 1977 Expiration Table

1978—EXPIRATION TABLE—1978

Day	Jan	Feb	Mar	Apr	May	Jun	Jul	Aug	Sep	Oct	Nov	Dec	Day
1	12785	12816	12844	12875	12905	12936	12966	12997	13028	13058	13089	13119	1
2	12786	12817	12845	12876	12906	12937	12967	12998	13029	13059	13090	13120	2
3	12787	12818	12846	12877	12907	12938	12968	12999	13030	13060	13091	13121	3
4	12788	12819	12847	12878	12908	12939	12969	13000	13031	13061	13092	13122	4
5	12789	12820	12848	12879	12909	12940	12971	13001	13032	13062	13093	13123	5
6	12790	12821	12849	12880	12910	12941	12971	13002	13033	13063	13094	13124	6
7	12791	12822	12850	12881	12911	12942	12972	13003	13034	13064	13095	13125	7
8	12792	12823	12851	12882	12912	12943	12973	13004	13035	13065	13096	13126	8
9	12793	12824	12852	12883	12913	12944	12974	13005	13036	13066	13097	13127	9
10	12794	12825	12853	12884	12914	12945	12976	13006	13037	13067	13098	13128	10
11	12795	12826	12854	12885	12915	12946	12976	13007	13038	13068	13099	13129	11
12	12796	12827	12855	12886	12916	12947	12977	13008	13039	13069	13100	13130	12
13	12797	12828	12856	12887	12917	12948	12978	13009	13040	13070	13101	13131	13
14	12798	12829	12857	12888	12918	12949	12979	13010	13041	13071	13102	13132	14
15	12799	12830	12858	12889	12919	12950	12980	13011	13042	13072	13103	13133	15
16	12800	12831	12859	12890	12920	12951	12981	13012	13043	13073	13104	13134	16
17	12801	12832	12860	12891	12921	12952	12982	13013	13044	13074	13105	13135	17
18	12802	12833	12861	12892	12922	12953	12983	13014	13045	13075	13106	13136	18
19	12803	12834	12862	12893	12923	12954	12984	13015	13046	13076	13107	13137	19
20	12804	12835	12863	12894	12924	12955	12985	13016	13047	13077	13108	13138	20
21	12805	12836	12864	12895	12925	12956	12986	13017	13048	13078	13109	13139	21
22	12806	12837	12865	12896	12926	12957	12987	13018	13049	13079	13110	13140	22
23	12807	12838	12866	12897	12927	12958	12988	13019	13050	13080	13111	13141	23
24	12808	12839	12867	12898	12928	12959	12989	13020	13051	13081	13112	13142	24
25	12809	12840	12868	12899	12929	12960	12990	13021	13052	13082	13113	13143	25
26	12810	12841	12869	12900	12930	12961	12991	13022	13053	13083	13114	13144	26
27	12811	12842	12870	12901	12931	12962	12992	13023	13054	13084	13115	13145	27
28	12812	12843	12871	12902	12932	12963	12993	13024	13055	13085	13116	13146	28
29	12813	xxxxx	12872	12903	12933	12964	12994	13025	13056	13086	13117	13147	29
30	12814	xxxxx	12873	12904	12934	12965	12995	13026	13057	13087	13118	13148	30
31	12815	xxxxx	12874	xxxxx	12935	xxxxx	12996	13027	xxxxx	13088	xxxxx	13149	31

Figure T-29. 1978 Expiration Table

1979—EXPIRATION TABLE—1979

Day	Jan	Feb	Mar	Apr	May	Jun	Jul	Aug	Sep	Oct	Nov	Dec	Day
1	13150	13181	13209	13240	13270	13301	13331	13362	13393	13423	13454	13484	1
2	13151	13182	13210	13241	13271	13302	13332	13363	13394	13424	13455	13485	2
3	13152	13183	13211	13242	13272	13303	13333	13364	13395	13425	13456	13486	3
4	13153	13184	13212	13243	13273	13304	13334	13365	13396	13426	13457	13487	4
5	13154	13185	13213	13244	13274	13305	13335	13366	13397	13427	13458	13488	5
6	13155	13186	13214	13245	13275	13306	13336	13367	13398	13428	13459	13489	6
7	13156	13187	13215	13246	13276	13307	13337	13368	13399	13429	13460	13490	7
8	13157	13188	13216	13247	13277	13308	13338	13369	13400	13430	13461	13491	8
9	13158	13189	13217	13248	13278	13309	13339	13370	13401	13431	13462	13492	9
10	13159	13190	13218	13249	13279	13310	13340	13371	13402	13432	13463	13493	10
11	13160	13191	13219	13250	13280	13311	13341	13372	13403	13433	13464	13494	11
12	13161	13192	13220	13251	13281	13312	13342	13373	13404	13434	13465	13495	12
13	13162	13193	13221	13252	13282	13313	13343	13374	13405	13435	13466	13496	13
14	13163	13194	13222	13253	13283	13314	13344	13375	13406	13436	13467	13497	14
15	13164	13195	13223	13254	13284	13315	13345	13376	13407	13437	13468	13498	15
16	13165	13196	13224	13255	13285	13316	13346	13377	13408	13438	13469	13499	16
17	13166	13197	13225	13256	13286	13317	13347	13378	13409	13439	13470	13500	17
18	13167	13198	13226	13257	13287	13318	13348	13379	13410	13440	13471	13501	18
19	13168	13199	13227	13258	13288	13319	13349	13380	13411	13441	13472	13502	19
20	13169	13200	13228	13259	13289	13320	13350	13381	13412	13442	13473	13503	20
21	13170	13201	13229	13260	13290	13321	13351	13382	13413	13443	13474	13504	21
22	13171	13202	13230	13261	13291	13322	13352	13383	13414	13444	13475	13505	22
23	13172	13203	13231	13262	13292	13323	13353	13384	13415	13445	13476	13506	23
24	13173	13204	13232	13263	13293	13324	13354	13385	13416	13446	13477	13507	24
25	13174	13205	13233	13264	13294	13325	13355	13386	13417	13447	13478	13508	25
26	13175	13206	13234	13265	13295	13326	13356	13387	13418	13448	13479	13509	26
27	13176	13207	13235	13266	13296	13327	13357	13388	13419	13449	13480	13510	27
28	13177	13208	13236	13267	13297	13328	13358	13389	13420	13450	13481	13511	28
29	13178	xxxxx	13237	13268	13298	13329	13359	13390	13421	13451	13482	13512	29
30	13179	xxxxx	13238	13269	13299	13330	13360	13391	13422	13452	13483	13513	30
31	13180	xxxxx	13239	xxxxx	13300	xxxxx	13361	13392	xxxxx	13453	xxxxx	13514	31

Figure T-30. 1979 Expiration Table

Day	Jan	Feb	Mar	Apr	May	Jun	Jul	Aug	Sep	Oct	Nov	Dec	Day
1	13515	15546	13575	13606	13636	13667	13697	13728	13759	13789	13820	13850	1
2	13516	13547	13576	13607	13637	13668	13698	13729	13760	13790	13821	13851	2
3	13517	13548	13577	13608	13638	13669	13699	13730	13761	13791	13822	13852	3
4	13518	13549	13578	13609	13639	13670	13700	13731	13762	13792	13823	13853	4
5	13519	13550	13579	13610	13640	13671	13701	13732	13763	13793	13824	13854	5
6	13520	13551	13580	13611	13641	13672	13702	13733	13764	13794	13825	13855	6
7	13521	13552	13581	13612	13642	13673	13703	13734	13765	13795	13826	13856	7
8	13522	13553	13582	13613	13643	13674	13704	13735	13766	13796	13827	13857	8
9	13523	13554	13583	13614	13644	13675	13705	13736	13767	13797	13828	13858	9
10	13524	13555	13584	13615	13645	13676	13706	13737	13768	13798	13829	13859	10
11	13525	13556	13585	13616	13646	13677	13707	13738	13769	13799	13830	13860	11
12	13526	13557	13586	13617	13647	13678	13708	13739	13770	13800	13831	13861	12
13	13527	13558	13587	13618	13648	13679	13709	13740	13771	13801	13832	13862	13
14	13528	13559	13588	13619	13649	13680	13710	13741	13772	13802	13833	13863	14
15	13529	13560	13589	13620	13650	13681	13711	13742	13773	13803	13834	13864	15
16	13530	13561	13590	13621	13651	13682	13712	13743	13774	13804	13835	13865	16
17	13531	13562	13591	13622	13652	13683	13713	13744	13775	13805	13836	13866	17
18	13532	13563	13592	13623	13653	13684	13714	13745	13776	13806	13837	13867	18
19	13533	13564	13593	13624	13654	13685	13715	13746	13777	13807	13838	13868	19
20	13534	13565	13594	13625	13655	13686	13716	13747	13778	13808	13839	13869	20
21	13535	13566	13595	13626	13656	13687	13717	13748	13779	13809	13840	13870	21
22	13536	13567	13596	13627	13657	13688	13718	13749	13780	13810	13841	13871	22
23	13537	13568	13597	13628	13658	13689	13719	13750	13781	13811	13842	13872	23
24	13538	13569	13598	13629	13659	13690	13720	13751	13782	13812	13843	13873	24
25	13539	13570	13599	13630	13660	13691	13721	13752	13783	13813	13844	13874	25
26	13540	13571	13600	13631	13661	13692	13722	13753	13784	13814	13845	13875	26
27	13541	13572	13601	13632	13662	13693	13723	13754	13785	13815	13846	13876	27
28	13542	13573	13602	13633	13663	13694	13724	13755	13786	13816	13847	13877	28
29	13543	13574	13603	13634	13664	13695	13725	13756	13787	13817	13848	13878	29
30	13544	xxxxx	13604	13635	13665	13696	13726	13757	13788	13818	13849	13879	30
31	13545	xxxxx	13605	xxxxx	13666	xxxxx	13727	13758	xxxxx	13819	xxxxx	13880	31

Figure T-31. 1980 Expiration Table

Day	Jan	Feb	Mar	Apr	May	Jun	Jul	Aug	Sep	Oct	Nov	Dec	Day
1	13881	13912	13940	13971	14001	14032	14062	14093	14124	14154	14185	14215	1
2	13882	13913	13941	13972	14002	14033	14063	14094	14125	14155	14186	14216	2
3	13883	13914	13942	13973	14003	14034	14064	14095	14126	14156	14187	14217	3
4	13884	13915	13943	13974	14004	14035	14065	14096	14127	14157	14188	13218	4
5	13885	13916	13944	13975	14005	14036	14066	14097	14128	14158	14189	14219	5
6	13886	13917	13945	13976	14006	14037	14067	14098	14129	14159	14190	14220	6
7	13887	13918	13946	13977	14007	14038	14068	14099	14130	14160	14191	14221	7
8	13888	13919	13947	13978	14008	14039	14069	14100	14131	14161	14192	14222	8
9	13889	13920	13948	13979	14009	14040	14070	14101	14132	14162	14193	14223	9
10	13890	13921	13949	13980	14010	14041	14071	14102	14133	14163	14194	14224	10
11	13891	13922	13950	13981	14011	14042	14072	14103	14134	14164	14195	14225	11
12	13892	13923	13951	13982	14012	14043	14073	14104	14135	14165	14196	14226	12
13	13893	13924	13952	13983	14013	14044	14074	14105	14136	14166	14197	14227	13
14	13894	13925	13953	13984	14014	14045	14075	14106	14137	14167	14198	14228	14
15	13895	13926	13954	13985	14015	14046	14076	14107	14138	14168	14199	14229	15
16	13896	13927	13955	13986	14016	14047	14077	14108	14139	14169	14200	14230	16
17	13897	13928	13956	13987	14017	14048	14078	14109	14140	14170	14201	14231	17
18	13898	13929	13957	13988	14018	14049	14079	14110	14141	14171	14202	14232	18
19	13899	13930	13958	13989	14019	14050	14080	14111	14142	14172	14203	14233	19
20	13900	13931	13959	13990	14020	14051	14081	14112	14143	14173	14204	14234	20
21	13901	13932	13960	13991	14021	14052	14082	14113	14144	14174	14205	14235	21
22	13902	13933	13961	13992	14022	14053	14083	14114	14145	14175	14206	14236	22
23	13903	13934	13962	13993	14023	14054	14084	14115	14146	14176	14207	14237	23
24	13904	13935	13963	13994	14024	14055	14085	14116	14147	14177	14208	14238	24
25	13905	13936	13964	13995	14025	14056	14086	14117	14148	14178	14209	14239	25
26	13906	13937	13965	13996	14026	14057	14087	14118	14149	14179	14210	14240	26
27	13907	13938	13966	13997	14027	14058	14088	14119	14150	14180	14211	14241	27
28	13908	13939	13967	13998	14028	14059	14089	14120	14151	14181	14212	14242	28
29	13909	xxxxx	13968	13999	14029	14060	14090	14121	14152	14182	14213	14243	29
30	13910	xxxxx	13969	14000	14030	14061	14091	14122	14153	14183	14214	14244	30
31	13911	xxxxx	13970	xxxxx	14031	xxxxx	14092	14123	xxxxx	14184	xxxxx	14245	31

Figure T-32. 1981 Expiration Table

Day	Jan	Feb	Mar	Apr	May	Jun	Jul	Aug	Sep	Oct	Nov	Dec	Day
1	14246	14277	14305	14336	14366	14397	14427	14458	14489	14519	14550	14580	1
2	14247	14278	14306	14337	14367	14398	14428	14459	14490	14520	14551	14581	2
3	14248	14279	14307	14338	14368	14399	14429	14460	14491	14521	14552	14582	3
4	14249	14280	14308	14339	14369	14400	14430	14461	14492	14522	14553	14583	4
5	14250	14281	14309	14340	14370	14401	14431	14462	14493	14523	14554	14584	5
6	14251	14282	14310	14341	14371	14402	14432	14463	14494	14524	14555	14585	6
7	14252	14283	14311	14342	14372	14403	14433	14464	14495	14525	14556	14586	7
8	14253	14284	14312	14343	14373	14404	14434	14465	14496	14526	14557	14587	8
9	14254	14285	14313	14344	14374	14405	14435	14466	14497	14527	14558	14588	9
10	14255	14286	14314	14345	14375	14406	14436	14467	14498	14528	14559	14589	10
11	14256	14287	14315	14346	14376	14407	14437	14468	14499	14529	14560	14590	11
12	14257	14288	14316	14347	14377	14408	14438	14469	14500	14530	14561	14591	12
13	14258	14289	14317	14348	14378	14409	14439	14470	14501	14531	14562	14592	13
14	14259	14290	14318	14349	14379	14410	14440	14471	14502	14532	14563	14593	14
15	14260	14291	14319	14350	14380	14411	14441	14472	14503	14533	14564	14594	15
16	14261	14292	14320	14351	14381	14412	14442	14473	14504	14534	14565	14595	16
17	14262	14293	14321	14352	14382	14413	14443	14474	14505	14535	14566	14596	17
18	14263	14294	14322	14353	14383	14414	14444	14475	14506	14536	14567	14597	18
19	14264	14295	14323	14354	14384	14415	14445	14476	14507	14537	14568	14598	19
20	14265	14296	14324	14355	14385	14416	14446	14477	14508	14538	14569	14599	20
21	14266	14297	14325	14356	14386	14417	14447	14478	14509	14539	14570	14600	21
22	14267	14298	14326	14357	14387	14418	14448	14479	14510	14540	14571	14601	22
23	14268	14299	14327	14358	14388	14419	14449	14480	14511	14541	14572	14602	23
24	14269	14300	14328	14359	14389	14420	14450	14481	14512	14542	14573	14603	24
25	14270	14301	14329	14360	14390	14421	14451	14482	14513	14543	14574	14604	25
26	14271	14302	14330	14361	14391	14422	14452	14483	14514	14544	14575	14605	26
27	14272	14303	14331	14362	14392	14423	14453	14484	14515	14545	14576	14606	27
28	14273	14304	14332	14363	14393	14424	14454	14485	14516	14546	14577	14607	28
29	14274	xxxxx	14333	14364	14394	14425	14455	14486	14517	14547	14578	14608	29
30	14275	xxxxx	14334	14365	14395	14426	14456	14487	14518	14548	14579	14609	30
31	14276	xxxxx	14335	xxxxx	14396	xxxxx	14457	14488	xxxxx	14549	xxxxx	14610	31

Figure T-33. 1982 Expiration Table

1983—EXPIRATION TABLE—1983

Day	Jan	Feb	Mar	Apr	May	Jun	Jul	Aug	Sep	Oct	Nov	Dec	Day
1	14611	14642	14670	14701	14731	14762	14792	14823	14854	14884	14915	14945	1
2	14612	14643	14671	14702	14732	14763	14793	14824	14855	14885	14916	14946	2
3	14613	14644	14672	14703	14733	14764	14794	14825	14856	14886	14917	14947	3
4	14614	14645	14673	14704	14734	14765	14795	14826	14857	14887	14918	14948	4
5	14615	14646	14674	14705	14735	14766	14796	14827	14858	14888	14919	14949	5
6	14616	14647	14675	14706	14736	14767	14797	14828	14859	14889	14920	14950	6
7	14617	14648	14676	14707	14737	14768	14798	14829	14860	14890	14921	14951	7
8	14618	14649	14677	14708	14738	14769	14799	14830	14861	14891	14922	14952	8
9	14619	14650	14678	14709	14739	14770	14800	14831	14862	14892	14923	14953	9
10	14620	14651	14679	14710	14740	14771	14801	14832	14863	14893	14924	14954	10
11	14621	14652	14680	14711	14741	14772	14802	14833	14864	14894	14925	14955	11
12	14622	14653	14681	14712	14742	14773	14803	14834	14865	14895	14926	14956	12
13	14623	14654	14682	14713	14743	14774	14804	14835	14866	14896	14927	14957	13
14	14624	14655	14683	14714	14744	14775	14805	14836	14867	14897	14928	14958	14
15	14625	14656	14684	14715	14745	14776	14806	14837	14868	14898	14929	14959	15
16	14626	14657	14685	14716	14746	14777	14807	14838	14869	14899	14930	14960	16
17	14627	14658	14686	14717	14747	14778	14808	14839	14870	14900	14931	14961	17
18	14628	14659	14687	14718	14748	14779	14809	14840	14871	14901	14932	14962	18
19	14629	14660	14688	14719	14749	14780	14810	14841	14872	14902	14933	14963	19
20	14630	14661	14689	14720	14750	14781	14811	14842	14873	14903	14934	14964	20
21	14631	14662	14690	14721	14751	14782	14812	14843	14874	14904	14935	14965	21
22	14632	14663	14691	14722	14752	14783	14813	14844	14875	14905	14936	14966	22
23	14633	14664	14692	14723	14753	14784	14814	14845	14876	14906	14937	14967	23
24	14634	14665	14693	14724	14754	14785	14815	14846	14877	14907	14938	14968	24
25	14635	14666	14694	14725	14755	14786	14816	14847	14878	14908	14939	14969	25
26	14636	14667	14695	14726	14756	14787	14817	14848	14879	14909	14940	14970	26
27	14637	14668	14696	14727	14757	14788	14818	14849	14880	14910	14941	14971	27
28	14638	14669	14697	14728	14758	14789	14819	14850	14881	14911	14942	14972	28
29	14639	xxxxx	14698	14729	14759	14790	14820	14851	14882	14912	14943	14973	29
30	14640	xxxxx	14699	14730	14760	14791	14821	14852	14883	14913	14944	14974	30
31	14641	xxxxx	14700	xxxxx	14761	xxxxx	14822	14853	xxxxx	14914	xxxxx	14975	31

Figure T-34. 1983 Expiration Table

1984—EXPIRATION TABLE—1984

Day	Jan	Feb	Mar	Apr	May	Jun	Jul	Aug	Sep	Oct	Nov	Dec	Day
1	14976	15007	15036	15067	15097	15128	15158	15189	15220	15250	15281	15311	1
2	14977	15008	15037	15068	15098	15129	15159	15190	15221	15251	15282	15312	2
3	14978	15009	15038	15069	15099	15130	15160	15191	15222	15252	15283	15313	3
4	14979	15010	15039	15070	15100	15131	15161	15192	15223	15253	15284	15314	4
5	14980	15011	15040	15071	15101	15132	15162	15193	15224	15254	15285	15315	5
6	14981	15012	15041	15072	15102	15133	15163	15194	15225	15255	15286	15316	6
7	14982	15013	15042	15073	15103	15134	15164	15195	15226	15256	15287	15317	7
8	14983	15014	15043	15074	15104	15135	15165	15196	15227	15257	15288	15318	8
9	14984	15015	15044	15075	15105	15136	15166	16197	15228	15258	15289	15319	9
10	14985	15016	15045	15076	15106	15137	15167	15198	15229	15259	15290	15320	10
11	14986	15017	15046	15077	15107	15138	15168	15199	15230	15260	15291	15321	11
12	14987	15018	15047	15078	15108	15139	15169	15200	15231	15261	15292	15322	12
13	14988	15019	15048	15079	15109	15140	15170	15201	15232	15262	15293	15323	13
14	14989	15020	15049	15080	15110	15141	15171	15202	15233	15263	15294	15324	14
15	14990	15021	15050	15081	15111	15142	15172	15203	15234	15264	15295	15325	15
16	14991	15022	15051	15082	15112	15143	15173	15204	15235	15265	15296	15326	16
17	14992	15023	15052	15083	15113	15144	15174	15205	15236	15266	15297	15327	17
18	14993	15024	15053	15084	15114	15145	15175	15206	15237	15267	15298	15328	18
19	14994	15025	15054	15085	15115	15146	15176	15207	15238	15268	15299	15329	19
20	14995	15026	15055	15086	15116	15147	15177	15208	15239	15269	15300	15330	20
21	14996	15027	15056	15087	15117	15148	15178	15209	15240	15270	15301	15331	21
22	14997	15028	15057	15088	15118	15149	15179	15210	15241	15271	15302	15332	22
23	14998	15029	15058	15089	15119	15150	15180	15211	15242	15272	15303	15333	23
24	14999	15030	15059	15090	15120	15151	15181	15212	15243	15273	15304	15334	24
25	15000	15031	15060	15091	15121	15152	15182	15213	15244	15274	15305	15335	25
26	15001	15032	15061	15092	15122	15153	15183	15214	15245	15275	15306	15336	26
27	15002	15033	15062	15093	15123	15154	15184	15215	15246	15276	15307	15337	27
28	15003	15034	15063	15094	15124	15155	15185	15216	15247	15277	15308	15338	28
29	15004	15035	15064	15095	15125	15156	15186	15217	15248	15278	15309	15339	29
30	15005	xxxxx	15065	15096	15126	15157	15187	15218	15249	15279	15310	15340	30
31	15006	xxxxx	15066	xxxxx	15127	xxxxx	15188	15219	xxxxx	15280	xxxxx	15341	31

Figure T-35. 1984 Expiration Table

Day	Jan	Feb	Mar	Apr	May	Jun	Jul	Aug	Sep	Oct	Nov	Dec	Day
1	15342	15373	15401	15432	15462	15493	15523	15554	15585	15615	15646	15676	1
2	15343	15374	15402	15433	15463	15494	15524	15555	15586	15616	15647	15677	2
3	15344	15375	15403	15434	15464	15495	15525	15556	15587	15617	15648	15678	3
4	15345	15376	15404	15435	15465	15496	15526	15557	15588	15618	15649	15679	4
5	15346	15377	15405	15436	15466	15497	15527	15558	15589	15619	15650	15680	5
6	15347	15378	15406	15437	15467	15498	15528	15559	15590	15620	15651	15681	6
7	15348	15379	15407	15438	15468	15499	15529	15560	15591	15021	15652	15682	7
8	15349	15380	15408	15439	15469	15500	15530	15561	15592	15622	15653	15683	8
9	15350	15381	15409	15440	15470	15501	15531	15562	15593	15623	15654	15684	9
10	15351	15382	15410	15441	15471	15502	15532	15563	15594	15624	15655	15685	10
11	15352	15383	15411	15442	15472	15503	15533	15564	15595	15625	15656	15686	11
12	15353	15384	15412	15443	15473	15504	15534	15565	15596	15626	15657	15687	12
13	15354	15385	15413	15444	15474	15505	15535	15566	15597	15627	15658	15688	13
14	15355	15386	15414	15445	15475	15506	15536	15567	15598	15628	15659	15689	14
15	15356	15387	15415	15446	15476	15507	15537	15568	15599	15629	15660	15690	15
16	15357	15388	15416	15447	15477	15508	15538	15569	15600	15630	15661	15691	16
17	15358	15389	15417	15448	15478	15509	15539	15570	15601	15631	15662	15692	17
18	15359	15390	15418	15449	15479	15510	15540	15571	15602	15632	15663	15693	18
19	15360	15391	15419	15450	15480	15511	15541	15572	15603	15633	15664	15694	19
20	15361	15392	15420	15451	15481	15512	15542	15573	15604	15634	15665	15695	20
21	15362	15393	15421	15452	15482	15513	15543	15574	15605	15635	15666	15696	21
22	15363	15394	15422	15453	15483	15514	15544	15575	15606	15636	15667	15697	22
23	15364	15395	15423	15454	15484	15515	15545	15576	15607	15637	15668	15698	23
24	15365	15396	15424	15455	15485	15516	15546	15577	15608	15638	15669	15699	24
25	15366	15397	15425	15456	15486	15517	15547	15578	15609	15639	15670	15700	25
26	15367	15398	15426	15457	15487	15518	15548	15579	15610	15640	15671	15701	26
27	15368	15399	15427	15458	15488	15519	15549	15580	15611	15641	15672	15702	27
28	15369	15400	15428	15459	15489	15520	15550	15581	15612	15642	15673	15703	28
29	15370	xxxxx	15429	15460	15490	15521	15551	15582	15613	15643	15674	15704	29
30	15371	xxxxx	15430	15461	15491	15522	15552	15583	15614	15644	15675	15705	30
31	15372	xxxxx	15431	xxxxx	15492	xxxxx	15553	15584	xxxxx	15645	xxxxx	15706	31

Figure T-36. 1985 Expiration Table

Day	Jan	Feb	Mar	Apr	May	Jun	Jul	Aug	Sep	Oct	Nov	Dec	Day
1	15707	15738	15766	15797	15827	15858	15888	15919	15950	15980	16011	16041	1
2	15708	15739	15767	15798	15828	15859	15889	15920	15951	15981	16012	16042	2
3	15709	15740	15768	15799	15829	15860	15890	15921	15952	15982	16013	16043	3
4	15710	15741	15769	15800	15830	15861	15891	15922	15953	15983	16014	16044	4
5	15711	15742	15770	15801	15831	15862	15892	15928	15954	15984	16015	16045	5
6	15712	15743	15771	15802	15832	15863	15893	15924	15955	15985	16016	16046	6
7	15713	15744	15772	15803	15833	15864	15894	15925	15956	15986	16017	16047	7
8	15714	15745	15773	15804	15834	15865	15895	15926	15957	15987	16018	16048	8
9	15715	15746	15774	15805	15835	15866	15896	15927	15958	15988	16019	16049	9
10	15716	15747	15775	15806	15836	15867	15897	15928	15959	15989	16020	16050	10
11	15717	15748	15776	15807	15837	15868	15898	15929	15960	15990	16021	16051	11
12	15718	15749	15777	15808	15838	15869	15899	15930	15961	15991	16022	16052	12
13	15719	15750	15778	15809	15839	15870	15900	15931	15962	15992	16023	16053	13
14	15720	15751	15779	15810	15840	15871	15901	15932	15963	15993	16024	16054	14
15	15721	15752	15780	15811	15841	15872	15902	15933	15964	15994	16025	16055	15
16	15722	15753	15781	15812	15842	15873	15903	15934	15965	15995	16026	16056	16
17	15723	15754	15782	15813	15843	15874	15904	15935	15966	15996	16027	16057	17
18	15724	15755	15783	15814	15844	15875	15905	15936	15967	15997	16028	16058	18
19	15725	15756	15784	15815	15845	15876	15906	15937	15968	15998	16029	16059	19
20	15726	15757	15785	15816	15846	15877	15907	15938	15969	15999	16030	16060	20
21	15727	15758	15786	15817	15847	15878	15908	15939	15970	16000	16031	16061	21
22	15728	15759	15787	15818	15848	15879	15909	15940	15971	16001	16032	16062	22
23	15729	15760	15789	15819	15849	15880	15910	15941	15972	16002	16034	16063	23
24	15730	15761	15789	15820	15850	15881	15911	15942	15973	16003	16034	16064	24
25	15731	15762	15790	15821	15851	15882	15912	15943	15974	16004	16035	16065	25
26	15732	15763	15791	15822	15852	15883	15913	15944	15975	16005	16036	16066	26
27	15733	15764	15792	15823	15853	15884	15914	15945	15976	16006	16037	16067	27
28	15734	15765	15793	15824	15854	15885	15915	15946	15977	16007	16038	16068	28
29	15735	xxxxx	15794	15825	15855	15886	15916	15947	15978	16008	16039	16069	29
30	15736	xxxxx	15795	15826	15856	15887	15917	15948	15979	16009	16040	16070	30
31	15737	xxxxx	15796	xxxxx	15857	xxxxx	15918	15949	xxxxx	16010	xxxxx	16071	31

Figure T-37. 1986 Expiration Table

Day	Jan	Feb	Mar	Apr	May	Jun	Jul	Aug	Sep	Oct	Nov	Dec	Day
1	16072	16103	16131	16162	16192	16223	16253	16284	16315	16345	16376	16406	1
2	16073	16104	16132	16163	16193	16224	16254	16285	16316	16346	16377	16407	2
3	16074	16105	16133	16164	16194	16225	16255	16286	16317	16347	16378	16408	3
4	16075	16106	16134	16165	16195	16226	16256	16287	16318	16348	16379	16409	4
5	16076	16107	16135	16166	16196	16227	16257	16288	16319	16349	16380	16410	5
6	16077	16108	16136	16167	16197	16228	16258	16289	16320	16350	16381	16411	6
7	16078	16109	16137	16168	16198	16229	16259	16290	16321	16351	16382	16412	7
8	16079	16110	16138	16169	16199	16230	16260	16291	16322	16352	16383	16413	8
9	16080	16111	16139	16170	16200	16231	16261	16292	16323	16353	16384	16414	9
10	16081	16112	16140	16171	16201	16232	16262	16293	16324	16354	16385	16415	10
11	16082	16113	16141	16172	16202	16233	16263	16294	16325	16355	16386	16416	11
12	16083	16114	16142	16173	16203	16234	16264	16295	16326	16356	16387	16417	12
13	16084	16115	16143	16174	16204	16235	16265	16296	16327	16357	16388	16418	13
14	16085	16116	16144	16175	16205	16236	16266	16297	16328	16358	16389	16419	14
15	16086	16117	16145	16176	16296	16237	16267	16298	16329	16359	16390	16420	15
16	16087	16118	16146	16177	16207	16238	16268	16299	16330	16360	16391	16421	16
17	16088	16119	16147	16178	16208	16239	16269	16300	16331	16361	16392	16422	17
18	16089	16120	16148	16179	16209	16240	16270	16301	16332	16362	16393	16423	18
19	16090	16121	16149	16180	16210	16241	16271	16302	16333	16363	16394	16424	19
20	16091	16122	16150	16181	16211	16242	16272	16303	16334	16364	16395	16425	20
21	16092	16123	16151	16182	16212	16243	16273	16304	16335	16365	16396	16426	21
22	16093	16124	16152	16183	16213	16244	16274	16305	16336	16366	16397	16427	22
23	16094	16125	16153	16184	16214	16245	16275	16306	16337	16367	16398	16428	23
24	16095	16126	16154	16185	16215	16246	16276	16307	16338	16368	16399	16429	24
25	16096	16127	16155	16186	16216	16247	16277	16308	16339	16369	16400	16430	25
26	16097	16128	16156	16187	16217	16248	16278	16309	16340	16370	16401	16431	26
27	16098	16129	16157	16188	16218	16249	16279	16310	16341	16371	16402	16432	27
28	16099	16130	16158	16189	16219	16250	16280	16311	16342	16372	16403	16433	28
29	16100	xxxxx	16159	16190	16220	16251	16281	16312	16343	16373	16404	16434	29
30	16101	xxxxx	16160	16191	16221	16252	16282	16313	16344	16374	16405	16435	30
31	16102	xxxxx	16161	xxxxx	16222	xxxxx	16283	16314	xxxxx	16375	xxxxx	16436	31

Figure T-38. 1987 Expiration Table

Day	Jan	Feb	Mar	Apr	May	Jun	Jul	Aug	Sep	Oct	Nov	Dec	Day
1	16437	16468	16497	16528	16558	16589	16619	16650	16681	16711	16742	16772	1
2	16438	16469	16498	16529	16559	16590	16620	16651	16682	16712	16743	16773	2
3	16439	16470	16499	16530	16560	16591	16621	16652	16683	16713	16744	16774	3
4	16440	16471	16500	16531	16561	16592	16622	16653	16684	16714	16745	16775	4
5	16441	16472	16501	16532	16562	16593	16623	16654	16685	16715	16746	16776	5
6	16442	16473	16502	16533	16563	16594	16624	16655	16686	16716	16747	16777	6
7	16443	16474	16503	16534	16564	16595	16625	16656	16687	16717	16748	16778	7
8	16444	16475	16504	16535	16565	16596	16626	16657	16688	16718	16749	16779	8
9	16445	16476	16505	16536	16566	16597	16627	16658	16689	16719	16750	16780	9
10	16446	16477	16506	16537	16567	16598	16628	16659	16690	16720	16751	16781	10
11	16447	16478	16507	16538	16568	16599	16629	16660	16691	16721	16752	16782	11
12	16448	16479	16508	16539	16569	16600	16630	16661	16692	17622	16753	16783	12
13	16449	16480	16509	16540	16570	16601	16631	16662	16693	16723	16754	16784	13
14	16450	16481	16510	16541	16571	16602	16632	16663	16694	16724	16755	16785	14
15	16451	16482	16511	16542	16572	16603	16633	16664	16695	16725	16756	16786	15
16	16452	16483	16512	16543	16573	16604	16634	16665	16696	16726	16757	16787	16
17	16453	16484	16513	16544	16574	16605	16635	16666	16697	16727	16758	16788	17
18	16454	16485	16514	16545	16575	16606	16636	16667	16698	16728	16759	16789	18
19	16455	16486	16515	16546	16576	16607	16637	16668	16699	16729	16760	16790	19
20	16456	16487	16516	16547	16577	16608	16638	16669	16700	16730	16761	16791	20
21	16457	16488	16517	16548	16578	16609	16639	16670	16701	16731	16762	16792	21
22	16458	16489	16518	16549	16579	16610	16640	16671	16702	16732	16763	16793	22
23	16459	16490	16519	16550	16580	16611	16641	16672	16703	16733	16764	16794	23
24	16460	16491	16520	16551	16581	16612	16642	16673	16704	16734	16765	16795	24
25	16461	16492	16521	16552	16582	16613	16643	16674	16705	16735	16766	16796	25
26	16462	16493	16522	16553	16583	16614	16644	16675	16706	16736	16767	16797	26
27	16463	16494	16523	16554	16584	16615	16645	16676	16707	16737	16768	16798	27
28	16464	16495	16524	16555	16585	16616	16646	16677	16708	16738	16769	16799	28
29	16465	16496	16525	16556	16586	16617	16647	16678	16709	16739	16770	16800	29
30	16466	xxxxx	16526	16557	16587	16618	16648	16679	16710	16740	16771	16801	30
31	16467	xxxxx	16527	xxxxx	16588	xxxxx	16649	16680	xxxxx	16741	xxxxx	16802	31

Figure T-39. 1988 Expiration Table

1989—EXPIRATION TABLE—1989

Day	Jan	Feb	Mar	Apr	May	Jun	Jul	Aug	Sep	Oct	Nov	Dec	Day
1	16803	16834	16862	16893	16923	16954	16984	17015	17046	17076	17107	17137	1
2	16804	16835	16863	16894	16924	16955	16985	17016	17047	17077	17108	17138	2
3	16805	16836	16864	16895	16925	16956	16986	17017	17048	17078	17109	17139	3
4	16806	16837	16865	16896	16926	16957	16987	17018	17049	17079	17110	17140	4
5	16807	16838	16866	16897	16927	16958	16988	17019	17050	17080	17111	17141	5
6	16808	16839	16867	16898	16928	16959	16989	17020	17051	17081	17112	17142	6
7	16809	16840	16868	16899	16929	16960	16990	17021	17052	17082	17113	17143	7
8	16810	16841	16869	16900	16930	16961	16991	17022	17053	17083	17114	17144	8
9	16811	16842	16870	16901	16931	16962	16992	17023	17054	17084	17115	17145	9
10	16812	16843	16871	16902	16932	16963	16993	17024	17055	17085	17116	17146	10
11	16813	16844	16872	16903	16933	16964	16994	17025	17056	17086	17117	17147	11
12	16814	16845	16873	16904	16934	16965	16995	17026	17057	17087	17118	17148	12
13	16815	16846	16874	16905	16935	16966	16996	17027	17058	17088	17119	17149	13
14	16816	16847	16875	16906	16936	16967	16997	17028	17059	17089	17120	17150	14
15	16817	16848	16876	16907	16937	16968	16998	17029	17060	17090	17121	17151	15
16	16818	16849	16877	16908	16938	16969	16999	17030	17061	17091	17122	17152	16
17	16819	16850	16878	16909	16939	16970	17000	17031	17062	17092	17123	17153	17
18	16820	16851	16879	16910	16940	16971	17001	17032	17063	17093	17124	17154	18
19	16821	16852	16880	16911	16941	16972	17002	17033	17064	17094	17125	17155	19
20	16822	16853	16881	16912	16942	16973	17003	17034	17065	17095	17126	17156	20
21	16823	16854	16882	16913	16943	16974	17004	17035	17066	17096	17127	17157	21
22	16824	16855	16883	16914	16944	16975	17005	17036	17067	17097	17128	17158	22
23	16825	16856	16884	16915	16945	16976	17006	17037	17068	17098	17129	17159	23
24	16826	16857	16885	16916	16946	16977	17007	17038	17069	17099	17130	17160	24
25	16827	16858	16886	16917	16947	16978	17008	17039	17070	17100	17131	17161	25
26	16828	16859	16887	16918	16948	16979	17009	17040	17071	17101	17132	17162	26
27	16829	16860	16888	16919	16949	16980	17010	17041	17072	17102	17133	17163	27
28	16830	16861	16889	16920	16950	16981	17011	17042	17073	17103	17134	17164	28
29	16831	xxxxx	16890	16921	16951	16982	17012	17043	17074	17104	17135	17165	29
30	16832	xxxxx	16891	16922	16952	16983	17013	17044	17075	17105	17136	17166	30
31	16833	xxxxx	16892	xxxxx	16953	xxxxx	17014	17045	xxxxx	17106	xxxxx	17167	31

Figure T-40. 1989 Expiration Table

Day	Jan	Feb	Mar	Apr	May	Jun	Jul	Aug	Sep	Oct	Nov	Dec	Day
1	17168	17199	17227	17258	17288	17319	17349	17380	17411	17441	17472	17502	1
2	17169	17200	17228	17259	17289	17320	17350	17381	17412	17442	17473	17503	2
3	17170	17201	17229	17260	17290	17321	17351	17382	17413	17443	17474	17504	3
4	17171	17202	17230	17261	17291	17322	17352	17383	17414	17444	17475	17505	4
5	17172	17203	17231	17262	17292	17323	17353	17384	17415	17445	17476	17506	5
6	17173	17204	17232	17263	17293	17324	17354	17385	17416	17446	17477	17507	6
7	17174	17205	17233	17264	17294	17325	17355	17386	17417	17447	17478	17508	7
8	17175	17206	17234	17265	17295	17326	17356	17387	17418	17448	17479	17509	8
9	17176	17207	17235	17266	17296	17327	17357	17388	17419	17449	17480	17510	9
10	17177	17208	17236	17267	17297	17328	17358	17389	17420	17450	17481	17511	10
11	17178	17209	17237	17268	17298	17329	17359	17390	17421	17451	17482	17512	11
12	17179	17210	17238	17269	17299	17330	17360	17391	17422	17452	17483	17513	12
13	17180	17211	17239	17270	17300	17331	17361	17392	17423	17453	17484	17514	13
14	17181	17212	17240	17271	17301	17332	17362	17393	17424	17454	17485	17515	14
15	17182	17213	17241	17272	17302	17333	17363	17394	17425	17455	17486	17516	15
16	17183	17214	17242	17273	17303	17334	17364	17395	17426	17456	17487	17517	16
17	17184	17215	17243	17274	17304	17335	17365	17396	17427	17457	17488	17518	17
18	17185	17216	17244	17275	17305	17336	17366	17397	17428	17458	17489	17519	18
19	17186	17217	17245	17276	17306	17337	17367	17398	17429	17459	17490	17520	19
20	17187	17218	17246	17277	17307	17338	17368	17399	17430	17460	17491	17521	20
21	17188	17219	17247	17278	17308	17339	17369	17400	17431	17461	17492	17522	21
22	17189	17220	17248	17279	17309	17340	17370	17401	17432	17462	17493	17523	22
23	17190	17221	17249	17280	17310	17341	17371	17402	17433	17463	17494	17524	23
24	17191	17222	17250	17281	17311	17342	17372	17403	17434	17464	17495	17525	24
25	17192	17223	17251	17282	17312	17343	17373	17404	17435	17465	17496	17526	25
26	17193	17224	17252	17283	17313	17344	17374	17405	17436	17466	17497	17527	26
27	17194	17225	17253	17284	17314	17345	17375	17406	17437	17467	17498	17528	27
28	17195	17226	17254	17285	17315	17346	17376	17407	17438	17468	17499	17529	28
29	17196	xxxxx	17255	17286	17316	17347	17377	17408	17439	17469	17500	17530	29
30	17197	xxxxx	17256	17287	17317	17348	17378	17409	17440	17470	17501	17531	30
31	17198	xxxxx	17257	xxxxx	17318	xxxxx	17379	17410	xxxxx	17471	xxxxx	17532	31

Figure T-41. 1990 Expiration Table

1991—EXPIRATION TABLE—1991

Day	Jan	Feb	Mar	Apr	May	Jun	Jul	Aug	Sep	Oct	Nov	Dec	Day
1	17533	17564	17592	17623	17653	17684	17714	17745	17776	17806	17837	17867	1
2	17534	17565	17593	17624	17654	17685	17715	17746	17777	17807	17838	17868	2
3	17535	17566	17594	17625	17655	17686	17716	17747	17778	17808	17839	17869	3
4	17536	17567	17595	17626	17656	17687	17717	17748	17779	17809	17840	17870	4
5	17537	17568	17596	17627	17657	17688	17718	17749	17780	17810	17841	17871	5
6	17538	17569	17597	17628	17658	17689	17719	17750	17781	17811	17842	17872	6
7	17539	17570	17598	17629	17659	17690	17720	17751	17782	17812	17843	17873	7
8	17540	17571	17599	17630	17660	17691	17721	17752	17783	17813	17844	17874	8
9	17541	17572	17600	17631	17661	17692	17722	17753	17784	17814	17845	17875	9
10	17542	17573	17601	17632	17662	17693	17723	17754	17785	17815	17846	17876	10
11	17543	17574	17602	17633	17663	17694	17724	17755	17786	17816	17847	17877	11
12	17544	17575	17603	17634	17664	17695	17725	17756	17787	17817	17848	17878	12
13	17545	17576	17604	17635	17665	17696	17726	17757	17788	17818	17849	17879	13
14	17546	17577	17605	17636	17666	17697	17727	17758	17789	17819	17850	17880	14
15	17547	17578	17606	17637	17667	17698	17728	17759	17790	17820	17851	17881	15
16	17548	17579	17607	17638	17668	17699	17729	17760	17791	17821	17852	17882	16
17	17549	17580	17608	17639	17669	17700	17730	17761	17792	17822	17853	17883	17
18	17550	17581	17609	17640	17670	17701	17731	17762	17793	17823	17854	17884	18
19	17551	17582	17610	17641	17671	17702	17732	17763	17794	17824	17855	17885	19
20	17552	17583	17611	17642	17672	17703	17733	17764	17795	17825	17856	17886	20
21	17553	17584	17612	17643	17673	17704	17734	17765	17796	17826	17857	17887	21
22	17554	17585	17613	17644	17674	17705	17735	17766	17797	17827	17858	17888	22
23	17555	17586	17614	17645	17675	17706	17736	17767	17798	17828	17859	17889	22
24	17556	17587	17615	17646	17676	17707	17737	17768	17799	17829	17860	17890	24
25	17557	17588	17616	17647	17677	17708	17738	17769	17800	17830	17861	17891	25
26	17558	17589	17617	17648	17678	17709	17739	17770	17801	17831	17862	17892	26
27	17559	17590	17618	17649	17679	17710	17740	17771	17802	17832	17863	17893	27
28	17560	17591	17619	17650	17680	17711	17741	17772	17803	17833	17864	17894	28
29	17561	xxxxx	17620	17651	17681	17712	17742	17773	17804	17834	17865	17895	29
30	17562	xxxxx	17621	17652	17682	17713	17743	17774	17805	17835	17866	17896	30
31	17563	xxxxx	17622	xxxxx	17683	xxxxx	17744	17775	xxxxx	17836	xxxxx	17897	31

Figure T-42. 1991 Expiration Table

Day	Jan	Feb	Mar	Apr	May	Jun	Jul	Aug	Sep	Oct	Nov	Dec	Day
1	17898	17929	17958	17989	18019	18050	18080	18111	18142	18172	18203	18233	1
2	17899	17930	17959	17990	18020	18051	18081	18112	18143	18173	18204	18234	2
3	17900	17931	17960	17991	18021	18052	18082	18113	18144	18174	18205	18235	3
4	17901	17932	17961	17992	18022	18053	18083	18114	18145	18175	18206	18236	4
5	17902	17933	17962	17993	18023	18054	18084	18115	18146	18176	18207	18237	5
6	17903	17934	17963	17994	18024	18055	18085	18116	18147	18177	18208	18238	6
7	17904	17935	17964	17995	18025	18056	18086	18117	18148	18178	18209	18239	7
8	17905	17936	17965	17996	18026	18057	18087	18118	18149	18179	18210	18240	8
9	17906	17937	17966	17997	18027	18058	18088	18119	18150	18180	18211	18241	9
10	17907	17938	17967	17998	18028	18059	18089	18120	18151	18181	18212	18242	10
11	17908	17939	17968	17999	18029	18060	18090	18121	18152	18182	18213	18243	11
12	17909	17940	17969	18000	18030	18061	18091	18122	18153	18183	18214	18244	12
13	17910	17941	17970	18001	18031	18062	18092	18123	18154	18184	18215	18245	13
14	17911	17942	17971	18002	18032	18063	18093	18124	18155	18185	18216	18246	14
15	17912	17943	17972	18003	18033	18064	18094	18125	18156	18186	18217	18247	15
16	17913	17944	17973	18004	18034	18065	18095	18126	18157	18187	18218	18248	16
17	17914	17945	17974	18005	18035	18066	18096	18127	18158	18188	18219	18249	17
18	17915	17946	17975	18006	18036	18067	18097	18128	18159	18189	18220	18250	18
19	17916	17947	17976	18007	18037	18068	18098	18129	18160	18190	18221	18251	19
20	17917	17948	17977	18008	18038	18069	18099	18130	18161	18191	18222	18252	20
21	17918	17949	17978	18009	18039	18070	18100	18131	18162	18192	18223	18253	21
22	17919	17950	17979	18010	18040	18071	18101	18132	18163	18193	18224	18254	22
23	17920	17951	17980	18011	18041	18072	18102	18133	18164	18194	18225	18255	23
24	17921	17952	17981	18012	18042	18073	18103	18134	18165	18195	18226	18256	24
25	17922	17953	17982	18013	18043	18074	18104	18135	18166	18196	18227	18257	25
26	17923	17954	17983	18014	18044	18075	18105	18136	18167	18197	18228	18258	26
27	17924	17955	17984	18015	18045	18076	18106	18137	18168	18198	18229	18259	27
28	17925	17956	17985	18016	18046	18077	18107	18138	18169	18199	18230	18260	28
29	17926	17957	17986	18017	18047	18078	18108	18139	18170	18200	18231	18261	29
30	17927	xxxxx	17987	18018	18048	18079	18109	18140	18171	18201	18232	18262	30
31	17928	xxxxx	17988	xxxxx	18049	xxxxx	18110	18141	xxxxx	18202	xxxxx	18263	31

Figure T-43. 1992 Expiration Table

Day	Jan	Feb	Mar	Apr	May	Jun	Jul	Aug	Sep	Oct	Nov	Dec	Day
1	18264	18295	18323	18354	18384	18415	18445	18476	18507	18537	18568	18598	1
2	18265	18296	18324	18355	18385	18416	18446	18477	18508	18538	18569	18599	2
3	18266	18297	18325	18356	18386	18417	18447	18478	18509	18539	18570	18600	3
4	18267	18298	18326	18357	18387	18418	18448	18479	18510	18540	18571	18601	4
5	18268	18299	18327	18358	18388	18419	18449	18480	18511	18541	18572	18602	5
6	18269	18300	18328	18359	18389	18420	18450	18481	18512	18542	18573	18603	6
7	18270	18301	18329	18360	18390	18421	18451	18482	18513	18543	18574	18604	7
8	18271	18302	18330	18361	18391	18422	18452	18483	18514	18544	18575	18605	8
9	18272	18303	18331	18362	18392	18423	18453	18484	18515	18545	18576	18606	9
10	18273	18304	18332	18363	18393	18424	18454	18485	18516	18546	18577	18607	10
11	18274	18305	18333	18364	18394	18425	18455	18486	18517	18547	18578	18608	11
12	18275	18306	18334	18365	18395	18426	18456	18487	18518	18548	18579	18609	12
13	18276	18307	18335	18366	18396	18427	18457	18488	18519	18549	18580	18610	13
14	18277	18308	18336	18367	18397	18428	18458	18489	18520	18550	18581	18611	14
15	18278	18309	18337	18368	18398	18429	18459	18490	18521	18551	18582	18612	15
16	18279	18310	18338	18369	18399	18430	18460	18491	18522	18552	18583	18613	16
17	18280	18311	18339	18370	18400	18431	18461	18492	18523	18553	18584	18614	17
18	18281	18312	18340	18371	18401	18432	18462	18493	18524	18554	18585	18615	18
19	18282	18313	18341	18372	18402	18433	18463	18494	18525	18555	18586	18616	19
20	18283	18314	18342	18373	18403	18434	18464	18495	18526	18556	18587	18617	20
21	18284	18315	18343	18374	18404	18435	18465	18496	18527	18557	18588	18618	21
22	18285	18316	18344	18375	18405	18436	18466	18497	18528	18558	18589	18619	22
23	18286	18317	18345	18376	18406	18437	18467	18498	18529	18559	18590	18620	23
24	18287	18318	18346	18377	18407	18438	18468	18499	18530	18560	18591	18621	24
25	18288	18319	18347	18378	18408	18439	18469	18500	18531	18561	18592	18622	25
26	18289	18320	18348	18379	18409	18440	18470	18501	18532	18562	18593	18623	26
27	18290	18321	18349	18380	18410	18441	18471	18502	18533	18563	18594	18624	27
28	18291	18322	18350	18381	18411	18442	18472	18503	18534	18564	18595	18625	28
29	18292	xxxxx	18351	18382	18412	18443	18473	18504	18535	18565	18596	18626	29
30	18293	xxxxx	18352	18383	18413	18444	18474	18505	18536	18566	18597	18627	30
31	18294	xxxxx	18353	xxxxx	18414	xxxxx	18475	18506	xxxxx	18567	xxxxx	18628	31

Figure T-44. 1993 Expiration Table

Day	Jan	Feb	Mar	Apr	May	Jun	Jul	Aug	Sep	Oct	Nov	Dec	Day
1	18629	18660	18688	18719	18749	18780	18810	18841	18872	18902	18933	18963	1
2	18630	18661	18689	18720	18750	18781	18811	18842	18873	18903	18934	18964	2
3	18631	18662	18690	18721	18751	18782	18812	18843	18874	18904	18935	18965	3
4	18632	18663	18691	18722	18752	18783	18813	18844	18875	18905	18936	18966	4
5	18633	18664	18692	18723	18753	18784	18814	18845	18876	18906	18937	18967	5
6	18634	18665	18693	18724	18754	18785	18815	18846	18877	18907	18938	18968	6
7	18635	18666	18694	18725	18755	18786	18816	18847	18878	18908	18939	18969	7
8	18636	18667	18695	18726	18756	18787	18817	18848	18879	18909	18940	18970	8
9	18637	18668	18696	18727	18757	18788	18818	18849	18880	18910	18941	18971	9
10	18638	18669	18697	18728	18758	18789	18819	18850	18881	18911	18942	18972	10
11	18639	18670	18698	18729	18759	18790	18820	18851	18882	18912	18943	18973	11
12	18640	18671	18699	18730	18760	18791	18821	18852	18883	18913	18944	18974	12
13	18641	18672	18700	18731	18761	18792	18822	18853	18884	18914	18945	18975	13
14	18642	18673	18701	18732	18762	18793	18823	18854	18885	18915	18946	18976	14
15	18643	18674	18702	18733	18763	18794	18824	18855	18886	18916	18947	18977	15
16	18644	18675	18703	18734	18764	18795	18825	18856	18887	18917	18948	18978	16
17	18645	18676	18704	18735	18765	18796	18826	18857	18888	18918	18949	18979	17
18	18646	18677	18705	18736	18766	18797	18827	18858	18889	18919	18950	18980	18
19	18647	18678	18706	18737	18767	18798	18828	18859	18890	18920	18951	18981	19
20	18648	18679	18707	18738	18768	18799	18829	18860	18891	18921	18952	18982	20
21	18649	18680	18708	18739	18769	18800	18830	18861	18892	18922	18953	18983	21
22	18650	18681	18709	18740	18770	18801	18831	18862	18893	18923	18954	18984	22
23	18651	18682	18710	18741	18771	18802	18832	18863	18894	18924	18955	18985	23
24	18652	18683	18711	18742	18772	18803	18833	18864	18895	18925	18956	18986	24
25	18653	18684	18712	18743	18773	18804	18834	18865	18896	18926	18957	18987	25
26	18654	18685	18713	18744	18774	18805	18835	18866	18897	18927	18958	18988	26
27	18655	18686	18714	18745	18775	18806	18836	18867	18898	18928	18959	18989	27
28	18656	18687	18715	18746	18776	18807	18837	18868	18899	18929	18960	18990	28
29	18657	xxxxx	18716	18747	18777	18808	18838	18869	18900	18930	18961	18991	29
30	18658	xxxxx	18717	18748	18778	18809	18839	18870	18901	18931	18962	18992	30
31	18659	xxxxx	18718	xxxxx	18779	xxxxx	18840	18871	xxxxx	18932	xxxxx	18993	31

Figure T-45. 1994 Expiration Table

Day	Jan	Feb	Mar	Apr	May	Jun	Jul	Aug	Sep	Oct	Nov	Dec	Day
1	18994	19025	19053	19084	19114	19145	19175	19206	19237	19267	19298	19328	1
2	18995	19026	19054	19085	19115	19146	19176	19207	19238	19268	19299	10329	2
3	18996	19027	19055	19086	19116	19147	19177	19208	19239	19269	19300	19330	3
4	18997	19028	19056	19087	19117	19148	19178	19209	19240	19270	19301	19331	4
5	18998	19029	19057	19088	19118	19149	19179	19210	19241	19271	19302	19332	5
6	18999	19030	19058	19089	19119	19150	19180	19211	19242	19272	19303	19333	6
7	19000	19031	19059	19090	19120	19151	19181	19212	19243	19273	19304	19334	7
8	19001	19032	19060	19091	19121	19152	19182	19213	19244	19274	19305	19335	8
9	19002	19033	19061	19092	19122	19153	19183	19214	19245	19275	19306	19336	9
10	19003	19034	19062	19093	19123	19154	19184	19215	19246	19276	19307	19337	10
11	19004	19035	19063	19094	19124	19155	19185	19216	19247	19277	19308	19338	11
12	19005	19036	19064	19095	19125	19156	19186	19217	19248	19278	19309	19339	12
13	19006	19037	19065	19096	19126	19157	19187	19218	19249	19279	19310	19340	13
14	19007	19038	19066	19097	19127	19158	19188	19219	19250	19280	19311	19341	14
15	19008	19039	19067	19098	19128	19159	19189	19220	19251	19281	19312	19342	15
16	19009	19040	19068	19099	19129	19160	19190	19221	19252	19282	19313	19343	16
17	19010	19041	19069	19100	19130	19161	19191	19222	19253	19283	19314	19344	17
18	19011	19042	19070	19101	19131	19162	19192	19223	19254	19284	19315	19345	18
19	19012	19043	19071	19102	19132	19163	19193	19224	19255	19285	19316	19346	19
20	19013	19044	19072	19103	19133	19164	19194	19225	19256	19286	19317	19347	20
21	19014	19045	19073	19104	19134	19165	19195	19226	19257	19287	19318	19348	21
22	19015	19046	19074	19105	19135	19166	19196	19227	19258	19288	19319	19349	22
23	19016	19047	19075	19106	19136	19167	19197	19228	19259	19289	19320	19350	23
24	19017	19048	19076	19107	19137	19168	19198	19229	19260	19290	19321	19351	24
25	19018	19049	19077	19108	19138	19169	19199	19230	19261	19291	19322	19352	25
26	19019	19050	19078	19109	19139	19170	19200	19231	19262	19292	19323	19353	26
27	19020	19051	19079	19110	19140	19171	19201	19232	19263	19293	19324	19354	27
28	19021	19252	19080	19111	19141	19172	19202	19233	19264	19294	19325	19355	28
29	19022	-------	19081	19112	19142	19173	19203	19234	19265	19295	19326	19356	29
30	19023	-------	19082	19113	19143	19174	19204	19235	19266	19296	19327	19357	30
31	19024	-------	19083	-------	19144	-------	19205	19236	-------	19297	-------	19358	31

Figure T-46. 1995 Expiration Table

1996 Expiration Table 1996

Day	Jan	Feb	Mar	Apr	May	Jun	Jul	Aug	Sep	Oct	Nov	Dec	Day
1	19359	19390	19419	19450	19480	19511	19541	19572	19603	19633	19664	19694	1
2	19360	19391	19420	19451	19481	19512	19542	19573	19604	19634	19665	19695	2
3	19361	19392	19421	19452	19482	19513	19543	19574	19605	19635	19666	19696	3
4	19362	19393	19422	19453	19483	19514	19544	19575	19606	19636	19667	19697	4
5	19363	19394	19423	19454	19484	19515	19545	19576	19607	19637	19668	19698	5
6	19364	19395	19424	19455	19485	19516	19546	19577	19608	19638	19669	19699	6
7	19365	19396	19425	19456	19486	19517	19547	19578	19609	19639	19670	19700	7
8	19366	19397	19426	19457	19487	19518	19548	19579	19610	19640	19671	19701	8
9	19367	19398	19427	19458	19488	19519	19549	19580	19611	19641	19672	19702	9
10	19368	19399	19428	19459	19489	19520	19550	19581	19612	19642	19673	19703	10
11	19369	19400	19429	19460	19490	19521	19551	19582	19613	19643	19674	19704	11
12	19370	19401	19430	19461	19491	19522	19552	19583	19614	19644	19675	19705	12
13	19371	19402	19431	19462	19492	19523	19553	19584	19615	19645	19676	19706	13
14	19372	19403	19432	19463	19493	19524	19554	19585	19616	19646	19677	19707	14
15	19373	19404	19433	19464	19494	19525	19555	19586	19617	19647	19678	19708	15
16	19374	19405	19434	19465	19495	19526	19556	19587	19618	19648	19679	19709	16
17	19375	19406	19435	19466	19496	19527	19557	19588	19619	19649	19680	19710	17
18	19376	19407	19436	19467	19497	19528	19558	19589	19620	19650	19681	19711	18
19	19377	19408	19437	19468	19498	19529	19559	19590	19621	19651	19682	19712	19
20	19378	19409	19438	19469	19499	19530	19560	19591	19622	19652	19683	19713	20
21	19379	19410	19439	19470	19500	19531	19561	19592	19623	19653	19684	19714	21
22	19380	19411	19440	19471	19501	19532	19562	19593	19624	19654	19685	19715	22
23	19381	19412	19441	19472	19502	19533	19563	19594	19625	19655	19686	19716	23
24	19382	19413	19442	19473	19503	19534	19564	19595	19626	19656	19687	19717	24
25	19383	19414	19443	19474	19504	19535	19565	19596	19627	19657	19688	19718	25
26	19384	19415	19444	19475	19505	19536	19566	19597	19628	19658	19689	19719	26
27	19385	19416	19445	19476	19506	19537	19567	19598	19629	19659	19690	19720	27
28	19386	19417	19446	19477	19507	19538	19568	19599	19630	19660	19691	19721	28
29	19387	19418	19447	19478	19508	19539	19569	19600	19631	19661	19692	19722	29
30	19388	-------	19448	19479	19509	19540	19570	19601	19632	19662	19693	19723	30
31	19389	-------	19449	-------	19510	-------	19571	19602	-------	19663	-------	19724	31

Figure T-47. 1996 Expiration Table

1997 Expiration Table 1997

Day	Jan	Feb	Mar	Apr	May	Jun	Jul	Aug	Sep	Oct	Nov	Dec	Day
1	19725	19756	19784	19815	19845	19876	19906	19937	19968	19998	20029	20059	1
2	19726	19757	19785	19816	19846	19877	19907	19938	19969	19999	20030	20060	2
3	19727	19758	19786	19817	19847	19878	19908	19939	19970	20000	20031	20061	3
4	19728	19759	19787	19818	19848	19879	19909	19940	19971	20001	20032	20062	4
5	19729	19760	19788	19819	19849	19880	19910	19941	19972	20002	20033	20063	5
6	19730	19761	19789	19820	19850	19881	19911	19942	19973	20003	20034	20064	6
7	19731	19762	19790	19821	19851	19882	19912	19943	19974	20004	20035	20065	7
8	19732	19763	19791	19822	19852	19883	19913	19944	19975	20005	20036	20066	8
9	19733	19764	19792	19823	19853	19884	19914	19945	19976	20006	20037	20067	9
10	19734	19765	19793	19824	19854	19885	19915	19946	19977	20007	20038	20068	10
11	19735	19766	19794	19825	19855	19886	19916	19947	19978	20008	20039	20069	11
12	19736	19767	19795	19826	19856	19887	19917	19948	19979	20009	20040	20070	12
13	19737	19768	19796	19827	19857	19888	19918	19949	19980	20010	20041	20071	13
14	19738	19769	19797	19828	19858	19889	19919	19950	19981	20011	20042	20072	14
15	19739	19770	19798	19829	19859	19890	19920	19951	19982	20012	20043	20073	15
16	19740	19771	19799	19830	19860	19891	19921	19952	19983	20013	20044	20074	16
17	19741	19772	19800	19831	19861	19892	19922	19953	19984	20014	20045	20075	17
18	19742	19773	19801	19832	19862	19893	19923	19954	19985	20015	20046	20076	18
19	19743	19774	19802	19833	19863	19894	19924	19955	19986	20016	20047	20077	19
20	19744	19775	19803	19834	19864	19895	19925	19956	19987	20017	20048	20078	20
21	19745	19776	19804	19835	19865	19896	19926	19957	19988	20018	20049	20079	21
22	19746	19777	19805	19836	19866	19897	19927	19958	19989	20019	20050	20080	22
23	19747	19778	19806	19837	19867	19898	19928	19959	19990	20020	20051	20081	23
24	19748	19779	19807	19838	19868	19899	19929	19960	19991	20021	20052	20082	24
25	19749	19780	19808	19839	19869	19900	19930	19961	19992	20022	20053	20083	25
26	19750	19781	19809	19840	19870	19901	19931	19962	19993	20023	20054	20084	26
27	19751	19782	19810	19841	19871	19902	19932	19963	19994	20024	20055	20085	27
28	19752	19783	19811	19842	19872	19903	19933	19964	19995	20025	20056	20086	28
29	19753	....	19812	19843	19873	19904	19934	19965	19996	20026	20057	20087	29
30	19754	....	19813	19844	19874	19905	19935	19966	19997	20027	20058	20088	30
31	19755	....	19814	....	19875	....	19936	19967	....	20028	....	20089	31

Figure T-48. 1997 Expiration Table

1998 Expiration Table 1998

Day	Jan	Feb	Mar	Apr	May	Jun	Jul	Aug	Sep	Oct	Nov	Dec	Day
1	20090	20121	20149	20180	20210	20241	20271	20302	20333	20363	20394	20424	1
2	20091	20122	20150	20181	20211	20242	20272	20303	20334	20364	20395	20425	2
3	20092	20123	20151	20182	20212	20243	20273	20304	20335	20365	20396	20426	3
4	20093	20124	20152	20183	20213	20244	20274	20305	20336	20366	20397	20427	4
5	20094	20125	20153	20184	20214	20245	20275	20306	20337	20367	20398	20428	5
6	20095	20126	20154	20185	20215	20246	20276	20307	20338	20368	20399	20429	6
7	20096	20127	20155	20186	20216	20247	20277	20308	20330	20369	20400	20430	7
8	20097	20128	20156	20187	20217	20248	20278	20309	20340	20370	20401	20431	8
9	20098	20129	20157	20188	20218	20249	20279	20310	20341	20371	20402	20432	9
10	20099	20130	20158	20189	20219	20250	20280	20311	20342	20372	20403	20433	10
11	20100	20131	20159	20190	20220	20251	20281	20312	20343	20373	20404	20434	11
12	20101	20132	20160	20191	20221	20252	20282	20313	20344	20374	20405	20435	12
13	20102	20133	20161	20192	20222	20253	20283	20314	20345	20375	20406	20436	13
14	20103	20134	20162	20193	20223	20254	20284	20315	20346	20376	20407	20437	14
15	20104	20135	20163	20194	20224	20255	20285	20316	20347	20377	20408	20438	15
16	20105	20136	20164	20195	20225	20256	20286	20317	20348	20378	20409	20439	16
17	20106	20137	20165	20196	20226	20257	20287	20318	20349	20379	20410	20440	17
18	20107	20138	20166	20197	20227	20258	20288	20319	20350	20380	20411	20441	18
19	20108	20139	20167	20198	20228	20259	20289	20320	20351	20381	20412	20442	19
20	20109	20140	20168	20199	20229	20260	20290	20321	20352	20382	20413	20443	20
21	20110	20141	20169	20200	20230	20261	20291	20322	20353	20383	20414	20444	21
22	20111	20142	20170	20201	20231	20262	20292	20323	20354	20384	20415	20445	22
23	20112	20143	20171	20202	20232	20263	20293	20324	20355	20385	20416	20446	23
24	20113	20144	20172	20203	20233	20264	20294	20325	20356	20386	20417	20447	24
25	20114	20145	20173	20204	20234	20265	20295	20326	20357	20387	20418	20448	25
26	20115	20146	20174	20205	20235	20266	20296	20327	20358	20388	20419	20449	26
27	20116	20147	20175	20206	20236	20267	20297	20328	20359	20389	20420	20450	27
28	20117	20148	20176	20207	20237	20268	20298	20329	20360	20390	20421	20451	28
29	20118	-------	20177	20208	20238	20269	20299	20330	20361	20391	20422	20452	29
30	20119	-------	20178	20209	20239	20270	20300	20331	20362	20392	20423	20453	30
31	20120	-------	20179	-------	20240	-------	20301	20332	-------	20393	-------	20454	31

Figure T-49. 1998 Expiration Table

1999   Expiration Table   1999

Day	Jan	Feb	Mar	Apr	May	Jun	Jul	Aug	Sep	Oct	Nov	Dec	Day
1	20455	20486	20514	20545	20575	20606	20636	20667	20698	20728	20759	20789	1
2	20456	20487	20515	20546	20576	20607	20637	20668	20699	20729	20760	20790	2
3	20457	20488	20516	20547	20577	20608	20638	20669	20700	20730	20761	20791	3
4	20458	20489	20517	20548	20578	20609	20639	20670	20701	20731	20762	20792	4
5	20459	20490	20518	20549	20579	20610	20640	20671	20702	20732	20763	20793	5
6	20460	20491	20519	20550	20580	20611	20641	20672	20703	20733	20764	20794	6
7	20461	20492	20520	20551	20581	20612	20642	20673	20704	20734	20765	20795	7
8	20462	20493	20521	20552	20582	20613	20643	20674	20705	20735	20766	20796	8
9	20463	20494	20522	20553	20583	20614	20644	20675	20706	20736	20767	20797	9
10	20464	20495	20523	20554	20584	20615	20645	20676	20707	20737	20768	20798	10
11	20465	20496	20524	20555	20585	20616	20646	20677	20708	20738	20769	20799	11
12	20466	20497	20525	20556	20586	20617	20647	20678	20709	20739	20770	20800	12
13	20467	20498	20526	20557	20587	20618	20648	20679	20710	20740	20771	20801	13
14	20468	20499	20527	20558	20588	20619	20649	20680	20711	20741	20772	20802	14
15	20469	20500	20528	20559	20589	20620	20650	20681	20712	20742	20773	20803	15
16	20470	20501	20529	20560	20590	20621	20651	20682	20713	20743	20774	20804	16
17	20471	20502	20530	20561	20591	20622	20652	20683	20714	20744	20775	20805	17
18	20472	20503	20531	20562	20592	20623	20653	20684	20715	20745	20776	20806	18
19	20473	20504	20532	20563	20593	20624	20654	20685	20716	20746	20777	20807	19
20	20474	20505	20533	20564	20594	20625	20655	20686	20717	20747	20778	20808	20
21	20475	20506	20534	20565	20595	20626	20656	20687	20718	20748	20779	20809	21
22	20476	20507	20535	20566	20596	20627	20657	20688	20719	20749	20780	20810	22
23	20477	20508	20536	20567	20597	20628	20658	20689	20720	20750	20781	20811	23
24	20478	20509	20537	20568	20598	20629	20659	20690	20721	20751	20782	20812	24
25	20479	20510	20538	20569	20599	20630	20660	20691	20722	20752	20783	20813	25
26	20480	20511	20539	20570	20600	20631	20661	20692	20723	20753	20784	20814	26
27	20481	20512	20540	20571	20601	20632	20662	20693	20724	20754	20785	20815	27
28	20482	20513	20541	20572	20602	20623	20663	20694	20725	20755	20786	20816	28
29	20483	-------	20542	20573	20603	20634	20664	20695	20726	20756	20787	20817	29
30	20484	-------	20543	20574	20604	20635	20665	20696	20727	20757	20788	20818	30
31	20485	-------	20544	-------	20605	-------	20666	20697	-------	20758	-------	20819	31

Figure T-50. 1999 Expiration Table

2000 Expiration Table 2000

Day	Jan	Feb	Mar	Apr	May	Jun	Jul	Aug	Sep	Oct	Nov	Dec	Day
1	20820	20851	20880	20911	20941	20972	21002	21033	21064	21094	21125	21155	1
2	20821	20852	20881	20912	20942	20973	21003	21034	21065	21095	21126	21156	2
3	20822	20853	20882	20913	20943	20974	21004	21035	21066	21096	21127	21157	3
4	20823	20854	20883	20914	20944	20975	21005	21036	21067	21097	21128	21158	4
5	20824	20855	20884	20915	20945	20976	21006	21037	21068	21098	21129	21159	5
6	20825	20856	20885	20916	20946	20977	21007	21038	21069	21099	21130	21160	6
7	20826	20857	20886	20917	20947	20978	21008	21039	21070	21100	21131	21161	7
8	20827	20858	20887	20918	20948	20979	21009	21040	21071	21101	21132	21162	8
9	20828	20859	20888	20919	20949	20980	21010	21041	21072	21102	21133	21163	9
10	20829	20860	20889	20920	20950	20981	21011	21042	21073	21103	21134	21164	10
11	20830	20861	20890	20921	20951	20982	21012	21043	21074	21104	21135	21165	11
12	20831	20862	20891	20922	20952	20983	21013	21044	21075	21105	21136	21166	12
13	20832	20863	20892	20923	20953	20984	21014	21045	21076	21106	21137	21167	13
14	20833	20864	20893	20924	20954	20985	21015	21046	21077	21107	21138	21168	14
15	20834	20865	20894	20925	20955	20986	21016	21047	21078	21108	21139	21169	15
16	20835	20866	20895	20926	20956	20987	21017	21048	21079	21109	21140	21170	16
17	20836	20867	20896	20927	20957	20988	21018	21049	21080	21110	21141	21171	17
18	20837	20868	20897	20928	20958	20989	21019	21050	21081	21111	21142	21172	18
19	20838	20869	20898	20929	20959	20990	21020	21051	21082	21112	21143	21173	19
20	20839	20870	20899	20930	20060	20991	21021	21052	21083	21113	21144	21174	20
21	20840	20871	20900	20931	20061	20992	21022	21053	21084	21114	21145	21175	21
22	20841	20872	20901	20932	20962	20993	21023	21054	21085	21115	21146	21176	22
23	20842	20873	20902	20933	20963	20994	21024	21055	21086	21116	21147	21177	23
24	20843	20874	20903	20934	20064	20995	21025	21056	21087	21117	21148	21178	24
25	20844	20875	20904	20935	20965	20996	21026	21057	21088	21118	21149	21179	25
26	20845	20876	20905	20936	20966	20997	21027	21058	21089	21119	21150	21180	26
27	20846	20877	20906	20937	20967	20998	21028	21059	21090	21120	21151	21181	27
28	20847	20878	20907	20938	20968	20999	21029	21060	21091	21121	21152	21182	28
29	20848	20879	20908	20939	20969	21000	21030	21061	21092	21122	21153	21183	29
30	20849	-----	20909	20940	20970	21001	21031	21062	21093	21123	21154	21184	30
31	20850	-----	20910	-----	20971	-----	21032	21063	----	21124	-------	21185	31

Figure T-51. 2000 Expiration Table

	2001					Expiration Table			2001				
Day	Jan	Feb	Mar	Apr	May	Jun	Jul	Aug	Sep	Oct	Nov	Dec	Day
1	21186	21217	21245	21276	21306	21337	21367	21398	21429	21459	21490	21520	1
2	21187	21218	21246	21277	21307	21338	21368	21399	21430	21460	21491	21521	2
3	21188	21219	21247	21278	21308	21339	21369	21400	21431	21461	21492	21522	3
4	21189	21220	21248	21279	21309	21340	21370	21401	21432	21462	21493	21523	4
5	21190	21221	21249	21280	21310	21341	21371	21402	21433	21463	21494	21524	5
6	21191	21222	21250	21281	21311	21342	21372	21403	21434	21464	21495	21525	6
7	21192	21223	21251	21282	21312	21343	21373	21404	21435	21465	21496	21526	7
8	21193	21224	21252	21283	21313	21344	21374	21405	21436	21466	21497	21527	8
9	21194	21225	21253	21284	21314	21345	21375	21406	21437	21467	21498	21528	9
10	21195	21226	21254	21285	21315	21346	21376	21407	21438	21468	21499	21529	10
11	21196	21227	21255	21286	21316	21347	21377	21408	21439	21469	21500	21530	11
12	21197	21228	21256	21287	21317	21348	21378	21409	21440	21470	21501	21531	12
13	21198	21229	21257	21288	21318	21349	21379	21410	21441	21471	21502	21532	13
14	21199	21230	21258	21289	21319	21350	21380	21411	21442	21472	21503	21533	14
15	21200	21231	21259	21290	21320	21351	21381	21412	21443	21473	21504	21534	15
16	21201	21232	21260	21291	21321	21352	21382	21413	21444	21474	21505	21535	16
17	21202	21233	21261	21292	21322	21353	21383	21414	21445	21475	21506	21536	17
18	21203	21234	21262	21293	21323	21354	21384	21415	21446	21476	21507	21537	18
19	21204	21235	21263	21294	21324	21355	21385	21416	21447	21477	21508	21538	19
20	21205	21236	21264	21295	21325	21356	21386	21417	21448	21478	21509	21539	20
21	21206	21237	21265	21296	21326	21357	21387	21418	21449	21479	21510	21540	21
22	21207	21238	21266	21297	21327	21358	21388	21419	21450	21480	21511	21541	22
23	21208	21239	21267	21298	21328	21359	21389	21420	21451	21481	21512	21542	23
24	21209	21240	21268	21299	21329	21360	21390	21421	21452	21482	21513	21543	24
25	21210	21241	21269	21300	21330	21361	21391	21422	21453	21483	21514	21544	25
26	21211	21242	21270	21301	21331	21362	21392	21423	21454	21484	21515	21545	26
27	21212	21243	21271	21302	21332	21363	21393	21424	21455	21485	21516	21546	27
28	21213	21244	21272	21303	21333	21364	21394	21425	21456	21486	21517	21547	28
29	21214	-------	21273	21304	21334	21365	21395	21426	21457	21487	21518	21548	29
30	21215	-------	21274	21305	21335	21366	21396	21427	21458	21488	21519	21549	30
31	21216	-------	21275	-------	21336	-------	21397	21428	-------	21489	-------	21550	31

Figure T-52. 2001 Expiration Table

Day	Jan	Feb	Mar	Apr	May	Jun	Jul	Aug	Sep	Oct	Nov	Dec	Day
1	21551	21582	21610	21641	21671	21702	21732	21763	21794	21824	21855	21885	1
2	21552	21583	21611	21642	21672	21703	21733	21764	21795	21825	21856	21886	2
3	21553	21584	21612	21643	21673	21704	21734	21765	21796	21826	21857	21887	3
4	21554	21585	21613	21644	21674	21705	21735	21766	21797	21827	21858	21888	4
5	21555	21586	21614	21645	21675	21706	21736	21767	21798	21828	21859	21889	5
6	21556	21587	21615	21646	21676	21707	21737	21768	21799	21829	21860	21890	6
7	21557	21588	21616	21647	21677	21708	21738	21769	21800	21830	21861	21891	7
8	21558	21589	21617	21648	21678	21709	21739	21770	21801	21831	21862	21892	8
9	21559	21590	21618	21649	21679	21710	21740	21771	21802	21832	21863	21893	9
10	21560	21591	21619	21650	21680	21711	21741	21772	21803	21833	21864	21894	10
11	21561	21592	21620	21651	21681	21712	21742	21773	21804	21834	21865	21895	11
12	21562	21593	21621	21652	21682	21713	21743	21774	21805	21835	21866	21896	12
13	21563	21594	21622	21653	21683	21714	21744	21775	21806	21836	21867	21897	13
14	21564	21595	21623	21654	21684	21715	21745	21776	21807	21837	21868	21898	14
15	21565	21596	21624	21655	21685	21716	21746	21777	21808	21838	21869	21899	15
16	21566	21597	21625	21656	21686	21717	21747	21778	21809	21839	21870	21900	16
17	21567	21598	21626	21657	21687	21718	21748	21779	21810	21840	21871	21901	17
18	21568	21599	21627	21658	21688	21719	21749	21780	21811	21841	21872	21902	18
19	21569	21600	21628	21659	21689	21720	21750	21781	21812	21842	21873	21903	19
20	21570	21601	21629	21660	21690	21721	21751	21782	21813	21843	21874	21904	20
21	21571	21602	21630	21661	21691	21722	21752	21783	21814	21844	21875	21905	21
22	21572	21603	21631	21662	21692	21723	21753	21784	21815	21845	21876	21906	22
23	21573	21604	21632	21663	21693	21724	21754	21785	21816	21846	21877	21907	23
24	21574	21605	21633	21664	21694	21725	21755	21786	21817	21847	21878	21908	24
25	21575	21606	21634	21665	21695	21726	21756	21787	21818	21848	21879	21909	25
26	21576	21607	21635	21666	21696	21727	21757	21788	21819	21849	21880	21910	26
27	21577	21608	21636	21667	21697	21728	21758	21789	21820	21850	21881	21911	27
28	21578	21609	21637	21668	21698	21729	21759	21790	21821	21851	21882	21912	28
29	21579	-------	21638	21669	21699	21730	21760	21791	21822	21852	21883	21913	29
30	21580	-------	21639	21670	21700	21731	21761	21792	21823	21853	21884	21914	30
31	21581	-------	21640	-------	21701	-------	21762	21793	-------	21854	-------	21915	31

Figure T-53. 2002 Expiration Table

Day	Jan	Feb	Mar	Apr	May	Jun	Jul	Aug	Sep	Oct	Nov	Dec	Day
1	21916	21947	21975	22006	22036	22067	22097	22128	22159	22189	22220	22250	1
2	21917	21948	21976	22007	22037	22068	22098	22129	22160	22190	22221	22251	2
3	21918	21949	21977	22008	22038	22069	22099	22130	22161	22191	22222	22252	3
4	21919	21950	21978	22009	22039	22070	22100	22131	22162	22192	22223	22253	4
5	21920	21951	21979	22010	22040	22071	22101	22132	22163	22193	22224	22254	5
6	21921	21952	21980	22011	22041	22072	22102	22133	22164	22194	22225	22255	6
7	21922	21953	21981	22012	22042	22073	22103	22134	22165	22195	22226	22256	7
8	21923	21954	21982	22013	22043	22074	22104	22135	22166	22196	22227	22257	8
9	21924	21955	21983	22014	22044	22075	22105	22136	22167	22197	22228	22258	9
10	21925	21956	21984	22015	22045	22076	22106	22137	22168	22198	22229	22259	10
11	21926	21957	21985	22016	22046	22077	22107	22138	22169	22199	22230	22260	11
12	21927	21958	21986	22017	22047	22078	22108	22139	22170	22200	22231	22261	12
13	21928	21959	21987	22018	22048	22079	22109	22140	22171	22201	22232	22262	13
14	21929	21960	21988	22019	22049	22080	22110	22141	22172	22202	22233	22263	14
15	21930	21961	21989	22020	22050	22081	22111	22142	22173	22203	22234	22264	15
16	21931	21962	21990	22021	22051	22082	22112	22143	22174	22204	22235	22265	16
17	21932	21963	21991	22022	22052	22083	22113	22144	22175	22205	22236	22266	17
18	21933	21964	21992	22023	22053	22084	22114	22145	22176	22206	22237	22267	18
19	21934	21965	21993	22024	22054	22085	22115	22146	22177	22207	22238	22268	19
20	21935	21966	21994	22025	22055	22086	22116	22147	22178	22208	22239	22269	20
21	21936	21967	21995	22026	22056	22087	22117	22148	22179	22209	22240	22270	21
22	21937	21968	21996	22027	22057	22088	22118	22149	22180	22210	22241	22271	22
23	21938	21969	21997	22028	22058	22089	22119	22150	22181	22211	22242	22272	23
24	21939	21970	21998	22029	22059	22090	22120	22151	22182	22212	22243	22273	24
25	21940	21971	21999	22030	22060	22091	22121	22152	22183	22213	22244	22274	25
26	21941	21972	22000	22031	22061	22092	22122	22153	22184	22214	22245	22275	26
27	21942	21973	22001	22032	22062	22093	22123	22154	22185	22215	22246	22276	27
28	21943	21974	22002	22033	22063	22094	22124	22155	22186	22216	22247	22277	28
29	21944	-------	22003	22034	22064	22095	22125	22156	22187	22217	22248	22278	29
30	21945	-------	22004	22035	22065	22096	22126	22157	22188	22218	22249	22279	30
31	21946	-------	22005	-------	22066	-------	22127	22158	-------	22219	-------	22280	31

Figure T-54. 2003 Expiration Table

2004   Expiration Table   2004

Day	Jan	Feb	Mar	Apr	May	Jun	Jul	Aug	Sep	Oct	Nov	Dec	Day
1	22281	22312	22341	22372	22402	22433	22463	22494	22525	22555	22586	22616	1
2	22282	22313	22342	22373	22403	22434	22464	22495	22526	22556	22587	22617	2
3	22283	22314	22343	22374	22404	22435	22465	22496	22527	22557	22588	22618	3
4	22284	22315	22344	22375	22405	22436	22466	22497	22528	22558	22589	22619	4
5	22285	22316	22345	22376	22406	22437	22467	22498	22529	22559	22590	22620	5
6	22286	22317	22346	22377	22407	22438	22468	22499	22530	22560	22591	22621	6
7	22287	22318	22347	22378	22408	22439	22469	22500	22531	22561	22592	22622	7
8	22288	22319	22348	22379	22409	22440	22470	22501	22532	22562	22593	22623	8
9	22289	22320	22349	22380	22410	22441	22471	22502	22533	22563	22594	22624	9
10	22290	22321	22350	22381	22411	22442	22472	22503	22534	22564	22595	22625	10
11	22291	22322	22351	22382	22412	22443	22473	22504	22535	22565	22596	22626	11
12	22292	22323	22352	22383	22413	22444	22474	22505	22536	22566	22597	22627	12
13	22293	22324	22353	22384	22414	22445	22475	22506	22537	22567	22598	22628	13
14	22294	22325	22354	22385	22415	22446	22476	22507	22538	22568	22599	22629	14
15	22295	22326	22355	22386	22416	22447	22477	22508	22539	22569	22600	22630	15
16	22296	22327	22356	22387	22417	22448	22478	22509	22540	22570	22601	22631	16
17	22297	22328	22357	22388	22418	22449	22479	22510	22541	22571	22602	22632	17
18	22298	22329	22358	22389	22419	22450	22480	22511	22542	22572	22603	22633	18
19	22299	22330	22359	22390	22420	22451	22481	22512	22543	22573	22604	22634	19
20	22300	22331	22360	22391	22421	22452	22482	22513	22544	22574	22605	22635	20
21	22301	22332	22361	22392	22422	22453	22483	22514	22545	22575	22606	22636	21
22	22302	22333	22362	22393	22423	22454	22484	22515	22546	22576	22607	22637	22
23	22303	22334	22363	22394	22424	22455	22485	22516	22547	22577	22608	22638	23
24	22304	22335	22364	22395	22425	22456	22486	22517	22548	22578	22609	22639	24
25	22305	22336	22365	22396	22426	22457	22487	22518	22549	22579	22610	22640	25
26	22306	22337	22366	22397	22427	22458	22488	22519	22550	22580	22611	22641	26
27	22307	22338	22367	22398	22428	22459	22489	22520	22551	22581	22612	22642	27
28	22308	22339	22368	22399	22429	22460	22490	22521	22552	22582	22613	22643	28
29	22309	22340	22369	22400	22430	22461	22491	22522	22553	22583	22614	22644	29
30	22310	-------	22370	22401	22431	22462	22492	22523	22554	22584	22615	22645	30
31	22311	-------	22371	-------	22432	-------	22493	22524	-------	22585	-------	22646	31

Figure T-55. 2004 Expiration Table

Day	Jan	Feb	Mar	Apr	May	Jun	Jul	Aug	Sep	Oct	Nov	Dec	Day
1	22647	22678	22706	22737	22767	22798	22828	22859	22890	22920	22951	22981	1
2	22648	22679	22707	22738	22768	22799	22829	22860	22891	22921	22952	22982	2
3	22649	22680	22708	22739	22769	22800	22830	22861	22892	22922	22953	22983	3
4	22650	22681	22709	22740	22770	22801	22831	22862	22893	22923	22954	22984	4
5	22651	22682	22710	22741	22771	22802	22832	22863	22894	22924	22955	22985	5
6	22652	22683	22711	22742	22772	22803	22833	22864	22895	22925	22956	22986	6
7	22653	22684	22712	22743	22773	22804	22834	22865	22896	22926	22957	22987	7
8	22654	22685	22713	22744	22774	22805	22835	22866	22897	22927	22958	22988	8
9	22655	22686	22714	22745	22775	22806	22836	22867	22898	22928	22959	22989	9
10	22656	22687	22715	22746	22776	22807	22837	22868	22899	22929	22960	22990	10
11	22657	22688	22716	22747	22777	22808	22838	22869	22900	22930	22961	22991	11
12	22658	22689	22717	22748	22778	22809	22839	22870	22901	22931	22962	22992	12
13	22659	22690	22718	22749	22779	22810	22840	22871	22902	22932	22963	22993	13
14	22660	22691	22719	22750	22780	22811	22841	22872	22903	22933	22964	22994	14
15	22661	22692	22720	22751	22781	22812	22842	22873	22904	22934	22965	22995	15
16	22662	22693	22721	22752	22782	22813	22843	22874	22905	22935	22966	22996	16
17	22663	22694	22722	22753	22783	22814	22844	22875	22906	22936	22967	22997	17
18	22664	22695	22723	22754	22784	22815	22845	22876	22907	22937	22968	22998	18
19	22665	22696	22724	22755	22785	22816	22846	22877	22908	22938	22969	22999	19
20	22666	22697	22725	22756	22786	22817	22847	22878	22909	22939	22970	23000	20
21	22667	22698	22726	22757	22787	22818	22848	22879	22910	22940	22971	23001	21
22	22668	22699	22727	22758	22788	22819	22849	22880	22911	22941	22972	23002	22
23	22669	22700	22728	22759	22789	22820	22850	22881	22912	22942	22973	23003	23
24	22670	22701	22729	22760	22790	22821	22851	22882	22913	22943	22974	23004	24
25	22671	22702	22730	22761	22791	22822	22852	22883	22914	22944	22975	23005	25
26	22672	22703	22731	22762	22792	22823	22853	22884	22915	22945	22976	23006	26
27	22673	22704	22732	22763	22793	22824	22854	22885	22916	22946	22977	23007	27
28	22674	22705	22733	22764	22794	22825	22855	22886	22917	22947	22978	23008	28
29	22675	-------	22734	22765	22795	22826	22856	22887	22918	22948	22979	23009	29
30	22676	-------	22735	22766	22796	22827	22857	22888	22919	22949	22980	23010	30
31	22677	-------	22736	-------	22797	-------	22858	22889	-------	22950	-------	23011	31

Figure T-56. 2005 Expiration Table

2006   Expiration Table   2006

Day	Jan	Feb	Mar	Apr	May	Jun	Jul	Aug	Sep	Oct	Nov	Dec	Day
1	23012	23043	23071	23102	23132	23163	23193	23224	23255	23285	23316	23346	1
2	23013	23044	23072	23103	23133	23164	23194	23225	23256	23286	23317	23347	2
3	23014	23045	23073	23104	23134	23165	23195	23226	23257	23287	23318	23348	3
4	23015	23046	23074	23105	23135	23166	23196	23227	23258	23288	23319	23349	4
5	23016	23047	23075	23106	23136	23167	23197	23228	23259	23289	23320	23350	5
6	23017	23048	23076	23107	23137	23168	23198	23229	23260	23290	23321	23351	6
7	23018	23049	23077	23108	23138	23169	23199	23230	23261	23291	23322	23352	7
8	23019	23050	23078	23109	23139	23170	23200	23231	23262	23292	23323	23353	8
9	23020	23051	23079	23110	23140	23171	23201	23232	23263	23293	23324	23354	9
10	23021	23052	23080	23111	23141	23172	23202	23233	23264	23294	23325	23355	10
11	23022	23053	23081	23112	23142	23173	23203	23234	23265	23295	23326	23356	11
12	23023	23054	23082	23113	23143	23174	23204	23235	23266	23296	23327	23357	12
13	23024	23055	23083	23114	23144	23175	23205	23236	23267	23297	23328	23358	13
14	23025	23056	23084	23115	23145	23176	23206	23237	23268	23298	23329	23359	14
15	23026	23057	23085	23116	23146	23177	23207	23238	23269	23299	23330	23360	15
16	23027	23058	23086	23117	23147	23178	23208	23239	23270	23300	23331	23361	16
17	23028	23059	23087	23118	23148	23179	23209	23240	23271	23301	23332	23362	17
18	23029	23060	23088	23119	23149	23180	23210	23241	23272	23302	23333	23363	18
19	23030	23061	23089	23120	23150	23181	23211	23242	23273	23303	23334	23364	19
20	23031	23062	23090	23121	23151	23182	23212	23243	23274	23304	23335	23365	20
21	23032	23063	23091	23122	23152	23183	23213	23244	23275	23305	23336	23366	21
22	23033	23064	23092	23123	23153	23184	23214	23245	23276	23306	23337	23367	22
23	23034	23065	23093	23124	23154	23185	23215	23246	23277	23307	23338	23368	23
24	23035	23066	23094	23125	23155	23186	23216	23247	23278	23308	23339	23369	24
25	23036	23067	23095	23126	23156	23187	23217	23248	23279	23309	23340	23370	25
26	23037	23068	23096	23127	23157	23188	23218	23249	23280	23310	23341	23371	26
27	23038	23069	23097	23128	23158	23189	23219	23250	23281	23311	23342	23372	27
28	23039	23070	23098	23129	23159	23190	23220	23251	23282	23312	23343	23373	28
29	23040	-------	23099	23130	23160	23191	23221	23252	23283	23313	23344	23374	29
30	23041	-------	23100	23131	23161	23192	23222	23253	23284	23314	23345	23375	30
31	23042	-------	23101	-------	23162	-------	23223	23254	-------	23315	-------	23376	31

Figure T-57. 2006 Expiration Table

2007 **Expiration Table** **2007**

Day	Jan	Feb	Mar	Apr	May	Jun	Jul	Aug	Sep	Oct	Nov	Dec	Day
1	23377	23408	23436	23467	23497	23528	23558	23589	23620	23650	23681	23711	1
2	23378	23409	23437	23468	23498	23529	23559	23590	23621	23651	23682	23712	2
3	23379	23410	23438	23469	23499	23530	23560	23591	23622	23652	23683	23713	3
4	23380	23411	23439	23470	23500	23531	23561	23592	23623	23653	23684	23714	4
5	23381	23412	23440	23471	23501	23532	23562	23593	23624	23654	23685	23715	5
6	23382	23413	23441	23472	23502	23533	23563	23594	23625	23655	23686	23716	6
7	23383	23414	23442	23473	23503	23534	23564	23595	23626	23656	23687	23717	7
8	23384	23515	23443	23474	23504	23535	23565	23596	23627	23657	23688	23718	8
9	23385	23416	23444	23475	23505	23536	23566	23597	23628	23658	23689	23719	9
10	23386	23417	23445	23476	23506	23537	23567	23598	23629	23659	23690	23720	10
11	23387	23418	23446	23477	23507	23538	23568	23599	23630	23660	23691	23721	11
12	23388	23419	23447	23478	23508	23539	23569	23600	23631	23661	23692	23722	12
13	23389	23420	23448	23479	23509	23540	23570	23601	23632	23662	23693	23723	13
14	23390	23421	23449	23480	23510	23541	23571	23602	23633	23663	23694	23724	14
15	23391	23422	23450	23481	23511	23542	23572	23603	23634	23664	23695	23725	15
16	23392	23423	23451	23482	23512	23543	23573	23604	23635	23665	23696	23726	16
17	23393	23424	23452	23483	23513	23544	23574	23605	23636	23666	23697	23727	17
18	23394	23425	23453	23484	23514	23545	23575	23606	23637	23667	23698	23728	18
19	23295	23426	23454	23485	23515	23546	23576	23607	23638	23668	23699	23729	19
20	23396	23427	23455	23486	23516	23547	23577	23608	23639	23669	23700	23730	20
21	23307	23428	23456	23487	23517	23548	23578	23609	23640	23670	23701	23731	21
22	23398	23429	23457	23488	23518	23549	23579	23610	23641	23671	23702	23732	22
23	23399	23430	23458	23489	23519	23550	23580	23611	23642	23672	23703	23733	23
24	23400	23431	23459	23490	23520	23551	23581	23612	23643	23673	23704	23734	24
25	23401	23432	23460	23491	23521	23552	23582	23613	23644	23674	23705	23735	25
26	23402	23433	23461	23492	23522	23553	23583	23614	23645	23675	23706	23736	26
27	23403	23434	23462	23493	23523	23554	23584	23615	23646	23676	23707	23737	27
28	23404	23435	23463	23494	23524	23555	23585	23616	23647	23677	23708	23738	28
29	23405	-------	23464	23495	23525	23556	23586	23617	23648	23678	23709	23739	29
30	23406	-------	23465	23496	23526	23557	23587	23618	23649	23679	23710	23740	30
31	23407	-------	23466	-------	23527	-------	23588	23619	-------	23680	-------	23741	31

Figure T-58. 2007 Expiration Table

2008   Expiration Table   2008

Day	Jan	Feb	Mar	Apr	May	Jun	Jul	Aug	Sep	Oct	Nov	Dec	Day
1	23742	23773	23802	23833	23863	23894	23924	23955	23986	24016	24047	24077	1
2	23743	23774	23803	23834	23864	23895	23925	23956	23987	24017	24048	24078	2
3	23744	23775	23804	23835	23865	23896	23926	23957	23988	24018	24049	24079	3
4	23745	23776	23805	23836	23866	23897	23927	23958	23989	24019	24050	24080	4
5	23746	23777	23806	23837	23867	23898	23928	23959	23990	24020	24051	24081	5
6	23747	23778	23807	23838	23868	23899	23929	23960	23991	24021	24052	24082	6
7	23748	23779	23808	23839	23869	23900	23930	23961	23992	24022	24053	24083	7
8	23749	23780	23809	23840	23870	23901	23931	23962	23993	24023	24054	24084	8
9	23750	23781	23810	23841	23871	23902	23932	23963	23994	24024	24055	24085	9
10	23751	23782	23811	23842	23872	23903	23933	23964	23995	24025	24056	24086	10
11	23752	23783	23812	23843	23873	23904	23934	23965	23996	24026	24057	24087	11
12	23753	23784	23813	23844	23874	23905	23935	23966	23997	24027	24058	24088	12
13	23754	23785	23814	23845	23875	23906	23936	23967	23998	24028	24059	24089	13
14	23755	23786	23815	23846	23876	23907	23937	23968	23999	24029	24060	24090	14
15	23756	23787	23816	23847	23877	23908	23938	23969	24000	24030	24061	24091	15
16	23757	23788	23817	23848	23878	23909	23939	23970	24001	24031	24062	24092	16
17	23758	23789	23818	23849	23879	23910	23940	23971	24002	24032	24063	24093	17
18	23759	23790	23819	23850	23880	23911	23941	23972	24003	24033	24064	24094	18
19	23760	23791	23820	23851	23881	23912	23942	23973	24004	24034	24065	24095	19
20	23761	23792	23821	23852	23882	23913	23943	23974	24005	24035	24066	24096	20
21	23762	23793	23822	23853	23883	23914	23944	23975	24006	24036	24067	24097	21
22	23763	23794	23823	23854	23884	23915	23945	23976	24007	24037	24068	24098	22
23	23764	23795	23824	23855	23885	23916	23946	23977	24008	24038	24069	24099	23
24	23765	23796	23825	23856	23886	23917	23947	23978	24009	24039	24070	24100	24
25	23766	23797	23826	23857	23887	23918	23948	23979	24010	24040	24071	24101	25
26	23767	23798	23827	23858	23888	23919	23949	23980	24011	24041	24072	24102	26
27	23768	23799	23828	23859	23889	23920	23950	23981	24012	24042	24073	24103	27
28	23769	23800	23829	23860	23890	23921	23951	23982	24013	24043	24074	24104	28
29	23770	23801	23830	23861	23891	23922	23952	23983	24014	24044	24075	24105	29
30	23771	-------	23831	23862	23892	23923	23953	23984	24015	24045	24076	24106	30
31	23772	-------	23832	-------	23893	-------	23954	23985	-------	24046	-------	24107	31

Figure T-59. 2008 Expiration Table

Day	Jan	Feb	Mar	Apr	May	Jun	Jul	Aug	Sep	Oct	Nov	Dec	Day
1	24108	24139	24167	24198	24228	24259	24289	24320	24351	24381	24412	24442	1
2	24109	24140	24168	24199	24229	24260	24290	24321	24352	24382	24413	24443	2
3	24110	24141	24169	24200	24230	24261	24291	24322	24353	24383	24414	24444	3
4	24111	24142	24170	24201	24231	24262	24292	24323	24354	24384	24415	24445	4
5	24112	24143	24171	24202	24232	24263	24293	24324	24355	24385	24416	24446	5
6	24113	24144	24172	24203	24233	24264	24294	24325	24356	24386	24417	24447	6
7	24114	24145	24173	24204	24234	24265	24295	24326	24357	24387	24418	24448	7
8	24115	24146	24174	24205	24235	24266	24296	24327	24358	24388	24419	24449	8
9	24116	24147	24175	24206	24236	24267	24297	24328	24359	24389	24420	24450	9
10	24117	24148	24176	24207	24237	24268	24298	24329	24360	24390	24421	24451	10
11	24118	24149	24177	24208	24238	24269	24299	24330	24361	24391	24422	24452	11
12	24119	24150	24178	24209	24239	24270	24300	24331	24362	24392	24423	24453	12
13	24120	24151	24179	24210	24240	24271	24301	24332	24363	24393	24424	24454	13
14	24121	24152	24180	24211	24241	24272	24302	24333	24364	24394	24425	24455	14
15	24122	24153	24181	24212	24242	24273	24303	24334	24365	24395	24426	24456	15
16	24123	24154	24182	24213	24243	24274	24304	24335	24366	24396	24427	24457	16
17	24124	24155	24183	24214	24244	24275	24305	24336	24367	24397	24428	24458	17
18	24125	24156	24184	24215	24245	24276	24306	24337	24368	24398	24429	24459	18
19	24126	24157	24185	24216	24246	24277	24307	24338	24369	24399	24430	24460	19
20	24127	24158	24186	24217	24247	24278	24308	24339	24370	24400	24431	24461	20
21	24128	24159	24187	24218	24248	24279	24309	24340	24371	24401	24432	24462	21
22	24129	24160	24188	24219	24249	24280	24310	24341	24372	24402	24433	24463	22
23	24130	24161	24189	24220	24250	24281	24311	24342	24373	24403	24434	24464	23
24	24131	24162	24190	24221	24251	24282	24312	24343	24374	24404	24435	24465	24
25	24132	24163	24191	24222	24252	24283	24313	24344	24375	24405	24436	24466	25
26	24133	24164	24192	24223	24253	24284	24314	24345	24376	24406	24437	24467	26
27	24134	24165	24193	24224	24254	24285	24315	24346	24377	24407	24438	24468	27
28	24135	24166	24194	24225	24255	24286	24316	24347	24378	24408	24439	24469	28
29	24136	-------	24195	24226	24256	24287	24317	24348	24379	24409	24440	24470	29
30	24137	-------	24196	24227	24257	24288	24318	24349	24380	24410	24441	24471	30
31	24138	-------	24197	-------	24258	-------	24319	24350	-------	24411	-------	24472	31

Figure T-60. 2009 Expiration Table

| | | 2010 | | | | Expiration Table | | | | 2010 | | | |
Day	Jan	Feb	Mar	Apr	May	Jun	Jul	Aug	Sep	Oct	Nov	Dec	Day
1	24473	24504	24532	24563	24593	24624	24654	24685	24716	24746	24777	24807	1
2	24474	24505	24533	24564	24594	24625	24655	24686	24717	24747	24778	24808	2
3	24475	24506	24534	24565	24595	24626	24656	24687	24718	24748	24779	24809	3
4	24476	24507	24535	24566	24596	24627	24657	24688	24719	24749	24780	24810	4
5	24477	24508	24536	24567	24597	24628	24658	24689	24720	24750	24781	24811	5
6	24478	24509	24537	24568	24598	24629	24659	24690	24721	24751	24782	24812	6
7	24479	24510	24538	24569	24599	24630	24660	24691	24722	24752	24783	24813	7
8	24480	24511	24539	24570	24600	24631	24661	24692	24723	24753	24784	24814	8
9	24481	24512	24540	24571	24601	24632	24662	24693	24724	24754	24785	24815	9
10	24482	24513	24541	24572	24602	24633	24663	24694	24725	24755	24786	24816	10
11	24483	24514	24542	24573	24603	24634	24664	24695	24726	24756	24787	24817	11
12	24484	24515	24543	24574	24604	24635	24665	24696	24727	24757	24788	24818	12
13	24485	24516	24544	24575	24605	24636	24666	24697	24728	24758	24789	24819	13
14	24486	24517	24545	24576	24606	24637	24667	24698	24729	24759	24790	24820	14
15	24487	24518	24546	24577	24607	24638	24668	24699	24730	24760	24791	24821	15
16	24488	24519	24547	24578	24608	24639	24669	24700	24731	24761	24792	24822	16
17	24489	24520	24548	24579	24609	24640	24670	24701	24732	24762	24793	24823	17
18	24490	24521	24549	24580	24610	24641	24671	24702	24733	24763	24794	24824	18
19	24491	24522	24550	24581	24611	24642	24672	24703	24734	24764	24795	24825	19
20	24492	24523	24551	24582	24612	24643	24673	24704	24735	24765	24796	24826	20
21	24493	24524	24552	24583	24613	24644	24674	24705	24736	24766	24797	24827	21
22	24494	24525	24553	24584	24614	24645	24675	24706	24737	24767	24798	24828	22
23	24495	24526	24554	24585	24615	24646	24676	24707	24738	24768	24799	24829	23
24	24496	24527	24555	24586	24616	24647	24677	24708	24739	24769	24800	24830	24
25	24497	24528	24556	24587	24617	24648	24678	24709	24740	24770	24801	24831	25
26	24498	24529	24557	24588	24618	24649	24679	24710	24741	24771	24802	24832	26
27	24499	24530	24558	24589	24619	24650	24680	24711	24742	24772	24803	24833	27
28	24500	24531	24559	24590	24620	24651	24681	24712	24743	24773	24804	24834	28
29	24501	....	24560	24591	24621	24652	24682	24713	24744	24774	24805	24835	29
30	24502	....	24561	24592	24622	24653	24683	24714	24745	24775	24806	24836	30
31	24503	....	24562	....	24623	....	24684	24715	....	24776	....	24837	31

Figure T-61. 2010 Expiration Table

Day	Jan	Feb	Mar	Apr	May	Jun	Jul	Aug	Sep	Oct	Nov	Dec	Day
1	24838	24869	24897	24928	24958	24989	25019	25050	25081	25111	25142	25172	1
2	24839	24870	24898	24929	24959	24990	25020	25051	25082	25112	25143	25173	2
3	24840	24871	24899	24930	24960	24991	25021	25052	25083	25113	25144	25174	3
4	24841	24872	24900	24931	24961	24992	25022	25053	25084	25114	25145	25175	4
5	24842	24873	24901	24932	24962	24993	25023	25054	25085	25115	25146	25176	5
6	24843	24874	24902	24933	24963	24994	25024	25055	25086	25116	25147	25177	6
7	24844	24875	24903	24934	24964	24995	25025	25056	25087	25117	25148	25178	7
8	24845	24876	24904	24935	24965	24996	25026	25057	25088	25118	25149	25179	8
9	24846	24877	24905	24936	24966	24997	25027	25058	25089	25119	25150	25180	9
10	24847	24878	24906	24937	24967	24998	25028	25059	25090	25120	25151	25181	10
11	24848	24879	24907	24938	24968	24999	25029	25060	25091	25121	25152	25182	11
12	24849	24880	24908	24939	24969	25000	25030	25061	25092	25122	25153	25183	12
13	24850	24881	24909	24940	24970	25001	25031	25062	25093	25123	25154	25184	13
14	24851	24882	24910	24941	24971	25002	25032	25063	25094	25124	25155	25185	14
15	24852	24883	24911	24942	24972	25003	25033	25064	25095	25125	25156	25186	15
16	24853	24884	24912	24943	24973	25004	25034	25065	25096	25126	25157	25187	16
17	24854	24885	24913	24944	24974	25005	25035	25066	25097	25127	25158	25188	17
18	24855	24886	24914	24945	24975	25006	25036	25067	25098	25128	25159	25189	18
19	24856	24887	24915	24946	24976	25007	25037	25068	25099	25129	25160	25190	19
20	24857	24888	24916	24947	24977	25008	25038	25069	25100	25130	25161	25191	20
21	24858	24889	24917	24948	24978	25009	25039	25070	25101	25131	25162	25192	21
22	24859	24890	24918	24949	24979	25010	25040	25071	25102	25132	25163	25193	22
23	24860	24891	24919	24950	24980	25011	25041	25072	25103	25133	25164	25194	23
24	24861	24892	24920	24951	24981	25012	25042	25073	25104	25134	25165	25195	24
25	24862	24893	24921	24952	24982	25013	25043	25074	25105	25135	25166	25196	25
26	24863	24894	24922	24953	24983	25014	25044	25075	25106	25136	25167	25197	26
27	24864	24895	24923	24954	24984	25015	25045	25076	25107	25137	25168	25198	27
28	24865	24896	24924	24955	24985	25016	25046	25077	25108	25138	25169	25199	28
29	24866	-------	24925	24956	24986	25017	25047	25078	25109	25139	25170	25200	29
30	24867	-------	24926	24957	24987	25018	25048	25079	25110	25140	25171	25201	30
31	24868	-------	24927	-------	24988	-------	25049	25080	-------	25141	-------	25202	31

Figure T-62. 2011 Expiration Table

Day	Jan	Feb	Mar	Apr	May	Jun	Jul	Aug	Sep	Oct	Nov	Dec	Day
1	25203	25234	25263	25294	25324	25355	25385	25416	25447	25477	25508	25538	1
2	25204	25235	25264	25295	25325	25356	25386	25417	25448	25478	25509	25539	2
3	25205	25236	25265	25296	25326	25357	25387	25418	25449	25479	25510	25540	3
4	25206	25237	25266	25297	25327	25358	25388	25419	25450	25480	25511	25541	4
5	25207	25238	25267	25298	25328	25359	25389	25420	25451	25481	25512	25542	5
6	25208	25239	25268	25299	25329	25360	25390	25421	25452	25482	25513	25543	6
7	25209	25240	25269	25300	25330	25361	25391	25422	25453	25484	25514	25544	7
8	25210	25241	25270	25301	25331	25362	25392	25423	25454	25484	25515	25545	8
9	25211	25242	25271	25302	25332	25363	25393	25424	25455	25485	25516	25546	9
10	25212	25243	25272	25303	25333	25364	25394	25425	25456	25486	25517	25547	10
11	25213	25244	25273	25304	25334	25365	25395	25426	25457	25487	25518	25548	11
12	25214	25245	25274	25305	25335	25366	25396	25427	25458	25488	25519	25549	12
13	25215	25246	25275	25306	25336	25367	25397	25428	25459	25489	25520	25550	13
14	25216	25247	25276	25307	25337	25368	25398	25429	25460	25490	25521	25551	14
15	25217	25248	25277	25308	25338	25369	25399	25430	25461	25491	25522	25552	15
16	25218	25249	25278	25309	25339	25370	25400	25431	25462	25492	25523	25553	16
17	25219	25250	25279	25310	25340	25371	25401	25432	25463	25494	25524	25554	17
18	25220	25251	25280	25311	25341	25372	25402	25433	25464	25494	25525	25555	18
19	25221	25252	25281	25312	25342	25373	25403	25434	25465	25495	25526	25556	19
20	25222	25253	25282	25313	25343	25374	25404	25435	25466	25496	25527	25557	20
21	25223	25254	25283	25314	25344	25375	25405	25436	25467	25497	25528	25558	21
22	25224	25255	25284	25315	25345	25376	25406	25437	25468	25498	25529	25559	22
23	25225	25256	25285	25316	25346	25377	25407	25438	25469	25499	25530	25560	23
24	25226	25257	25286	25317	25347	25378	25408	25439	25470	25500	25531	25561	24
25	25227	25258	25287	25318	25348	25379	25409	25440	25471	25501	25532	25562	25
26	25228	25259	25288	25319	25349	25380	25410	25441	25472	25502	25533	25563	26
27	25229	25260	25289	25320	25350	25381	25411	25442	25473	25503	25534	25564	27
28	25230	25261	25290	25321	25351	25382	25412	25443	25474	25504	25535	25565	28
29	25231	25262	25291	25322	25352	25383	25413	25444	25475	25505	25536	25566	29
30	25232	-------	25292	25323	25353	25384	25414	25445	25476	25506	25537	2557	30
31	25233	-------	25293	-------	25354	-------	25415	25446	-------	25507	-------	25568	31

Figure T-63. 2012 Expiration Table

Day	Jan	Feb	Mar	Apr	May	Jun	Jul	Aug	Sep	Oct	Nov	Dec	Day
1	25569	25600	25628	25659	25689	25720	25750	25781	25812	25842	25873	25903	1
2	25570	25601	25629	25660	25690	25721	25751	25782	25813	25843	25874	25904	2
3	25571	25602	25630	25661	25691	25722	25752	25783	25814	25844	25875	25905	3
4	25572	25603	25631	25662	25692	25723	25753	25784	25815	25845	25876	25906	4
5	25573	25604	25632	25663	25693	25724	25754	25785	25816	25846	25877	25907	5
6	25574	25605	25633	25664	25694	25725	25755	25786	25817	25847	25878	25908	6
7	25575	25606	25634	25665	25695	25726	25756	25787	25818	25848	25879	25909	7
8	25576	25607	25635	25666	25696	25727	25757	25788	25819	25849	25880	25910	8
9	25577	25608	25636	25667	25697	25728	25758	25789	25820	25850	25881	25911	9
10	25578	25609	25637	25668	25698	25729	25759	25790	25821	25851	25882	25912	10
11	25579	25610	25638	25669	25699	25730	25760	25791	25822	25852	25883	25913	11
12	25580	25611	25639	25670	25700	25731	25761	25792	25823	25853	25884	25914	12
13	25581	25612	25640	25671	25701	25732	25762	25793	25824	25854	25885	25915	13
14	25582	25613	25641	25672	25702	25733	25763	25794	25825	25855	25886	25916	14
15	25583	25614	25642	25673	25703	25734	25764	25795	25826	25856	25887	25917	15
16	25584	25615	25643	25674	25704	25735	25765	25796	25827	25857	25888	25918	16
17	25585	25616	25644	25675	25705	25736	25766	25797	25828	25858	25889	25919	17
18	25586	25617	25645	25676	25706	25737	25767	25798	25829	25859	25890	25920	18
19	25587	25618	25646	25677	25707	25738	25768	25799	25830	25860	25891	25921	19
20	25588	25619	25647	25678	25708	25739	25769	25800	25831	25861	25892	25922	20
21	25589	25620	25648	25679	25709	25740	25770	25801	25832	25862	25893	25923	21
22	25590	25621	25649	25680	25710	25741	25771	25802	25833	25863	25894	25924	22
23	25591	25622	25650	25681	25711	25742	25772	25803	25834	25864	25895	25925	23
24	25592	25623	25651	25682	25712	25743	25773	25804	25835	25865	25896	25926	24
25	25593	25624	25652	25683	25713	25744	25774	25805	25836	25866	25897	25927	25
26	25594	25625	25653	25684	25714	25745	25775	25806	25837	25867	25898	25928	26
27	25595	25626	25654	25685	25715	25746	25776	25807	25838	25868	25899	25929	27
28	25596	25627	25655	25686	25716	25747	25777	25808	25839	25869	25900	25930	28
29	25597	-------	25656	25687	25717	25748	25778	25809	25840	25870	25901	25931	29
30	25598	-------	25657	25688	25718	25749	25779	25810	25841	25871	25902	25932	30
31	25599	-------	25658	-------	25719	-------	25780	25811	-------	25872	-------	25933	31

Figure T-64. 2013 Expiration Table

Day	Jan	Feb	Mar	Apr	May	Jun	Jul	Aug	Sep	Oct	Nov	Dec	Day
1	25934	25965	25993	26024	26054	26085	26115	26146	26177	26207	26238	26268	1
2	25935	25966	25994	26025	26055	26086	26116	26147	26178	26208	26239	26269	2
3	25936	25967	25995	26026	26056	26087	26117	26148	26179	26209	26240	26270	3
4	25937	25968	25996	26027	26057	26088	26118	26149	26180	26210	26241	26271	4
5	25938	25969	25997	26028	26058	26089	26119	26150	26181	26211	26242	26272	5
6	25939	25970	25998	26029	26059	26090	26120	26151	26182	26212	26243	26273	6
7	25940	25971	25999	26030	26060	26091	26121	26152	26183	26213	26244	26274	7
8	25941	25972	26000	26031	26061	26092	26122	26153	26184	26214	26245	26275	8
9	25942	25973	26001	26032	26062	26093	26123	26154	26185	26215	26246	26276	9
10	25943	25974	26002	26033	26063	26094	26124	26155	26186	26216	26247	26277	10
11	25944	25975	26003	26034	26064	26095	26125	26156	26187	26217	26248	26278	11
12	25945	25976	26004	26035	26065	26096	26126	26157	26188	26218	26249	26279	12
13	25946	25977	26005	26036	26066	26097	26127	26158	26189	26219	26250	26280	13
14	25947	25978	26006	26037	26067	26098	26128	26159	26190	26220	26251	26281	14
15	25948	25979	26007	26038	26068	26099	26129	26160	26191	26221	25252	26282	15
16	25949	25980	26008	26039	26069	26100	26130	26161	26192	26222	26253	26283	16
17	25950	25981	26009	26040	26070	26101	26131	26162	26193	26223	26254	26284	17
18	25951	25982	26010	26041	26071	26102	26132	26163	26194	26224	26255	26285	18
19	25952	25983	26011	26042	26072	26103	26133	26164	26195	26225	26256	26286	19
20	25953	25984	26012	26043	26073	26104	26134	26165	26196	26226	26257	26287	20
21	25954	25985	26013	26044	26074	26105	26135	26166	26197	26227	26258	26288	21
22	25955	25986	26014	26045	26075	26106	26136	26167	26198	26228	26259	26289	22
23	25956	25987	26015	26046	26076	26107	26137	26168	26199	26229	26260	26290	23
24	25957	25988	26016	26047	26077	26108	26138	26169	26200	26230	26261	26291	24
25	25958	25989	26017	26048	26078	26109	26139	26170	26201	26231	26262	26292	25
26	25959	25990	26018	26049	26079	26110	26140	26171	26202	26232	26263	26293	26
27	25960	25991	26019	26050	26080	26111	26141	26172	26203	26233	26264	26294	27
28	25961	25992	26020	26051	26081	26112	26142	26173	26204	26234	26265	26295	28
29	25962	....	26021	26052	26082	26113	26143	26174	26205	26235	26266	26296	29
30	25963	....	26022	26053	26083	26114	26144	26175	26206	26236	26267	26297	30
31	25964	....	26023	....	26084	....	26145	26176	....	26237	....	26298	31

Figure T-65. 2014 Expiration Table

2015   **Expiration Table**   **2015**

Day	Jan	Feb	Mar	Apr	May	Jun	Jul	Aug	Sep	Oct	Nov	Dec	Day
1	26299	26330	26358	26389	26419	26450	26480	26511	26542	26572	26603	26633	1
2	26300	26331	26359	26390	26420	26451	26481	26512	26543	26573	26604	26634	2
3	26301	26332	26360	26391	26421	26452	26482	26513	26544	26574	26605	26635	3
4	26302	26333	26361	26392	26422	26453	26483	26514	26545	26575	26606	26636	4
5	26303	26334	26362	26393	26423	26454	26484	26515	26546	26576	26607	26637	5
6	26304	26335	26363	26394	26424	26455	26485	26516	26547	26577	26608	26638	6
7	26305	26336	26364	26395	26425	26456	26486	26517	26548	26578	26609	26639	7
8	26306	26337	26365	26396	26426	26457	26487	26518	26549	26579	26610	26640	8
9	26307	26338	26366	26397	26427	26458	26488	26519	26550	26580	26611	26641	9
10	26308	26339	26367	26398	26428	26459	26489	26520	26551	26581	26612	26642	10
11	26309	26340	26368	26399	26429	26460	26490	26521	26552	26582	26613	26643	11
12	26310	26341	26369	26400	26430	26461	26491	26522	26553	26583	26614	26644	12
13	26311	26342	26370	26401	26431	26462	26492	26523	26554	26584	26615	26645	13
14	26312	26343	26371	26402	26432	26463	26493	26524	26555	26585	26616	26646	14
15	26313	26344	26372	26403	26433	26464	26494	26525	26556	26586	26617	26647	15
16	26314	26345	26373	26404	26434	26465	26495	26526	26557	26587	26618	26648	16
17	26315	26346	26374	26405	26435	26466	26496	26527	26558	26588	26619	26649	17
18	26316	26347	26375	26406	26436	26467	26497	26528	26559	26589	26620	26650	18
19	26317	26348	26376	26407	26437	26468	26498	26529	26560	26590	26621	26651	19
20	26318	26349	26377	26408	26438	26469	26499	26530	26561	26591	26622	26652	20
21	26319	26350	26378	26409	26439	26470	26500	26531	26562	26592	26623	26653	21
22	26320	26351	26379	26410	26440	26471	26501	26532	26563	26593	26624	26654	22
23	26321	26352	26380	26411	26441	26472	26502	26533	26564	26594	26625	26655	23
24	26322	26353	26381	26412	26442	26473	26503	26534	26565	26595	26626	26656	24
25	26323	26354	26382	26413	26443	26474	26504	26535	26566	26596	26627	26657	25
26	26324	26355	26383	26414	26444	26475	26505	26536	26567	26597	26628	26658	26
27	26325	26356	26384	26415	26445	26476	26506	26537	26568	26598	26629	26659	27
28	26326	26357	26385	26416	26446	26477	26507	26538	26569	26599	26630	26660	28
29	26327	-------	26386	26417	26447	26478	26508	26539	26570	26600	26631	26661	29
30	26328	-------	26387	26418	26448	26479	26509	26540	26571	26601	26632	26662	30
31	26329	-------	26388	-------	26449	-------	26510	26541	-------	26602	-------	26663	31

Figure T-66. 2015 Expiration Table

2016   Expiration Table   2016

Day	Jan	Feb	Mar	Apr	May	Jun	Jul	Aug	Sep	Oct	Nov	Dec	Day
1	26664	26695	26724	26755	26785	26816	26846	26877	26908	26938	26969	26999	1
2	26665	26696	26725	26756	26786	26817	26847	26878	26909	26939	26970	27000	2
3	26666	26697	26726	26757	26787	26818	26848	26879	26910	26940	26971	27001	3
4	26667	26698	26727	26758	26788	26819	26849	26880	26911	26941	26972	27002	4
5	26668	26699	26728	26759	26789	26820	26850	26881	26912	26942	26973	27003	5
6	26669	26700	26729	26760	26790	26821	26851	26882	26913	26943	26974	27004	6
7	26670	26701	26730	26761	26791	26822	26852	26883	26914	26944	26975	27005	7
8	26671	26702	26731	26762	26792	26823	26853	26884	26915	26945	26976	27006	8
9	26672	26703	26732	26763	26793	26824	26854	26885	26916	26946	26977	27007	9
10	26673	26704	26733	26764	26794	26825	26855	26886	26917	26947	26978	27008	10
11	26674	26705	26734	26765	26795	26826	26856	26887	26918	26948	26979	27009	11
12	26675	26706	26735	26766	26796	26827	26857	26888	26919	26949	26980	27010	12
13	26676	26707	26736	26767	26797	26828	26858	26889	26920	26950	26981	27011	13
14	26677	26708	26737	26768	26798	26829	26859	26890	26921	26951	26982	27012	14
15	26678	26709	26738	26769	26799	26830	26860	26891	26922	26952	26983	27013	15
16	26679	26710	26739	26770	26800	26831	26861	26892	26923	26953	26984	27014	16
17	26680	26711	26740	26771	26801	26832	26862	26893	26924	26954	26985	27015	17
18	26681	26712	26741	26772	26802	26833	26863	26894	26925	26955	26986	27016	18
19	26682	26713	26742	26773	26803	26834	26864	26895	26926	26956	26987	27017	19
20	26683	26714	26743	26774	26804	26835	26865	26896	26927	26957	26988	27018	20
21	26684	26715	26744	26775	26805	26836	26866	26897	26928	26958	26989	27019	21
22	26685	26716	26745	26776	26806	26837	26867	26898	26929	26959	26990	27020	22
23	26686	26717	26746	26777	26807	26838	26868	26899	26930	26960	26991	27021	23
24	26687	26718	26747	26778	26808	26839	26869	26900	26931	26961	26992	27022	24
25	26688	26719	26748	26779	26809	26840	26870	26901	26932	26962	26993	27023	25
26	26689	26720	26749	26780	26810	26841	26871	26902	26933	26963	26994	27024	26
27	26690	26721	26750	26781	26811	26842	26872	26903	26934	26964	26995	27025	27
28	26691	26722	26751	26782	26812	26843	26873	26904	26935	26965	26996	27026	28
29	26692	26723	26752	26783	26813	26844	26874	26905	26936	26966	26997	27027	29
30	26693	-------	26753	26784	26814	26845	26875	26906	26937	26967	26998	27028	30
31	26694	-------	26754	-------	26815	-------	26876	26907	-------	26968	-------	27029	31

Figure T-67. 2016 Expiration Table

Day	Jan	Feb	Mar	Apr	May	Jun	Jul	Aug	Sep	Oct	Nov	Dec	Day
1	27030	27061	27089	27120	27150	27181	27211	27242	27273	27303	27334	27364	1
2	27031	27062	27090	27121	27151	27182	27212	27243	27274	27304	27335	27365	2
3	27032	27063	27091	27122	27152	27183	27213	27244	27275	27305	27336	27366	3
4	27033	27064	27092	27123	27153	27184	27214	27245	27276	27306	27337	27367	4
5	27034	27065	27093	27124	27154	27185	27215	27246	27277	27307	27338	27368	5
6	27035	27066	27094	27125	27155	27186	27216	27247	27278	27308	27339	27369	6
7	27036	27067	27095	27126	27156	27187	27217	27248	27279	27309	27340	27370	7
8	27037	27068	27096	27127	27157	27188	27218	27249	27280	27310	27341	27371	8
9	27038	27069	27097	27128	27158	27189	27219	27250	27281	27311	27342	27372	9
10	27039	27070	27098	27129	27159	27190	27220	27251	27282	27312	27343	27373	10
11	27040	27071	27099	27130	27160	27191	27221	27252	27283	27313	27344	27374	11
12	27041	27072	27100	27131	27161	27192	27222	27253	27284	27314	27345	27375	12
13	27042	27073	27101	27132	27162	27193	27223	27254	27285	27315	27346	27376	13
14	27043	27074	27102	27133	27163	27194	27224	27255	27286	27316	27347	27377	14
15	27044	27075	27103	27134	27164	27195	27225	27256	27287	27317	27348	27378	15
16	27045	27076	27104	27135	27165	27196	27226	27257	27288	27318	27349	27379	16
17	27046	27077	27105	27136	27166	27197	27227	27258	27289	27319	27350	27380	17
18	27047	27078	27106	27137	27167	27198	27228	27259	27290	27320	27351	27381	18
19	27048	27079	27107	27138	27168	27199	27229	27260	27291	27321	27352	27382	19
20	27049	27080	27108	27139	27169	27200	27230	27261	27292	27322	27353	27383	20
21	27050	27081	27109	27140	27170	27201	27231	27262	27293	27323	27354	27384	21
22	27051	27082	27110	27141	27171	27202	27232	27263	27294	27324	27355	27385	22
23	27052	27083	27111	27142	27172	27203	27233	27264	27295	27325	27356	27386	23
24	27053	27084	27112	27143	27173	27204	27234	27265	27296	27326	27357	27387	24
25	27054	27085	27113	27144	27174	27205	27235	27266	27297	27327	27358	27388	25
26	27055	27086	27114	27145	27175	27206	27236	27267	27298	27328	27359	27389	26
27	27056	27087	27115	27146	27176	27207	27237	27268	27299	27329	27360	27390	27
28	27057	27088	27116	27147	27177	27208	27238	27269	27300	27330	27361	27391	28
29	27058	-------	27117	27148	27178	27209	27239	27270	27301	27331	27362	27392	29
30	27059	-------	27118	27149	27179	27210	27240	27271	27302	27332	27363	27393	30
31	27060	-------	27119	-------	27180	-------	27241	27272	-------	27333	-------	27394	31

Figure T-68. 2017 Expiration Table

	2018				**Expiration Table**				**2018**				
Day	Jan	Feb	Mar	Apr	May	Jun	Jul	Aug	Sep	Oct	Nov	Dec	Day
1	27395	27426	27454	27485	27515	27546	27576	27607	27638	27668	27699	27729	1
2	27396	27427	27455	27486	27516	27547	27577	27608	27639	27669	27700	27730	2
3	27397	27428	27456	27487	27517	27548	27578	27609	27640	27670	27701	27731	3
4	27398	27429	27457	27488	27518	27549	27579	27610	27641	27671	27702	27732	4
5	27399	27430	27458	27489	27519	27550	27580	27611	27642	27672	27703	27733	5
6	27400	27431	27459	27490	27520	27551	27581	27612	27643	27673	27704	27734	6
7	27401	27432	27460	27491	27521	27552	27582	27613	27644	27674	27705	27735	7
8	27402	27433	27461	27492	27522	27553	27583	27614	27645	27675	27706	27736	8
9	27403	27434	27462	27493	27523	27554	27584	27615	27646	27676	27707	27737	9
10	27404	27435	27463	27494	27524	27555	27585	27616	27647	27677	27708	27738	10
11	27405	27436	27464	27495	27525	27556	27586	27617	27648	27678	27709	27739	11
12	27406	27437	27565	27496	27526	27557	27587	27618	27649	27679	27710	27740	12
13	27407	27438	27466	27497	27527	27558	27588	27619	27650	27680	27711	27741	13
14	27408	27439	27467	27498	27528	27559	27589	27620	27651	27681	27712	27742	14
15	27409	27440	27468	27499	27529	27560	27590	27621	27652	27682	27713	27743	15
16	27410	27441	27469	27500	27530	27561	27591	27622	27653	27683	27714	27744	16
17	27411	27442	27470	27501	27531	27562	27592	27623	27654	27684	27715	27745	17
18	27412	27443	27471	27502	27532	27563	27593	27624	27655	27685	27716	27746	18
19	27413	27444	27472	27503	27533	27564	27594	27625	27656	27686	27717	27747	19
20	27414	27445	27473	27504	27534	27565	27595	27626	27657	27687	27718	27748	20
21	27415	27446	27474	27505	27535	27566	27596	27627	27658	27688	27719	27749	21
22	27416	27447	27475	27506	27536	27567	27597	27628	27659	27689	27720	27750	22
23	27417	27448	27476	27507	27537	27568	27598	27629	27660	27690	27721	27751	23
24	27418	27449	27477	27508	27538	27569	27599	27630	27661	27691	27722	27752	24
25	27419	27450	27478	27509	27539	27570	27600	27631	27662	27692	27723	27753	25
26	27420	27451	27479	27510	27540	27571	27601	27632	27663	27693	27724	27754	26
27	27421	27452	27480	27511	27541	27572	27602	27633	27664	27694	27725	27755	27
28	27422	27453	27481	27512	27542	27573	27603	27634	27665	27695	27726	27756	28
29	27423	-------	27482	27513	27543	27574	27604	27635	27666	27696	27727	27757	29
30	27424	-------	27483	27514	27544	27575	27605	27636	27667	27697	27728	27758	30
31	27425	-------	27484	-------	27545	-------	27606	27637	-----	27698	-------	27759	31

Figure T-69. 2018 Expiration Table

2019 Expiration Table 2019

Day	Jan	Feb	Mar	Apr	May	Jun	Jul	Aug	Sep	Oct	Nov	Dec	Day
1	27760	27791	27819	27850	27880	27911	27941	27972	28003	28033	28064	28094	1
2	27761	27792	27820	27851	27881	27912	27942	27973	28004	28034	28065	28095	2
3	27762	27793	27821	27852	27882	27913	27943	27974	28005	28035	28066	28096	3
4	27763	27794	27822	27853	27883	27914	27944	27975	28006	28036	28067	28097	4
5	27764	27795	27823	27854	27884	27915	27945	27976	28007	28037	28068	28098	5
6	27765	27796	27824	27855	27885	27916	27946	27977	28008	28038	28069	28099	6
7	27766	27797	27825	27856	27886	27917	27947	27978	28009	28039	28070	28100	7
8	27767	27798	27826	27857	27887	27918	27948	27979	28010	28040	28071	28101	8
9	27768	27799	27827	27858	27888	27919	27949	27980	28011	28041	28072	28102	9
10	27769	27800	27828	27859	27889	27920	27950	27981	28012	28042	28073	28103	10
11	27770	27801	27829	27860	27890	27921	27951	27982	28013	28043	28074	28104	11
12	27771	27802	27830	27861	27891	27922	27952	27983	28014	28044	28075	28105	12
13	27772	27803	27831	27862	27892	27923	27953	27984	28015	28045	28076	28106	13
14	27773	27804	27832	27863	27893	27924	27954	27985	28016	28046	28077	28107	14
15	27774	27805	27833	27864	27894	27925	27955	27986	28017	28047	28078	28108	15
16	27775	27806	27834	27865	27895	27926	27956	27987	28018	28048	28079	28109	16
17	27776	27807	27835	27866	27896	27927	27957	27988	28019	28049	28080	28110	17
18	27777	27808	27836	27867	27897	27928	27958	27989	28020	28050	28081	28111	18
19	27778	27809	27837	27868	27898	27929	27959	27990	28021	28051	28082	28112	19
20	27779	27810	27838	27869	27899	27930	27960	27991	28022	28052	28083	28113	20
21	27780	27811	27839	27870	27900	27931	27961	27992	28023	28053	28084	28114	21
22	27781	27812	27840	27871	27901	27932	27962	27993	28024	28054	20885	28115	22
23	27782	27813	27841	27872	27902	27933	27963	27994	28025	28055	28086	28116	23
24	27783	27814	27842	27873	27903	27934	27964	27995	28026	28056	28087	28117	24
25	27784	27815	27843	27874	27904	27935	27965	27996	28027	28057	28088	28118	25
26	27785	27816	27844	27875	27905	27936	27966	27997	28028	28058	28089	28119	26
27	27786	27817	27845	27876	27906	27937	27967	27998	28029	28059	28090	28120	27
28	27787	27818	27846	27877	27907	27938	27968	27999	28030	28060	28091	28121	28
29	27788	....	27847	27878	27908	27939	27969	28000	28031	28061	28092	28122	29
30	27789	....	27848	27879	27909	27940	27970	28001	28032	28062	28093	28123	30
31	27790	....	27849	....	27910	....	27971	28002	....	28063	....	28124	31

Figure T-70. 2019 Expiration Table

2020 **Expiration Table** **2020**

Day	Jan	Feb	Mar	Apr	May	Jun	Jul	Aug	Sep	Oct	Nov	Dec	Day
1	28125	28156	28185	28216	28246	28277	28307	28338	28369	28399	28430	28460	1
2	28126	28157	28186	28217	28247	28278	28308	28339	28370	28400	28431	28461	2
3	28127	28158	28187	28218	28248	28279	28309	28340	28371	28401	28432	28462	3
4	28128	28159	28188	28219	28249	28280	28310	28341	28372	28402	28433	28463	4
5	28129	28160	28189	28120	28250	28281	28311	28342	28373	28403	28434	28464	5
6	28130	28161	28190	28221	28251	28282	28312	28343	28374	28404	28435	28465	6
7	28131	28162	28191	28222	28252	28283	28313	28344	28375	28405	28436	28466	7
8	28132	28163	28192	28223	28253	28284	28314	28345	28376	28406	28437	28467	8
9	28133	28164	28193	28224	28254	28285	28315	28346	28377	28407	28438	28468	9
10	28134	28165	28194	28225	28255	28286	28316	28347	28378	28408	28439	28469	10
11	28135	28166	28195	28226	28256	28287	28317	28348	28379	28409	28440	28470	11
12	28136	28167	28196	28227	28257	28288	28318	28349	28380	28410	28441	28471	12
13	28137	28168	28197	28228	28258	28289	28319	28350	28381	28411	28442	28472	13
14	28138	28169	28198	28229	28259	28290	28320	28351	28382	28412	28443	28473	14
15	28139	28170	28199	28230	28260	28291	28321	28352	28383	28413	28444	28474	15
16	28140	28171	28200	28231	28261	28292	28322	28353	28384	28414	28445	28475	16
17	28141	28172	28201	28232	28262	28293	28323	28354	28385	28415	28446	28476	17
18	28142	28173	28202	28233	28263	28294	28324	28355	28386	28416	28447	28477	18
19	28143	28174	28203	28234	28264	28295	28325	28356	28387	28417	28448	28478	19
20	28144	28175	28204	28235	28265	28296	28326	28357	28388	28418	28449	28479	20
21	28145	28176	28205	28236	28266	28297	28327	28358	28389	28419	28450	28480	21
22	28146	28177	28206	28237	28267	28298	28328	28359	28390	28420	28451	28481	22
23	28147	28178	28207	28238	28268	28299	28329	28360	28391	28421	28452	28482	23
24	28148	28179	28208	28239	28269	28300	28330	28361	28392	28422	28453	28483	24
25	28149	28180	28209	28240	28270	28301	28331	28362	28393	28423	28454	28484	25
26	28150	28181	28210	28241	28271	28302	28332	28363	28394	28424	28455	28485	26
27	28151	28182	28211	28242	28272	28303	28333	28364	28395	28425	28556	28486	27
28	28152	28183	28212	28243	28273	28304	28334	28365	28396	28426	28457	28487	28
29	28153	28184	28213	28244	28274	28305	28335	28366	28397	28427	28458	28488	29
30	28154	....	28214	28245	28275	28306	28336	28367	28398	28428	28459	28489	30
31	28155	....	28215	....	28276	....	28337	28368	....	28429	....	28490	31

Figure T-71. 2020 Expiration Table

<table>
<tr><td>Day</td><td>2021</td><td></td><td></td><td></td><td></td><td></td><td></td><td>Expiration Table</td><td></td><td></td><td>2021</td><td></td><td>Day</td></tr>
</table>

2021 Expiration Table 2021

Day	Jan	Feb	Mar	Apr	May	Jun	Jul	Aug	Sep	Oct	Nov	Dec	Day
1	28491	28522	28550	28581	28611	28642	28672	28703	28734	28764	28795	28825	1
2	28492	28523	28551	28582	28612	28643	28673	28704	28735	28765	28796	28826	2
3	28493	28524	28552	28583	28613	28644	28674	28705	28736	28766	28797	28827	3
4	28494	28525	28553	28584	28614	28645	28675	28706	28737	28767	28798	28828	4
5	28495	28526	28554	28585	28615	28646	28676	28707	28738	28768	28799	28829	5
6	28496	28527	28555	28586	28616	28647	28677	28708	28739	28769	28800	28830	6
7	28497	28528	28556	28587	28617	28648	28678	28709	28740	28770	28801	28831	7
8	28498	28529	28557	28588	28618	28649	28679	28710	28741	28771	28802	28832	8
9	28499	28530	28558	28589	28619	28650	28680	28711	28742	28772	28803	28833	9
10	28500	28531	28559	28590	28620	28651	28681	28712	28743	28773	28804	28834	10
11	28501	28532	28560	28591	28621	28652	28682	28713	28744	28774	28805	28835	11
12	28502	28533	28561	28592	28622	28653	28683	28714	28745	28775	28806	28836	12
13	28503	28534	28562	28593	28623	28654	28684	28715	28746	28776	28807	28837	13
14	28504	28535	28563	28594	28624	28655	28685	28716	28747	28777	28808	28838	14
15	28505	28536	28564	28595	28625	28656	28686	28717	28748	28778	28809	28839	15
16	28506	28537	28565	28596	28626	28657	28687	28718	28749	28779	28810	28840	16
17	28507	28538	28566	28597	28627	28658	28688	28719	28750	28780	28811	28841	17
18	28508	28539	28567	28598	28628	28659	28689	28720	28751	28781	28812	28842	18
19	28509	28540	28568	28599	28629	28660	28690	28721	28752	28782	28813	28843	19
20	28510	28541	28569	28600	28630	28661	28691	28722	28753	28783	28814	28844	20
21	28511	28542	28570	28601	28631	28662	28692	28723	28754	28784	28815	28845	21
22	28512	28543	28571	28602	28632	28663	28693	28724	28755	28785	28816	28846	22
23	28513	28544	28572	28603	28633	28664	28694	28725	28756	28786	28817	28847	23
24	28514	28545	28573	28604	28634	28665	28695	28726	28757	28787	28818	28848	24
25	28515	28546	28574	28605	28635	28666	28696	28727	28758	28788	28819	28849	25
26	28516	28547	28575	28606	28636	28667	28697	28728	28759	28789	28820	28850	26
27	28517	28548	28576	28607	28637	28668	28698	28729	28760	28790	28821	28851	27
28	28518	28549	28577	28608	28638	28669	28699	28730	28761	28791	28822	28852	28
29	28519	-------	28578	28609	28639	28670	28700	28731	28762	28792	28823	28853	29
30	28520	-------	28579	28610	28640	28671	28701	28732	28763	28793	28824	28854	30
31	28521	-------	28580	-------	28641	-------	28702	28733	-------	28794	-------	28855	31

Figure T-72. 2021 Expiration Table

Day	Jan	Feb	Mar	Apr	May	Jun	Jul	Aug	Sep	Oct	Nov	Dec	Day
1	28856	28887	28915	28946	28976	29007	29037	29068	29099	29129	29160	29190	1
2	28857	28888	28916	28947	28977	29008	29038	29069	29100	29130	29161	29191	2
3	28858	28889	28917	28948	28978	29009	29039	29070	29101	29131	29162	29192	3
4	28859	28890	28918	28949	28979	29010	29040	29071	29102	29132	29163	29193	4
5	28860	28891	28919	28950	28980	29011	29041	29072	29103	29133	29164	29194	5
6	28861	28892	28920	28951	28981	29012	29042	29073	29104	29134	29165	29195	6
7	28862	28893	28921	28952	28982	29013	29043	29074	29105	29135	29166	29196	7
8	28863	28894	28922	28953	28983	29014	29044	29075	29106	29136	29167	29197	8
9	28864	28895	28923	28954	28984	29015	29045	29076	29107	29137	29168	29198	9
10	28865	28896	28924	28955	28985	29016	29046	29077	29108	29138	29169	29199	10
11	28866	28897	28925	28956	28986	29017	29047	29078	29109	29139	29170	29200	11
12	28867	28898	28926	28957	28987	29018	29048	29079	29110	29140	29171	29201	12
13	28868	28899	28927	28958	28988	20010	29049	29080	29111	29141	29172	29202	13
14	28869	28900	28928	28959	28989	29020	29050	29081	29112	29142	29173	29203	14
15	28870	28901	28929	28960	28990	29021	29051	29082	29113	29143	29174	29204	15
16	28871	28902	28930	28961	28991	29022	29052	29083	29114	29144	29175	29205	16
17	28872	28903	28931	28962	28992	29023	29053	29084	29115	29145	29176	29206	17
18	28873	28904	28932	28963	28993	29024	29054	29085	29116	29146	29177	29207	18
19	28874	28905	28933	28964	28994	29025	29055	29086	29117	29147	29178	29208	19
20	28875	28906	28934	28965	28995	29026	29056	29087	29118	29148	29179	29209	20
21	28876	28907	28935	28966	28996	29027	29057	29088	29119	29149	29180	29210	21
22	28877	28908	28936	28967	28997	29028	29058	29089	29120	29150	29181	29211	22
23	28878	28909	28937	28968	28998	29029	29059	29090	29121	29151	29182	29212	23
24	28879	28910	28938	28969	28999	29030	29060	29091	29122	19252	29183	29213	24
25	28880	28911	28939	28970	29000	29031	29061	29092	29123	29153	29184	29214	25
26	28881	28912	28940	28971	29001	29032	29062	29093	29124	29154	29185	29215	26
27	28882	28913	28941	28972	29002	29033	29063	29094	29125	29155	29186	29216	27
28	28883	28914	28942	28973	29003	29034	29064	29095	29126	29156	29187	29217	28
29	28884	-------	28943	28974	29004	29035	29065	29096	29127	29157	29188	29218	29
30	28885	-------	28944	28975	29005	29036	29066	29097	29128	29158	29189	29219	30
31	28886	-------	28945	-------	29006	-------	29067	29098	-------	29159	-------	29220	31

Figure T-73. 2022 Expiration Table

2023   Expiration Table   2023

Day	Jan	Feb	Mar	Apr	May	Jun	Jul	Aug	Sep	Oct	Nov	Dec	Day
1	29221	29252	29280	29311	29341	29372	29402	29433	29464	29494	29525	29555	1
2	29222	29253	29281	29312	29342	29373	29403	29434	29465	29495	29526	29556	2
3	29223	29254	29282	29313	29343	29374	29404	29435	29466	29496	29527	29557	3
4	29224	29255	29283	29314	29344	29375	29405	29436	29467	29497	29528	29558	4
5	29225	29256	29284	29315	29345	29376	29406	29437	29468	29498	29529	29559	5
6	29226	29257	29285	29316	29346	29377	29407	29438	29469	29499	29530	29560	6
7	29227	29258	29286	29317	29347	29378	29408	29439	29470	29500	29531	29561	7
8	29228	29259	29287	29318	29348	29379	29409	29440	29471	29501	29532	29562	8
9	29229	29260	29288	29319	29349	29380	29410	29441	29472	29502	29533	29563	9
10	29230	29261	29289	29320	29350	29381	29411	29442	29473	29503	29534	29564	10
11	29231	29262	29290	29321	29351	29382	29412	29443	29474	29504	29535	29565	11
12	29232	29263	29291	29322	29352	29383	29413	29444	29475	29505	29536	29566	12
13	29233	29264	29292	29323	29353	29384	29414	29445	29476	29506	29537	29567	13
14	29234	29265	29293	29324	29354	29385	29415	29446	29477	29507	29538	29568	14
15	29235	29266	29294	29325	29355	29386	29416	29447	29478	29508	29539	29569	15
16	29236	29267	29295	29326	29356	29387	29417	29448	29479	29509	29540	29570	16
17	29237	29268	29296	29327	29357	29388	29418	29449	29480	29510	29541	29571	17
18	29238	29269	29297	29328	29358	29389	29419	29450	29481	29511	29542	29572	18
19	29239	29270	29298	29329	29359	29390	29420	29451	29482	29512	29543	29573	19
20	29240	29271	29299	29330	29360	29391	29421	29452	29483	29513	29544	29574	20
21	29241	29272	29300	29331	29361	29392	29422	29453	29484	29514	29545	29575	21
22	29242	29273	29301	29332	29362	29393	29423	29454	29485	29515	29546	29576	22
23	29243	29274	29302	29333	29363	29394	29424	29455	29486	29516	29547	29577	23
24	29244	29275	29303	29334	29364	29395	29425	29456	29487	29517	29548	29578	24
25	29245	29276	29304	29335	29365	29396	29426	29457	29488	29518	29549	29579	25
26	29246	29277	29305	29336	29366	29397	29427	29458	29489	29519	29550	29580	26
27	29247	29278	29306	29337	29367	29398	29428	29459	29490	29520	29551	29581	27
28	29248	29279	29307	29338	29368	29399	29429	29460	29491	29521	29552	29582	28
29	29249	-------	29308	29339	29369	29400	29430	29461	29492	29522	29553	29583	29
30	29250	-------	29309	29340	29370	29401	29431	29462	29493	29523	29554	29584	30
31	29251	-------	29310	-------	29371	-------	29432	29463	-------	29524	-------	29585	31

Figure T-74. 2023 Expiration Table

Day	Jan	Feb	Mar	Apr	May	Jun	Jul	Aug	Sep	Oct	Nov	Dec	Day
1	29586	29617	29646	29677	29707	29738	29768	29799	29830	29860	29891	29921	1
2	29587	29618	29647	29678	29708	29739	29769	29800	29831	29861	29892	29922	2
3	29588	29619	29648	29679	29709	29740	29770	29801	29832	29862	29893	29923	3
4	29589	29620	29649	29680	29710	29741	29771	29802	29833	29863	29894	29924	4
5	29590	29621	29650	29681	29711	29742	29772	29803	29834	29864	29895	29925	5
6	29591	29622	29651	29682	29712	29743	29773	29804	29835	29865	29896	29926	6
7	29592	29623	29652	29683	29713	29744	29774	29805	29836	29866	29897	29927	7
8	29593	29624	29653	29684	29714	29745	29775	29806	29837	29867	29898	29928	8
9	29594	29625	29654	29685	29715	29746	29776	29807	29838	29868	29899	29929	9
10	29595	29626	29655	29686	29716	29747	29777	29808	29839	29869	29900	29930	10
11	29596	29627	29656	29687	29717	29748	29778	29809	29840	29870	29901	29931	11
12	29597	29628	29657	29688	29718	29749	29779	29810	29841	29871	29902	29932	12
13	29598	29629	29658	29689	29719	29750	29780	29811	29842	29872	29903	29933	13
14	29599	29630	29659	29690	29720	29751	29781	29812	29843	29873	29904	29934	14
15	29600	29631	29660	29691	29721	29752	29782	29813	29844	29874	29905	29935	15
16	29601	29632	29661	29692	29722	29753	29783	29814	29845	29875	29906	29936	16
17	29602	29633	29662	29693	29723	29754	29784	29815	29846	29876	29907	29937	17
18	29603	29635	29663	29694	29724	29755	29785	29816	29847	29877	29908	29938	18
19	29604	29634	29664	29695	29725	29756	29786	29817	29848	29878	29909	29939	19
20	29605	29636	29665	29696	29726	29757	29787	29818	29849	29879	29910	29940	20
21	29606	29637	29666	29697	29727	29758	29788	29819	29850	29880	29911	29941	21
22	29607	29638	29667	29698	29728	29759	29789	29820	29851	29881	29912	29942	22
23	29608	29639	29668	29699	29729	29760	29790	29821	29852	29882	29913	29943	23
24	29609	29640	29669	29700	29730	29761	29791	29822	29853	29883	29914	29944	24
25	29610	29641	29670	29701	29731	29762	29792	29823	29854	29884	29915	29945	25
26	29611	29642	29671	29702	29732	29763	29793	29824	29855	29885	29916	29946	26
27	29612	29643	29672	29703	29733	29764	29794	29825	29856	29886	29917	29947	27
28	29613	29644	29673	29704	29734	29765	29795	29826	29857	29887	29918	29948	28
29	29614	29645	29674	29705	29735	29766	29796	29827	29858	29888	29919	29949	29
30	29615	-------	29675	29706	29736	29767	29797	29828	29859	29889	29920	29950	30
31	29616	-------	29676	-------	29737	-------	29798	29829	-------	29890	-------	29951	31

Figure T-75. 2024 Expiration Table

Day	Jan	Feb	Mar	Apr	May	Jun	Jul	Aug	Sep	Oct	Nov	Dec	Day
1	29952	29983	30011	30042	30072	30103	30133	30164	30195	30225	30256	30286	1
2	29953	29984	30012	30043	30073	30104	30134	30165	30196	30226	30257	30287	2
3	29954	29985	30013	30044	30074	30105	30135	30166	30197	30227	30258	30288	3
4	29955	29986	30014	30045	30075	30106	30136	30167	30198	30228	30259	30289	4
5	29956	29987	30015	30046	30076	30107	30137	30168	30199	30229	30260	30290	5
6	29957	29988	30016	30047	30077	30108	30138	30169	30200	30230	30261	30291	6
7	29958	29989	30017	30048	30078	30109	30139	30170	30201	30231	30262	30292	7
8	29959	29990	30018	30049	30079	30110	30140	30171	30202	30232	30263	30293	8
9	29960	29991	30019	30050	30080	30111	30141	30172	30203	30233	30264	30294	9
10	29961	29992	30020	30051	30081	30112	30142	30173	30204	30234	30265	30295	10
11	29962	29993	30021	30052	30082	30113	30143	30174	30205	30235	30266	30296	11
12	29963	29994	30022	30053	30083	30114	30144	30175	30206	30236	30267	30297	12
13	29964	29995	30023	30054	30084	30115	30145	30176	30207	30237	30268	30298	13
14	29965	29996	30024	30055	30085	30116	30146	30177	30208	30238	30269	30299	14
15	29966	29997	30025	30056	30086	30117	30147	30178	30209	30239	30270	30300	15
16	29967	29998	30026	30057	30087	30118	30148	30179	30210	30240	30271	30301	16
17	29968	29999	30027	30058	30088	30119	30149	30180	30211	30241	30272	30302	17
18	29969	30000	30028	30059	30089	30120	30150	30181	30212	30242	30273	30303	18
19	29970	30001	30029	30060	30090	30121	30151	30182	30213	30243	30274	30304	19
20	29971	30002	30030	30061	30091	30122	30152	30183	30214	30244	30275	30305	20
21	29972	30003	30031	30062	30092	30123	30153	30184	30215	30245	30276	30306	21
22	29973	30004	30032	30063	30093	30124	30154	30185	30216	30246	30277	30307	22
23	29974	30005	30033	30064	30094	30125	30155	30186	30217	30247	30278	30308	23
24	29975	30006	30034	30065	30095	30126	30156	30187	30218	30248	30279	30309	24
25	29976	30007	30035	30066	30096	30127	30157	30188	30219	30249	30280	30310	25
26	29977	30008	30036	30067	30097	30128	30158	30189	30220	30250	30281	30311	26
27	29978	30009	30037	30068	30098	30129	30159	30190	30221	30251	30282	30312	27
28	29979	30010	30038	30069	30099	30130	30160	30191	30222	30252	30283	30313	28
29	29980	-------	30039	30070	30100	30131	30161	30192	30223	30253	30284	30314	29
30	29981	-------	30040	30071	30101	30132	30162	30193	30224	30254	30285	30315	30
31	29982	-------	30041	-------	30102	-------	30163	30194	-------	30255	-------	30316	31

Figure T-76. 2025 Expiration Table

| | **2026** | | | | | **Expiration Table** | | | | **2026** | | | |
Day	Jan	Feb	Mar	Apr	May	Jun	Jul	Aug	Sep	Oct	Nov	Dec	Day
1	30317	30348	30376	30407	30437	30468	30498	30529	30560	30590	30621	30651	1
2	30318	30349	30377	30408	30438	30469	30499	30530	30561	30591	30622	30652	2
3	30319	30350	30378	30409	30439	30470	30500	30531	30562	30592	30623	30653	3
4	30320	30351	30379	30410	30440	30471	30501	30532	30563	30593	30624	30654	4
5	30321	30352	30380	30411	30441	30472	30502	30533	30564	30594	30625	30655	5
6	30322	30353	30381	30412	30442	30473	30503	30534	30565	30595	30626	30656	6
7	30323	30354	30382	30413	30443	30474	30504	30535	30566	30596	30627	30657	7
8	30324	30355	30383	30414	30444	30475	30505	30536	30567	30597	30628	30658	8
9	30325	30356	30384	30415	30445	30476	30506	30537	30568	30598	30629	30659	9
10	30326	30357	30385	30416	30446	30477	30507	30538	30569	30599	30630	30660	10
11	30327	30358	30386	30417	30447	30478	30508	30539	30570	30600	30631	30661	11
12	30328	30359	30387	30418	30448	30479	30509	30540	30571	30601	30632	30662	12
13	30329	30360	30388	30419	30449	30480	30510	30541	30572	30602	30633	30663	13
14	30330	30361	30389	30420	30450	30481	30511	30542	30573	30603	30634	30664	14
15	30331	30362	30390	30421	30451	30482	30512	30543	30574	30604	30635	30665	15
16	30332	30363	30391	30422	30452	30483	30513	30544	30575	30605	30636	30666	16
17	30333	30364	30392	30423	30453	30484	30514	30545	30576	30606	30637	30667	17
18	30334	30365	30393	30424	30454	30485	30515	30546	30577	30607	30638	30668	18
19	30335	30366	30394	30425	30455	30486	30516	30547	30578	30608	30639	30669	19
20	30336	30367	30395	30426	30456	30487	30517	30548	30579	30609	30640	30670	20
21	30337	30368	30396	30427	30457	30488	30518	30549	30580	30610	30641	30671	21
22	30338	30369	30397	30428	30458	30489	30519	30550	30581	30611	30642	30672	22
23	30339	30370	30398	30429	30459	30490	30520	30551	30582	30612	30643	30673	23
24	30340	30371	30399	30430	30460	30491	30521	30552	30583	30613	30644	30674	24
25	30341	30372	30400	30431	30461	30492	30522	30553	30584	30614	30645	30675	25
26	30342	30373	30401	30432	30462	30493	30523	30554	30585	30615	30646	30676	26
27	30343	30374	30402	30433	30463	30494	30524	30555	30586	30616	30647	30677	27
28	30344	30375	30403	30434	30464	30495	30525	30556	30587	30617	30648	30678	28
29	30345	-------	30404	30435	30465	30496	30526	30557	30588	30618	30649	30679	29
30	30346	-------	30405	30436	30466	30497	30527	30558	30589	30619	30650	30680	30
31	30347	-------	30406	-------	30467	-------	30528	30559	-------	30620	-------	30681	31

Figure T-77. 2026 Expiration Table

Day	Jan	Feb	Mar	Apr	May	Jun	Jul	Aug	Sep	Oct	Nov	Dec	Day
1	30682	30713	30741	30772	30802	30833	30863	30894	30925	30955	30986	31016	1
2	30683	30714	30742	30773	30803	30834	30864	30895	30926	30956	30987	31017	2
3	30684	30715	30743	30774	30804	30835	30865	30896	30927	30957	30988	31018	3
4	30685	30716	30744	30775	30805	30836	30866	30897	30928	30958	30989	31019	4
5	30686	30717	30745	30776	30806	30837	30867	30898	30929	30959	30990	31020	5
6	30687	30718	30746	30777	30807	30838	30868	30899	30930	30960	30991	31021	6
7	30688	30719	30747	30778	30808	30839	30869	30900	30931	30961	30992	31022	7
8	30689	30720	30748	30779	30809	30840	30870	30901	30932	30962	30993	31023	8
9	30690	30721	30749	30780	30810	30841	30871	30902	30933	30963	30994	31024	9
10	30691	30722	30750	30781	30811	30842	30872	30903	30934	30964	30995	31025	10
11	30692	30723	30751	30782	30812	30843	30873	30904	30935	30965	30996	31026	11
12	30693	30724	30752	30783	30813	30844	30874	30905	30936	30966	30997	31027	12
13	30694	30725	30753	30784	30814	30845	30875	30906	30937	30967	30998	31028	13
14	30695	30726	30754	30785	30815	30846	30876	30907	30938	30968	30999	31029	14
15	30696	30727	30755	30786	30816	30847	30877	30908	30939	30969	31000	31030	15
16	30697	30728	30756	30787	30817	30848	30878	30909	30940	30970	31001	31031	16
17	30698	30729	30757	30788	30818	30849	30879	30910	30941	30971	31002	31032	17
18	30699	30730	30758	30789	30819	30850	30880	30911	30942	30972	31003	31033	18
19	30700	30731	30759	30790	30820	30851	30881	30912	30943	30973	31004	31034	19
20	30701	30732	30760	30791	30821	30852	30882	30913	30944	30974	31005	31035	20
21	30702	30733	30761	30792	30822	30853	30883	30914	30945	30975	31006	31036	21
22	30703	30734	30762	30793	30823	30854	30884	30915	30946	30976	31007	31037	22
23	30704	30735	30763	30794	30824	30855	30885	30916	30947	30977	31008	31038	23
24	30705	30736	30764	30795	30825	30856	30886	30917	30948	30978	31009	31039	24
25	30706	30737	30765	30796	30826	30857	30887	30918	30949	30979	31040	31040	25
26	30707	30738	30766	30797	30827	30858	30888	30919	30950	30980	31011	31041	26
27	30708	30739	30767	30798	30828	30859	30889	30920	30951	30981	31012	31042	27
28	30709	30740	30768	30799	30829	30860	30890	30921	30952	30982	31013	31043	28
29	30710	-------	30769	30800	30830	30861	30891	30922	30953	30983	31014	31044	29
30	30711	-------	30770	30801	30831	30862	30892	30923	30954	30984	31015	31045	30
31	30712	-------	30771	-------	30832	-------	30893	30924	-------	30985	-------	31046	31

Figure T-78. 2027 Expiration Table

	2028				**Expiration Table**				**2028**				
Day	Jan	Feb	Mar	Apr	May	Jun	Jul	Aug	Sep	Oct	Nov	Dec	Day,
1	31047	31078	31107	31138	31168	31199	31229	31260	31291	31321	31352	31382	1
2	31048	31079	31108	31139	31169	31200	31230	31261	31292	31322	31353	31383	2
3	31049	31080	31109	31140	31170	31201	31231	31262	31293	31323	31354	31384	3
4	31050	31081	31110	31141	31171	31202	31232	31263	31294	31324	31355	31385	4
5	31051	31082	31111	31142	31172	31203	31233	31264	31295	31325	31356	31386	5
6	31052	31083	31112	31143	31173	31204	31234	31265	31296	31326	31357	31387	6
7	31053	31084	31113	31144	31174	31205	31235	31266	31297	31327	31358	31388	7
8	31054	31085	31114	31145	31175	31206	31236	31267	31298	31328	31359	31389	8
9	31055	31086	31115	31146	31176	31207	31237	31268	31299	31329	31360	31390	9
10	31056	31087	31116	31147	31177	31208	31238	31269	31300	31330	31361	31391	10
11	31057	31088	31117	31148	31178	31209	31239	31270	31301	31331	31362	31392	11
12	31058	31089	31118	31149	31179	31210	31240	31271	31302	31332	31363	31393	12
13	31059	31090	31119	31150	31180	31211	31241	31272	31303	31333	31364	31394	13
14	31060	31091	31120	31151	31181	31212	31242	31273	31304	31334	31365	31395	14
15	31061	31092	31121	31152	31182	31213	31243	31274	31305	31335	31366	31396	15
16	31062	31093	31122	31153	31183	31214	31244	31275	31306	31336	31367	31397	16
17	31063	31094	31123	31154	31184	31215	31245	31276	31307	31337	31368	31398	17
18	31064	31095	31124	31155	31185	31216	31246	31277	31308	31338	31369	31399	18
19	31065	31096	31125	31156	31186	31217	31247	31278	31309	31339	31370	31400	19
20	31066	31097	31126	31157	31187	31218	31248	31279	31310	31340	31371	31401	20
21	31067	31098	31127	31158	31188	31219	31249	31280	31311	31341	31372	31402	21
22	31068	31099	31128	31159	31189	31220	31250	31281	31312	31342	31373	31403	22
23	31069	31100	31129	31160	31190	31221	31251	31282	31313	31343	31374	31404	23
24	31070	31101	31130	31161	31191	31222	31252	31283	31314	31344	31375	31405	24
25	31071	31102	31131	31162	31192	31223	31253	31284	31315	31345	31376	31406	25
26	31072	31103	31132	31163	31193	31224	31254	31285	31316	31346	31377	31407	26
27	31073	31104	31133	31164	31194	31225	31255	31286	31317	31347	31378	31408	27
28	31074	31105	31134	31165	31195	31226	31256	31287	31318	31348	31379	31409	28
29	31075	31106	31135	31166	31196	31227	31257	31288	31319	31349	31380	31410	29
30	31076	-------	31136	31167	31197	31228	31258	31289	31320	31350	31381	31411	30
31	31077	-------	31137	-------	31198	-------	31259	31290	-------	31351	-------	31412	31

Figure T-79. 2028 Expiration Table

Day	Jan	Feb	Mar	Apr	May	Jun	Jul	Aug	Sep	Oct	Nov	Dec	Day
1	31413	31444	31472	31503	31533	31564	31594	31625	31656	31686	31717	31747	1
2	31414	31445	31473	31504	31534	31565	31595	31626	31657	31687	31718	31748	2
3	31415	31446	31474	31505	31535	31566	31596	31627	31658	31688	31719	31749	3
4	31416	31447	31475	31506	31536	31567	31597	31628	31659	31689	31720	31750	4
5	31417	31448	31476	31507	31537	31568	31598	31629	31660	31690	31721	31751	5
6	31418	31449	31477	31508	31538	31569	31599	31630	31661	31691	31722	31752	6
7	31419	31450	31478	31509	31539	31570	31600	31631	31662	31692	31723	31753	7
8	31420	31451	31479	31510	31540	31571	31601	31632	31663	31693	31724	31754	8
9	31421	31452	31480	31511	31541	31572	31602	31633	31664	31694	31725	31755	9
10	31422	31453	31481	31512	31542	31573	31603	31634	31665	31695	31726	31756	10
11	31423	31454	31482	31513	31543	31574	31604	31635	31666	31696	31727	31757	11
12	31424	31455	31483	31514	31544	31575	31605	31636	31667	31697	31728	31758	12
13	31425	31456	31484	31515	31545	31576	31606	31637	31668	31698	31729	31759	13
14	31426	31457	31485	31516	31546	31577	31607	31638	31669	31699	31730	31760	14
15	31427	31458	31486	31517	31547	31578	31608	31639	31670	31700	31731	31761	15
16	31428	31459	31487	31518	31548	31579	31609	31640	31671	31701	31732	31762	16
17	31429	31460	31488	31519	31549	31580	31610	31641	31672	31702	31733	31763	17
18	31430	31461	31489	31520	31550	31581	31611	31642	31673	31703	31734	31764	18
19	31431	31462	31490	31521	31551	31582	31612	31643	31674	31704	31735	31765	19
20	31432	31463	31491	31522	31552	31583	31613	31644	31675	31705	31736	31766	20
21	31433	31464	31492	31523	31553	31584	31614	31645	31676	31706	31737	31767	21
22	31434	31465	31493	31524	31554	31585	31615	31646	31677	31707	31738	31768	22
23	31435	31466	31494	31525	31555	31586	31616	31647	31678	31708	31739	31769	23
24	31436	31467	31495	31526	31556	31587	31617	31648	31679	31709	31740	31770	24
25	31437	31468	31496	31527	31557	31588	31618	31649	31680	31710	31741	31771	25
26	31438	31469	31497	31528	31558	31589	31619	31650	31681	31711	31742	31772	26
27	31439	31470	31498	31529	31559	31590	31620	31651	31682	31712	31743	31773	27
28	31440	31471	31499	31530	31560	31591	31621	31652	31683	31713	31744	31774	28
29	31441	-------	31500	31531	31561	31592	31622	31653	31684	31714	31745	31775	29
30	31442	-------	31501	31532	31562	31593	31623	31654	31685	31715	31746	31776	30
31	31443	-------	31502	-------	31563	-------	31624	31655	-------	31716	-------	31777	31

Figure T-80. 2029 Expiration Table

Day	Jan	Feb	Mar	Apr	May	Jun	Jul	Aug	Sep	Oct	Nov	Dec	Day
1	31778	31809	31837	31868	31898	31929	31959	31990	32021	32051	32082	32112	1
2	31779	31810	31838	31869	31899	31930	31960	31991	32022	32052	32083	32113	2
3	31780	31811	31839	31870	31900	31931	31961	31992	32023	32053	32084	32114	3
4	31781	31812	31840	31871	31901	31932	31962	31993	32024	32054	32085	32115	4
5	31782	31813	31841	31872	31902	31933	31963	31994	32025	32055	32086	32116	5
6	31783	31814	31842	31873	31903	31934	31964	31995	32026	32056	32087	32117	6
7	31784	31815	31843	31874	31904	31935	31965	31996	32027	32057	32088	32118	7
8	31785	31816	31844	31875	31905	31936	31966	31997	32028	32058	32089	32119	8
9	31786	31817	31845	31876	31906	31937	31967	31998	32029	32059	32090	32120	9
10	31787	31818	31846	31877	31907	31938	31968	31999	32030	32060	32091	32121	10
11	31788	31819	31847	31878	31908	31939	31969	32000	32031	32061	32092	32122	11
12	31789	31820	31848	31879	31909	31940	31970	32001	32032	32062	32093	32123	12
13	31790	31821	31849	31880	31910	31941	31971	32002	32033	32063	32094	32124	13
14	31791	31822	31850	31881	31911	31942	31972	32003	32034	32064	32095	32125	14
15	31792	31823	31851	31882	31912	31943	31973	32004	32035	32065	32096	32126	15
16	31793	31824	31852	31883	31913	31944	31974	32005	32036	32066	32097	32127	16
17	31794	31825	31853	31884	31914	31945	31975	32006	32037	32067	32098	32128	17
18	31795	31826	31854	31885	31915	31946	31976	32007	32038	32068	32099	32129	18
19	31796	31827	31855	31886	31916	31947	31977	32008	32039	32069	32100	32130	19
20	31797	31828	31856	31887	31917	31948	31978	32009	32040	32070	32101	32131	20
21	31798	31829	31857	31888	31918	31949	31979	32010	32041	32071	32102	32132	21
22	31799	31830	31858	31889	31919	31950	31980	32011	32042	32072	32103	32133	22
23	31800	31831	31859	31890	31920	31951	31981	32012	32043	32073	32104	32134	23
24	31801	31832	31860	31891	31921	31952	31982	32013	32044	32074	32105	32135	24
25	31802	31833	31861	31892	31922	31953	31983	32014	32045	32075	32106	32136	25
26	31803	31834	31862	31893	31923	31954	31984	32015	32046	32076	32107	32137	26
27	31804	31835	31863	31894	31924	31955	31985	32016	32047	32077	32108	32138	27
28	31805	31836	31864	31895	31925	31956	31986	32017	32048	32078	32109	32139	28
29	31806	_____	31865	31896	31926	31957	31987	32018	32049	32079	32110	32140	29
30	31807	_____	31866	31897	31927	31958	31988	32019	32050	32080	32111	32141	30
31	31808	_____	31867	_____	31928	_____	31989	32020	_____	32081	_____	32142	31

Figure T-81. 2030 Expiration Table

2031   Expiration Table   2031

Day	Jan	Feb	Mar	Apr	May	Jun	Jul	Aug	Sep	Oct	Nov	Dec	Day
1	32143	32174	32202	32233	32263	32294	32324	32355	32386	32416	32447	32477	1
2	32144	32175	32203	32234	32264	32295	32325	32356	32387	32417	32448	32478	2
3	32145	32176	32204	32235	32265	32296	32326	32357	32388	32418	32449	32479	3
4	32146	32177	32205	32236	32266	32297	32327	32358	32389	32419	32450	32480	4
5	32147	32178	32206	32237	32267	32298	32328	32359	32390	32420	32451	32481	5
6	32148	32179	32207	32238	32368	32299	32329	32360	32391	32421	32452	32482	6
7	32149	32180	32208	32239	32269	32300	32330	32361	32392	32422	32453	32483	7
8	32150	32181	32209	32240	32270	32301	32331	32362	32393	32423	32454	32484	8
9	32151	32182	32210	32241	32271	32302	32332	32363	32394	32424	32455	32485	9
10	32152	32183	32211	32242	32272	32303	32333	32364	32395	32425	32456	32486	10
11	32153	32184	32212	32243	32273	32304	32334	32365	32396	32426	32457	32487	11
12	32154	32185	32213	32244	32274	32305	32335	32366	32397	32427	32458	32488	12
13	32155	32186	32214	32245	32275	32306	32336	32367	32398	32428	32459	32489	13
14	32156	32187	32215	32246	32276	32307	32337	32368	32399	32429	32460	32490	14
15	32157	32188	32216	32247	32277	32308	32338	32369	32400	32430	32461	32491	15
16	32158	32189	32217	32248	32278	32309	32339	32370	32401	32431	32462	32492	16
17	32159	32190	32218	32249	32279	32310	32340	32371	32402	32432	32463	32493	17
18	32160	32191	32219	32250	32280	32311	32341	32372	32403	32433	32464	32494	18
19	32161	32192	32220	32251	32281	32312	32342	32373	32404	32434	32465	32495	19
20	32162	32193	32221	32252	32282	32313	32343	32374	32405	32435	32466	32496	20
21	32163	32194	32222	32253	32283	32314	32344	32375	32406	32436	32467	32497	21
22	32164	32195	32223	32254	32284	32315	32345	32376	32407	32437	32468	32498	22
23	32165	32196	32224	32255	32285	32316	32346	32377	32408	32438	32469	32499	23
24	32166	32197	32225	32256	32286	32317	32347	32378	32409	32439	32470	32500	24
25	32167	32198	32226	32257	32287	32318	32348	32379	32410	32440	32471	32501	25
26	32168	32199	32227	32258	32288	32319	32349	32380	32411	32441	32472	32502	26
27	32169	32200	32228	32259	32289	32320	32350	32381	32412	32442	32473	32503	27
28	32170	32201	32229	32260	32290	32321	32351	32382	32413	32443	32474	32504	28
29	32171	-------	32230	32261	32291	32322	32352	32383	32414	32444	32475	32505	29
30	32172	-------	32231	32262	32292	32323	32353	32384	32415	32445	32476	32506	30
31	32173	-------	32232	-------	32293	-------	32354	32385	-------	32446	-------	32507	31

Figure T-82. 2031 Expiration Table

Day	Jan	Feb	Mar	Apr	May	Jun	Jul	Aug	Sep	Oct	Nov	Dec	Day
1	32508	32539	32568	32599	32629	32660	32690	32721	32752	32782	32813	32843	1
2	32509	32540	32569	32600	32630	32661	32691	32722	32753	32783	32814	32844	2
3	32510	32541	32570	32601	32631	32662	32692	32723	32754	32784	32815	32845	3
4	32511	32542	32571	32602	32632	32663	32693	32724	32755	32785	32816	32846	4
5	32512	32543	32572	32603	32633	32664	32694	32725	32756	32786	32817	32847	5
6	32513	32544	32573	32604	32634	32665	32695	32726	32757	32787	32818	32848	6
7	32514	32545	32574	32605	32635	32666	32696	32727	32758	32788	32819	32849	7
8	32515	32546	32575	32606	32636	32667	32697	32728	32759	32789	32820	32850	8
9	32516	32547	32576	32607	32637	32668	32698	32729	32760	32790	32821	32851	9
10	32517	32548	32577	32608	32638	32669	32699	32730	32761	32791	32822	32852	10
11	32518	32549	32578	32609	32639	32670	32700	32731	32762	32792	32823	32853	11
12	32519	32550	32579	32610	32640	32671	32701	32732	32763	32793	32824	32854	12
13	32520	32551	32580	32611	32641	32672	32702	32733	32764	32794	32825	32855	13
14	32521	32552	32581	32612	32642	32673	32703	32734	32765	32795	32826	32856	14
15	32522	32553	32582	32613	32643	32674	32704	32735	32766	32796	32827	32857	15
16	32523	32554	32583	32614	32644	32675	32705	32736	32767	32797	32828	32858	16
17	32524	32555	32584	32615	32645	32676	32706	32737	32768	32798	32829	32859	17
18	32525	32556	32585	32616	32646	32677	32707	32738	32769	32799	32830	32860	18
19	32526	32557	32586	32617	32647	32678	32708	32739	32770	32800	32831	32861	19
20	32527	32558	32587	32618	32648	32679	32709	32740	32771	32801	32832	32862	20
21	32528	32559	32588	32619	32649	32680	32710	32741	32772	32802	32833	32863	21
22	32529	32560	32589	32620	32650	32681	32711	32742	32773	32803	32834	32864	22
23	32530	32561	32590	32621	32651	32682	32712	32743	32774	32804	32835	32865	23
24	32531	32562	32591	32622	32652	32683	32713	32744	32775	32805	32836	32866	24
25	32532	32563	32592	32623	32653	32684	32714	32745	32776	32806	32837	32867	25
26	32533	32564	32593	32624	32654	32685	32715	32746	32777	32807	32838	32868	26
27	32534	32565	32594	32625	32655	32686	32716	32747	32778	32808	32839	32869	27
28	32535	32566	32595	32626	32656	32687	32717	32748	32779	32809	32840	32870	28
29	32536	32567	32596	32627	32657	32688	32718	32749	32780	32810	32841	32871	29
30	32537	-------	32597	32628	32658	32689	32719	32750	32781	32811	32842	32872	30
31	32538	-------	32598	-------	32659	-------	32720	32751	-------	32812	-------	32873	31

Figure T-83. 2032 Expiration Table

Day	Jan	Feb	Mar	Apr	May	Jun	Jul	Aug	Sep	Oct	Nov	Dec	Day
1	32874	32905	32933	32964	32994	33025	33055	33086	33117	33147	33178	33208	1
2	32875	32906	32934	32965	32995	33026	33056	33087	33118	33148	33179	33209	2
3	32876	32907	32935	32966	32996	33027	33057	33088	33119	33149	33180	33210	3
4	32877	32908	32936	32967	32997	33028	33058	33089	33120	33150	33181	33211	4
5	32878	32909	32937	32968	32998	33029	33059	33090	33121	33151	33182	33212	5
6	32879	32910	32938	32969	32999	33030	33060	33091	33122	33152	33183	33213	6
7	32880	32911	32939	32970	33000	33031	33061	33092	33123	33153	33184	33214	7
8	32881	32912	32940	32971	33001	33032	33062	33093	33124	33154	33185	33215	8
9	32882	32913	32941	32972	33002	33033	33063	33094	33125	33155	33186	33216	9
10	32883	32914	32942	32973	33003	33034	33064	33095	33126	33156	33187	33217	10
11	32884	32915	32943	32974	33004	33035	33065	33096	33127	33157	33188	33218	11
12	32885	32916	32944	32975	33005	33036	33066	33097	33128	33158	33189	33219	12
13	32886	32917	32945	32976	33006	33037	33067	33098	33129	33159	33190	33220	13
14	32887	32918	32946	32977	33007	33038	33068	33099	33130	33160	33191	33221	14
15	32888	32919	32947	32978	33008	33039	33069	33100	33131	33161	33192	33222	15
16	32889	32920	32948	32979	33009	33040	33070	33101	33132	33162	33193	33223	16
17	32890	32921	32949	32980	33010	33041	33071	33102	33133	33163	33194	33224	17
18	32891	32922	32950	32981	33011	33042	33072	33103	33134	33164	33195	33225	18
19	32892	32923	32951	32982	33012	33043	33073	33104	33135	33165	33196	33226	19
20	32893	32924	32952	32983	33013	33044	33074	33105	33136	33166	33197	33227	20
21	32894	32925	32953	32984	33014	33045	33075	33106	33137	33167	33198	33228	21
22	32895	32926	32954	32985	33015	33046	33076	33107	33138	33168	33199	33229	22
23	32896	32927	32955	32986	33016	33047	33077	33108	33139	33169	33200	33230	23
24	32897	32928	32956	32987	33017	33048	33078	33109	33140	33170	33201	33231	24
25	32898	32929	32957	32988	33018	33049	33079	33110	33141	33171	33202	33232	25
26	32899	32930	32958	32989	33019	33050	33080	33111	33142	33172	33203	33233	26
27	32900	32931	32959	32990	33020	33051	33081	33112	33143	33173	33204	33234	27
28	32901	32932	32960	32991	33021	33052	33082	33113	33144	33174	33205	33235	28
29	32902	-------	32961	32992	33022	33053	33083	33114	33145	33175	33206	33236	29
30	32903	-------	32962	32993	33023	33054	33084	33115	33146	33176	33207	33237	30
31	32904	-------	32963	-------	33024	-------	33085	33116	-------	33177	-------	33238	31

Figure T-84. 2033 Expiration Table

Day	Jan	Feb	Mar	Apr	May	Jun	Jul	Aug	Sep	Oct	Nov	Dec	Day
1	33239	33270	33298	33329	33359	33390	33420	33451	33482	33512	33543	33573	1
2	33240	33271	33299	33330	33360	33391	33421	33452	33483	33513	33544	33574	2
3	33241	33272	33300	33331	33361	33392	33422	33453	33484	33514	33545	33575	3
4	33242	33273	33301	33332	33362	33393	33423	33454	33485	33515	33546	33576	4
5	33243	33274	33302	33333	33363	33394	33424	33455	33486	33516	33547	33577	5
6	33244	33275	33303	33334	33364	33395	33425	33456	33487	33517	33548	33578	6
7	33245	33276	33304	33335	33365	33396	33426	33457	33488	33518	33549	33579	7
8	33246	33277	33305	33336	33366	33397	33427	33458	33489	33519	33550	33580	8
9	33247	33278	33306	33337	33367	33398	33428	33459	33490	33520	33551	33581	9
10	33248	33279	33307	33338	33368	33399	33429	33460	33491	33521	33552	33582	10
11	33249	33280	33308	33339	33369	33400	33430	33461	33492	33522	33553	33583	11
12	33250	33281	33309	33340	33370	33401	33431	33462	33493	33523	33554	33584	12
13	33251	33282	33310	33341	33371	33402	33432	33463	33494	33524	33555	33585	13
14	33252	33283	33311	33342	33372	33403	33433	33464	33495	33525	33556	33586	14
15	33253	33284	33312	33343	33373	33404	33434	33465	33496	33526	33557	33587	15
16	33254	33285	33313	33344	33374	33405	33435	33466	33497	33527	33558	33588	16
17	33255	33286	33314	33345	33375	33406	33436	33467	33498	33528	33559	33589	17
18	33256	33287	33315	33346	33376	33407	33437	33468	33499	33529	33560	33590	18
19	33257	33288	33316	33347	33377	33408	33438	33469	33500	33530	33561	33591	19
20	33258	33289	33317	33348	33378	33409	33439	33470	33501	33531	33562	33592	20
21	33259	33290	33318	33349	33379	33410	33440	33471	33502	33532	33563	33593	21
22	33260	33291	33319	33350	33380	33411	33441	33472	33503	33533	33564	33594	22
23	33261	33292	33320	33351	33381	33412	33442	33473	33504	33534	33565	33595	23
24	33262	33293	33321	33352	33382	33413	33443	33474	33505	33535	33566	33596	24
25	33263	33294	33322	33353	33383	33414	33444	33475	33506	33536	33567	33597	25
26	33264	33295	33323	33354	33384	33415	33445	33476	33507	33537	33568	33598	26
27	33265	33296	33324	33355	33385	33416	33446	33477	33508	33538	33569	33599	27
28	33266	33297	33325	33356	33386	33417	33447	33478	33509	33539	33570	33600	28
29	33267	-------	33326	33357	33387	33418	33448	33479	33510	33540	33571	33601	29
30	33268	-------	33327	33358	33388	33419	33449	33480	33511	33541	33572	33602	30
31	33269	-------	33328	-------	33389	-------	33450	33481	-------	33542	-------	33603	31

Figure T-85. 2034 Expiration Table

Day	Jan	Feb	Mar	Apr	May	Jun	Jul	Aug	Sep	Oct	Nov	Dec	Day
1	33604	33635	33663	33694	33724	33755	33785	33816	33847	33877	33908	33938	1
2	33605	33636	33664	33695	33725	33756	33786	33817	33848	33878	33909	33939	2
3	33606	33637	33665	33696	33726	33757	33787	33818	33849	33879	33910	33940	3
4	33607	33638	33666	33697	33727	33758	33788	33819	33850	33880	33911	33941	4
5	33608	33639	33667	33698	33728	33759	33789	33820	33851	33881	33912	33942	5
6	33609	33640	33668	33699	33729	33760	33790	33821	33852	33882	33913	33943	6
7	33610	33641	33669	33700	33730	33761	33791	33822	33853	33883	33914	33944	7
8	33611	33642	33670	33701	33731	33762	33792	33823	33854	33884	33915	33945	8
9	33612	33643	33671	33702	33732	33763	33793	33824	33855	33885	33916	33946	9
10	33613	33644	33672	33703	33733	33764	33794	33825	33856	33886	33917	33947	10
11	33614	33645	33673	33704	33734	33765	33795	33826	33857	33887	33918	33948	11
12	33615	33646	33674	33705	33735	33766	33796	33827	33858	33888	33919	33949	12
13	33616	33647	33675	33706	33736	33767	33797	33828	33859	33889	33920	33950	13
14	33617	33648	33676	33707	33737	33768	33798	33829	33860	33890	33921	33951	14
15	33618	33649	33677	33708	33738	33769	33799	33830	33861	33891	33922	33952	15
16	33619	33650	33678	33709	33739	33770	33800	33831	33862	33892	33923	33953	16
17	33620	33651	33679	33710	33740	33771	33801	33832	33863	33893	33924	33954	17
18	33621	33652	33680	33711	33741	33772	33802	33833	33864	33894	33925	33955	18
19	33622	33653	33681	33712	33742	33773	33803	33834	33865	33895	33926	33956	19
20	33623	33654	33682	33713	33743	33774	33804	33835	33866	33896	33927	33957	20
21	33624	33655	33683	33714	33744	33775	33805	33836	33867	33897	33928	33958	21
22	33625	33656	33684	33715	33745	33776	33806	33837	33868	33898	33929	33959	22
23	33626	33657	33685	33716	33746	33777	33807	33838	33869	33899	33930	33960	23
24	33627	33658	33686	33717	33747	33778	33808	33839	33870	33900	33931	33961	24
25	33628	33659	33687	33718	33748	33779	33809	33840	33871	33901	33932	33962	25
26	33629	33660	33688	33719	33749	33780	33810	33841	33872	33902	33933	33963	26
27	33630	33661	33689	33720	33750	33781	33811	33842	33873	33903	33934	33964	27
28	33631	33662	33690	33721	33751	33782	33812	33843	33874	33904	33935	33965	38
29	33632	-------	33691	33722	33752	33783	33813	33844	33875	33905	33936	33966	29
30	33633	-------	33692	33723	33753	33784	33814	33845	33876	33906	33937	33967	30
31	33634	-------	33693	-------	33754	-------	33815	33846	-------	33907	-------	33968	31

Figure T-86. 2035 Expiration Table

	2036			**Expiration Table**					**2036**				
Day	*Jan*	*Feb*	*Mar*	*Apr*	*May*	*Jun*	*Jul*	*Aug*	*Sep*	*Oct*	*Nov*	*Dec*	*Day*
1	33969	34000	34029	34060	34090	34121	34151	34182	34213	34243	34274	34304	1
2	33970	34001	34030	34061	34091	34122	34152	34183	34214	34244	34275	34305	2
3	33971	34002	34031	34062	34092	34123	34153	34184	34215	34245	34276	34306	3
4	33972	34003	34032	34063	34093	34124	34154	34185	34216	34246	34277	34307	4
5	33973	34004	34033	34064	34094	34125	34155	34186	34217	34247	34278	34308	5
6	33974	34005	34034	34065	34095	34126	34156	34187	34218	34248	34279	34309	6
7	33975	34006	34035	34066	34096	34127	34157	34188	34219	34249	34280	34310	7
8	33976	34007	34036	34067	34097	34128	34158	34189	34220	34250	24281	34311	8
9	33977	34008	34037	34068	34098	34129	34159	34190	34221	34251	34282	34312	9
10	33978	34009	34038	34069	34099	34130	34160	34191	34222	34252	34283	34313	10
11	33979	34010	34039	34070	34100	34131	34161	34192	34223	34253	34284	34314	11
12	33980	34011	34040	34071	34101	34132	34162	34193	34224	34254	34285	34315	12
13	33981	34012	34041	34072	34102	34133	34163	34194	34225	34255	34286	34316	13
14	33982	34013	34042	34073	34103	34134	34164	34195	34226	34256	34287	34317	14
15	33983	34014	34043	34074	34104	34135	34165	34196	34227	34257	34288	34318	15
16	33984	34015	34044	34075	34105	34136	34166	34197	34228	34258	34289	34319	16
17	33985	34016	34045	34076	34106	34137	34167	34198	34229	34259	34290	34320	17
18	33986	34017	34046	34077	34107	34138	34168	34199	34230	34260	34291	34321	18
19	33987	34018	34047	34078	34108	34139	34169	34200	34231	34261	34292	34322	19
20	33988	34019	34048	34079	34109	34140	34170	34201	34232	34262	34293	34323	20
21	33989	34020	34049	34080	34110	34141	34171	34202	34233	34263	34294	34324	21
22	33990	34021	34050	34081	34111	34142	34172	34203	34234	34264	34295	34325	22
23	33991	34022	34051	34082	34112	34143	34173	34204	34235	34265	34296	34326	23
24	33992	34023	34052	34083	34113	34144	34174	34205	34236	34266	34297	34327	24
25	33993	34024	34053	34084	34114	34145	34175	34206	34237	34267	34298	34328	25
26	33994	34025	34054	34085	34115	34146	34176	34207	34238	34268	34299	34329	26
27	33995	34026	34055	34086	34116	34147	34177	34208	34239	34269	34300	34330	27
28	33996	34027	34056	34087	34117	34148	34178	34209	34240	34270	34301	34331	28
29	33997	34028	34057	34088	34118	34149	34179	34210	34241	34271	34302	34332	29
30	33998	....	34058	34089	34119	34150	34180	34211	34242	34272	34303	34333	30
31	33999	....	34059	....	34120	....	34181	34212	....	34273	....	34334	31

Figure T-87. 2036 Expiration Table

Day	Jan	Feb	Mar	Apr	May	Jun	Jul	Aug	Sep	Oct	Nov	Dec	Day
1	34335	34366	34394	34425	34455	34486	34516	34547	34578	34608	34639	34669	1
2	34336	34367	34395	34426	34456	34487	34517	34548	34579	34609	34640	34670	2
3	34337	34368	34396	34427	34457	34488	34518	34549	34580	34610	34641	34671	3
4	34338	34369	34397	34428	34458	34489	34519	34550	34581	34611	34642	34672	4
5	34339	34370	34398	34429	34459	34490	34520	34551	34582	34612	34643	34673	5
6	34340	34371	34399	34430	34460	34491	34521	34552	34583	34613	34644	34674	6
7	34341	34372	34400	34431	34461	34492	34522	34553	34584	34614	34645	34675	7
8	34342	34373	34401	34432	34462	34493	34523	34554	34585	34615	34646	34676	8
9	34343	34374	34402	34433	34463	34494	34524	34555	34586	34616	34647	34677	9
10	34344	34375	34403	34434	34464	34495	34525	34556	34587	34617	34648	34678	10
11	34345	34376	34404	34435	34465	34496	34526	34557	34588	34618	34649	34679	11
12	34346	34377	34405	34436	34466	34497	34527	34558	34589	34619	34650	34680	12
13	34347	34378	34406	34437	34467	34498	34528	34559	34590	34620	34651	34681	13
14	34348	34379	34407	34438	34468	34499	34529	34560	34591	34621	34652	34682	14
15	34349	34380	34408	34439	34469	34500	34530	34561	34592	34622	34653	34683	15
16	34350	34381	34409	34440	34470	34501	34531	34562	34593	34623	34654	34684	16
17	34351	34382	34410	34441	34471	34502	34532	34563	34594	34624	34655	34685	17
18	34352	34383	34411	34442	34472	34503	34533	34564	34595	34625	34656	34686	18
19	34353	34384	34412	34443	34473	34504	34534	34565	34596	34626	34657	34687	19
20	34354	34385	34413	34444	34474	34505	34535	34566	34597	34627	34658	34688	20
21	34355	34386	34414	34445	34475	34506	34536	34567	34598	34628	34659	34689	21
22	34356	34387	34415	34446	34476	34507	34537	34568	34599	34629	34660	34690	22
23	34357	34388	34416	34447	34477	34508	34538	34569	34600	34630	34661	34691	23
24	34358	34389	34417	34448	34478	34509	34539	34570	34601	34631	34662	34692	24
25	34359	34390	34418	34449	34479	34510	34540	34571	34602	34632	34663	34693	25
26	34360	34391	34419	34450	34480	34511	34541	34572	34603	34633	34664	34694	26
27	34361	34392	34420	34451	34481	34512	34542	34573	34604	34634	34665	34695	27
28	34362	34393	34421	34452	34482	34513	34543	34574	34605	34635	34666	34696	28
29	34363	-------	34422	34453	34483	34514	34544	34575	34606	34636	34667	34697	29
30	34364	-------	34423	34454	34484	34515	34545	34576	34607	34637	34668	34698	30
31	34365	-------	34424	-------	34485	-------	34546	34577	-------	34638	-------	34699	31

Figure T-88. 2037 Expiration Table

Day	Jan	Feb	Mar	Apr	May	Jun	Jul	Aug	Sep	Oct	Nov	Dec	Day
1	34700	34731	34759	34790	34820	34851	34881	34912	34943	34973	35004	35034	1
2	34701	34732	34760	34791	34821	34852	34882	34913	34944	34974	35005	35035	2
3	34702	34733	34761	34792	34822	34853	34883	34914	34945	34975	35006	35036	3
4	34703	34734	34762	34793	34823	34854	34884	34915	34946	34976	35007	35037	4
5	34704	34735	34763	34794	34824	34855	34885	34916	34947	34077	35008	35038	5
6	34705	34736	34764	34795	34825	34856	34886	34917	34948	34978	35009	35039	6
7	34706	34737	34766	34796	34826	34857	34887	34918	34949	34979	35010	35040	7
8	34707	34738	34766	34797	34827	34858	34888	34919	34950	34980	35011	35041	8
9	34708	34739	34767	34798	34828	34859	34889	34920	34951	34981	35012	35042	9
10	34709	34740	34768	34799	34829	34860	34890	34921	34952	34982	35013	35043	10
11	34710	34741	34769	34800	34830	34861	34891	34922	34953	34983	35014	35044	11
12	34711	34742	34770	34801	34831	34862	34892	34923	34954	34984	35015	35045	12
13	34712	34743	34771	34802	34832	34863	34893	34924	24955	34985	35016	35046	13
14	34713	34744	34772	34803	34833	34864	34894	34925	34956	34986	35017	35047	14
15	34714	34745	34773	34804	34834	34865	34895	34926	34957	34987	35018	35048	15
16	34715	34746	34774	34805	34835	34866	34896	34927	34958	34988	35019	35049	16
17	34716	34747	34776	34806	34836	34867	34897	34928	34959	34989	35020	35050	17
18	34717	34748	34776	34807	34837	34868	34898	34929	34960	34990	35021	35051	18
19	34718	34749	34777	34808	34838	34869	34899	34930	34961	34991	35022	35052	19
20	34719	34750	34778	34809	34839	34870	34900	34931	34962	34992	35023	35053	20
21	34720	34751	34779	34810	34840	34871	34901	34932	34963	34993	35024	35054	21
22	34721	34752	34780	34811	34841	34872	34902	34933	34964	34994	35025	35055	22
23	34722	34753	34781	34812	34842	34873	34903	34934	34965	34995	35026	35056	23
24	34723	34754	34782	34813	34843	34874	34904	34935	34966	34996	35027	35057	24
25	34724	34755	34783	34814	34844	34875	34905	34936	34967	34997	35028	35058	25
26	34725	34756	34784	34815	34845	34876	34906	34937	34968	34998	35029	35059	26
27	34726	34757	34785	34816	34846	34877	34907	34938	34969	34999	35030	35060	27
28	34727	34758	34786	34817	34847	34878	34908	34939	34970	35000	35031	35061	28
29	34728	....	34787	34818	34848	34879	34909	34940	34971	35001	35032	35062	29
30	34729	....	34788	34819	34849	34880	34910	34941	34972	35002	35033	35063	30
31	34730	....	34789	....	34850	....	34911	34942	....	35003	....	35064	31

Figure T-89. 2038 Expiration Table

2039   Expiration Table   2039

Day	Jan	Feb	Mar	Apr	May	Jun	Jul	Aug	Sep	Oct	Nov	Dec	Day
1	35065	35096	35124	35155	35185	35216	35246	35277	35308	35338	35369	35399	1
2	35066	35097	35125	35156	35186	35217	35247	35278	35309	35339	35370	35400	2
3	35067	35098	35126	35157	35187	35218	35248	35279	35310	35340	35371	35401	3
4	35068	35099	35127	35158	35188	35219	35249	35280	35311	35341	35372	35402	4
5	35069	35100	35128	35159	35189	35220	35250	35281	35312	35342	35373	35403	5
6	35070	35101	35129	35160	35190	35221	35251	35282	35313	35343	35374	35404	6
7	35071	35102	35130	35161	35191	35222	35252	35283	35314	35344	35375	35405	7
8	35072	35103	35131	35162	35192	35223	35253	35284	35315	35345	35376	35406	8
9	35073	35104	35132	35163	35193	35224	35254	35285	35316	35346	35377	35407	9
10	35074	35105	35133	35164	35194	35225	35255	35286	35317	35347	35378	35408	10
11	35075	35106	35134	35165	35195	35226	35256	35287	35318	35348	35379	35409	11
12	35076	35107	35135	35166	35196	35227	35257	35288	35319	35349	35380	35410	12
13	35077	35108	35136	35167	35197	35228	35258	35289	35320	35350	35381	35411	13
14	35078	35109	35137	35168	35198	35229	35259	35290	35321	35351	35382	35412	14
15	35079	35110	35138	35169	35199	35230	35260	35291	35322	35352	35383	35413	15
16	35080	35111	35139	35170	35200	35231	35261	35292	35323	35353	35384	35414	16
17	35081	35112	35140	35171	35201	35232	35262	35293	35324	35354	35385	35415	17
18	35082	35113	35141	35172	35202	35233	35263	35294	35325	35355	35386	35416	18
19	35083	35114	35142	35173	35203	35234	35264	35295	35226	35356	35387	35417	19
20	35084	35115	35143	35174	35204	35235	35265	35296	35327	35357	35388	35418	20
21	35085	35116	35144	35175	35205	35236	35266	35297	35328	35358	35389	35419	21
22	35086	35117	35145	35176	35206	35237	35267	35298	35329	35359	35390	35420	22
23	35087	35118	35146	35177	35207	35238	35268	35299	35330	35360	35391	35421	23
24	35088	35119	35147	35178	35208	35239	35269	35300	35331	35361	35392	35422	24
25	35089	35120	35148	35179	35209	35240	35270	35301	35332	35362	35393	35423	25
26	35090	35121	35149	35180	35210	35241	35271	35302	35333	35363	35394	35424	26
27	35091	35122	35150	35181	35211	35242	35272	35303	35334	35364	35395	35425	27
28	35092	35123	35151	35182	35212	35243	35273	35304	35335	35365	35396	35426	28
29	35093	-------	35152	35183	35213	35244	35274	35305	35336	35366	35397	35427	29
30	35094	-------	35153	35184	35214	35245	35275	35306	35337	35367	35398	35428	30
31	35095	-------	35154	-------	35215	-------	35276	35307	-------	35368	-------	35429	31

Figure T-90. 2039 Expiration Table

		2040			**Expiration Table**				2040				
Day	Jan	Feb	Mar	Apr	May	Jun	Jul	Aug	Sep	Oct	Nov	Dec	Day
1	35430	35461	35490	35521	35551	35582	35612	35643	35674	35704	35735	35765	1
2	35431	35462	35491	35522	35552	35583	35613	35644	35675	35705	35736	35766	2
3	35432	35463	35492	35523	35553	35584	35614	35645	35676	35706	35737	35767	3
4	35433	35464	35493	35524	35554	35585	35615	35646	35677	35707	35738	35768	4
5	35434	35465	35494	35525	35555	35586	35616	35647	35678	35708	35739	35769	5
6	35435	35466	35495	35526	35556	35587	35617	35648	35679	35709	35740	35770	6
7	35436	35467	35496	35527	35557	35588	35618	35649	35680	35710	35741	35771	7
8	35437	35468	35497	35528	35558	35589	35619	35650	35681	35711	35742	35772	8
9	35438	35469	35498	35529	35559	35590	35620	35651	35682	35712	35743	35773	9
10	35439	35470	35499	35530	35560	35591	35621	35652	35683	35713	35744	35774	10
11	35440	35471	35500	35531	35561	35592	35622	35653	35684	35714	35745	35775	11
12	35441	35472	35501	35532	35562	35593	35623	35654	35685	35715	35746	35776	12
13	35442	35473	35502	35533	35563	35594	35624	35655	35686	35716	35747	35777	13
14	35443	35474	35503	35534	35564	35595	35625	35656	35687	35717	35748	35778	14
15	35444	35475	35504	35535	35565	35596	35626	35657	35688	35718	35749	35779	15
16	35445	35476	35505	35536	35566	35597	35627	35658	35689	35719	35750	35780	16
17	35446	35477	35506	35537	35567	35598	35628	35659	35690	35720	35751	35781	17
18	35447	35478	35507	35538	35568	35599	35629	35660	35691	35721	35752	35782	18
19	35448	35479	35508	35539	35569	35600	35630	35661	35692	35722	35753	35783	19
20	35449	35480	35509	35540	35570	35601	35631	35662	35693	35723	35754	35784	20
21	35450	35481	35510	35541	35571	35602	35632	35663	35694	35724	35755	35785	21
22	35451	35482	35511	35542	35572	35603	35633	35664	35695	35725	35756	35786	22
23	35452	35483	35512	35543	35573	35604	35634	35665	35696	35726	35757	35787	23
24	35453	35484	35513	35544	35574	35605	35635	35666	35697	35727	35758	35788	24
25	35454	35485	35514	35545	35575	35606	35636	35667	35698	35728	35759	35789	25
26	35455	35486	35515	35546	35576	35607	35637	35668	35699	35729	35760	35790	26
27	35456	35487	35516	35547	35577	35608	35638	35669	35700	35730	35761	35791	27
28	35457	35488	35517	35548	35578	35609	35639	35670	35701	35731	35762	35792	28
29	35458	35489	35518	35549	35579	35610	35640	35671	35702	35732	35763	35793	29
30	35459	-------	35519	35550	35580	35611	35641	35672	35703	35733	35764	35794	30
31	35460	-------	35520	-------	35581	-------	35642	35673	-------	35734	-------	35795	31

Figure T-91. 2040 Expiration Table

2041 Expiration Table 2041

Day	Jan	Feb	Mar	Apr	May	Jun	Jul	Aug	Sep	Oct	Nov	Dec	Day
1	35796	35827	35855	35886	35916	35947	35977	36008	36039	36069	36100	36130	1
2	35797	35828	35856	35887	35917	35948	35978	36009	36040	36070	36101	36131	2
3	35798	35829	35857	35888	35918	35949	35979	36010	36041	36071	36102	36132	3
4	35799	35830	35858	35889	35919	35950	35980	36011	36042	36072	36103	36133	4
5	35800	35831	35859	35890	35920	35951	35981	36012	36043	36073	36104	36134	5
6	35801	35832	35860	35891	35921	35952	35982	36013	36044	36074	36105	36135	6
7	35802	35833	35861	35892	35922	35953	35983	36014	36045	36075	36106	36136	7
8	35803	35834	35862	35893	35923	35954	35984	36015	36046	36076	36107	36137	8
9	35804	35835	35863	35894	35924	35955	35985	36016	36047	36077	36108	36138	9
10	35805	35836	35864	35895	35925	35956	35986	36017	36048	36078	36109	36139	10
11	35806	35837	35865	35896	35926	35957	35987	36018	36049	36079	36110	36140	11
12	35807	35838	35866	35897	35927	35958	35988	36019	36050	36080	36111	36141	12
13	35808	35839	35867	35898	35928	35959	35989	36020	36051	36081	36112	36142	13
14	35809	35840	35868	35899	35929	35960	35990	36021	36052	36082	36113	36143	14
15	35810	35841	35869	35900	35930	35961	35991	36022	36052	36083	36114	36144	15
16	35811	35842	35870	35901	35931	35962	35992	36023	36054	36084	36115	36145	16
17	35812	35843	35871	35902	35932	35963	35993	36024	36055	36085	36116	36146	17
18	35813	35844	35872	35903	35933	35964	35994	36025	36056	36086	36117	36147	18
19	35814	35845	35873	35904	35934	35965	35995	36026	36057	36087	36118	36148	19
20	35815	35846	35874	35905	35935	35966	35996	36027	36058	36088	36119	36149	20
21	35816	35847	35875	35906	35936	35967	35997	36028	36059	36089	36120	36150	21
22	35817	35848	35876	35907	35937	35968	35998	36029	36060	36090	36121	36151	22
23	35818	35849	35877	35908	35938	35969	35999	36030	36061	36091	36122	36152	23
24	35819	35850	35878	35909	35939	35970	36000	36031	36062	36092	36123	36153	24
25	35820	35851	35879	35910	35940	35971	36001	36032	36063	36093	36124	36154	25
26	35821	35852	35880	35911	35941	35972	36002	36033	36064	36094	36125	36155	26
27	35822	35853	35881	35912	35942	35973	36003	36034	36065	36095	36126	36156	27
28	35823	35854	35882	35913	35943	35974	36004	36035	36066	36096	36127	36157	28
29	35824	-------	35883	35914	35944	35975	36005	36036	36067	36097	36128	36158	29
30	35825	-------	35884	35915	35945	35976	36006	36037	36068	36098	36129	36159	30
31	35826	-------	35885	-------	35946	-------	36007	36038	-------	36099	-------	36160	31

Figure T-92. 2041 Expiration Table

2042   Expiration Table   2042

Day	Jan	Feb	Mar	Apr	May	Jun	Jul	Aug	Sep	Oct	Nov	Dec	Day
1	36161	36192	36220	36251	36281	36312	36342	36373	36404	36434	36465	36495	1
2	36162	36193	36221	36252	36282	36313	36343	36374	36405	36435	36466	36496	2
3	36163	36194	36222	36253	36283	36314	36344	36375	36406	36436	36467	36497	3
4	36164	36195	36223	36254	36284	36315	36345	36376	36407	36437	36468	36498	4
5	36165	36196	36224	36255	36285	36316	36346	36377	36408	36438	36469	36499	5
6	36166	36197	36225	36256	36286	36317	36347	36378	36409	36439	36470	36500	6
7	36167	36198	36226	36257	36287	36318	36348	36379	36410	36440	36471	36501	7
8	36168	36199	36227	36258	36288	36319	36349	36380	36411	36441	36472	36502	8
9	36169	36200	36228	36259	36289	36320	36350	36381	36412	36442	36473	36503	9
10	36170	36201	36229	36360	36290	36321	36351	36382	36413	36443	36474	36504	10
11	36171	36202	36230	36261	36291	36322	36352	36383	36414	36444	36475	36505	11
12	36172	36203	36231	36262	36292	36323	36353	36384	36415	36445	36476	36506	12
13	36173	36204	36232	36263	36293	36324	36354	36385	36416	36446	36477	36507	13
14	36174	36205	36233	36264	36294	36325	36355	36386	36417	36447	36478	36508	14
15	36175	36206	36234	36265	36295	36326	36356	36387	36418	36448	36479	36509	15
16	36176	36207	36235	36266	36296	36327	36357	36388	36419	36449	36480	36510	16
17	36177	36208	36236	36267	36297	36328	36358	36389	36420	36450	36481	36511	17
18	36178	36209	36237	36268	36298	36329	36359	36390	36421	36451	36482	36512	18
19	36179	36210	36238	36269	36299	36330	36360	36391	36422	36452	36483	36513	19
20	36180	36211	36239	36270	36300	36331	36361	36392	36423	36453	36484	36514	20
21	36181	36212	36240	36271	36301	36332	36362	36393	36424	36454	36485	36515	21
22	36182	36213	36241	36272	36302	36333	36363	36394	36425	36455	36486	36516	22
23	36183	36214	36242	36273	36303	36334	36364	36395	36426	36456	36487	36517	23
24	36184	36215	36243	36274	36304	36335	36365	36396	36427	36457	36488	36518	24
25	36185	36216	36244	36275	36305	36336	36366	36397	36428	36458	36489	36519	25
26	36186	36217	36245	36276	36306	36337	36367	36398	36429	36459	36490	36520	26
27	36187	36218	36246	36277	36307	36338	36368	36399	36430	36460	36491	36521	27
28	36188	36219	36247	36278	36308	36339	36369	36400	36431	36461	36492	36522	28
29	36189	-------	36248	36279	36309	36340	36370	36401	36432	36462	36493	36523	29
30	36190	-------	36249	36280	36310	36341	36371	36402	36433	36463	36494	36524	30
31	36191	-------	36250	-------	36311	-------	36372	36403	-------	36464	-------	36525	31

Figure T-93. 2042 Expiration Table

2043 Expiration Table 2043

Day	Jan	Feb	Mar	Apr	May	Jun	Jul	Aug	Sep	Oct	Nov	Dec	Day
1	36526	36557	36585	36616	36646	36677	36707	36738	36769	36799	36830	36860	1
2	36527	36558	36586	36617	36647	36678	36708	36739	36770	36800	36831	36861	2
3	36528	36559	36587	36618	36648	36679	36709	36740	36771	36801	36832	36862	3
4	36529	36560	36588	36619	36649	36680	36710	36741	36772	36802	36833	36863	4
5	36530	36561	36589	36620	36650	36681	36711	36742	36773	36803	36834	36864	5
6	36531	36562	36590	36621	36651	36682	36712	36743	36774	36804	36835	36865	6
7	36532	36563	36591	36622	36652	36683	36713	36744	36775	36805	36836	36866	7
8	36533	36564	36592	36623	36653	36684	36714	36745	36776	36806	36837	36867	8
9	36534	36565	36593	36624	36654	36685	36715	36746	36777	36807	36838	36868	9
10	36535	36566	36594	36625	36655	36686	36716	36747	36778	36808	36839	36869	10
11	36536	36567	36595	36626	36656	36687	36717	36748	36779	36809	36840	36870	11
12	36537	36568	36596	36627	36657	36688	36718	36749	36780	36810	36841	36871	12
13	36538	36569	36597	36628	36658	36689	36719	36750	36781	36811	36842	36872	13
14	36539	36570	36598	36629	36659	36690	36720	36751	36782	36812	36843	36873	14
15	36540	36571	36599	36630	36660	36691	36721	36752	36783	36813	36844	36874	15
16	36541	36572	36600	36631	36661	36692	36722	36753	36784	36814	36845	36875	16
17	36542	36573	36601	36632	36662	36693	36723	36754	36785	36815	36846	36876	17
18	36543	36574	36602	36633	36663	36694	36724	36755	36786	36816	36847	36877	18
19	36544	36575	36603	36634	36664	36695	36725	36756	36787	36817	36848	36878	19
20	36545	36576	36604	36635	36665	36696	36726	36757	36788	36818	36849	36879	20
21	36546	36577	36605	36636	36666	36697	36727	36758	36789	36819	36850	36880	21
22	36547	36578	36606	36637	36667	36698	36728	36759	36790	36820	36851	36881	22
23	36548	36579	36607	36638	36668	36699	36729	36760	36791	36821	36852	36882	23
24	36549	36580	36608	36639	36669	36700	36730	36761	36792	36822	36853	36883	24
25	36550	36581	36609	36640	36670	36701	36731	36762	36793	36823	36854	36884	25
26	36551	36582	36610	36641	36671	36702	36732	36763	36794	36824	36855	36885	26
27	36552	36583	36611	36642	36672	36703	36733	36764	36795	36825	36856	36886	27
28	36553	36584	36612	36643	36673	36704	36734	36765	36796	36826	36857	36887	28
29	36554	....	36613	36644	36674	36705	36735	36766	36797	36827	36858	36888	29
30	36555	....	36614	36645	36675	36706	36736	36767	36798	36828	36859	36889	30
31	36556	....	36615	....	36676	....	36737	36768	....	36829	....	36890	31

Figure T-94. 2043 Expiration Table

Figure T-95. 2044 Expiration Table

Day	Jan	Feb	Mar	Apr	May	Jun	Jul	Aug	Sep	Oct	Nov	Dec	Day
1	36891	36922	36951	36982	37012	37043	37073	37104	37135	37165	37196	37226	1
2	36892	36923	36952	36983	37013	37044	37074	37105	37136	37166	37197	37227	2
3	36893	36924	36953	36984	37014	37045	37075	37106	37137	37167	37198	37228	3
4	36894	36925	36954	36985	37015	37046	37076	37107	37138	37168	37199	37229	4
5	36805	36926	36955	36986	37016	37047	37077	37108	37139	37169	37200	37230	5
6	36896	36927	36956	36987	37017	37048	37078	37109	37140	37170	37201	37231	6
7	36897	36928	36957	36988	37018	37049	37079	37110	37141	37171	37202	37232	7
8	36898	36929	36958	36989	37019	37050	37080	37111	37142	37172	37203	37233	8
9	36899	36930	36959	36990	37020	37051	37081	37112	37143	37173	37204	37234	9
10	36900	36931	36960	36991	37021	37052	37082	37113	37144	37174	37205	32735	10
11	36901	36932	36961	36992	37022	37053	37083	37114	37145	37175	37206	32736	11
12	36902	36933	36962	36993	37023	37054	37084	37115	37146	37176	37207	37237	12
13	36903	36934	36963	36994	37024	37055	37085	37116	37147	37177	37208	37238	13
14	36904	36935	36964	36995	37025	37056	37086	37117	37148	37178	37209	37239	14
15	30905	36936	36965	36996	37026	37057	37087	37118	37149	37179	37210	37240	15
16	36906	36937	36966	36997	37027	37058	37088	37119	37150	37180	37211	37241	16
17	36907	36938	36967	36998	37028	37059	37089	37120	37151	37181	37212	37242	17
18	36908	36939	36968	36999	37029	37060	37090	37121	37152	37182	37213	37243	18
19	36909	36940	36969	37000	37030	37061	37091	37122	37153	37183	37214	37244	19
20	36910	36941	36970	37001	37031	37062	37092	37123	37154	37184	37215	37245	20
21	36911	36942	36971	37002	37032	37063	37093	37124	37155	37185	37216	37246	21
22	36912	36943	36972	37003	37033	37064	37094	37125	37156	37186	37217	37247	22
23	36913	36944	36973	37004	37034	37065	37095	37126	37157	37187	37218	37248	23
24	36914	36945	36974	37005	37035	37066	37096	37127	37158	37188	37219	37249	24
25	36915	36946	36975	37006	37036	37067	37097	37128	37159	37189	37220	37250	25
26	36916	36947	36976	37007	37037	37068	37098	37129	37160	37190	37221	37251	26
27	36917	36948	36977	37008	37038	37069	37099	37130	37161	37191	37222	37252	27
28	36918	36949	36978	37009	37039	37070	37100	37131	37162	37192	37223	37253	28
29	36919	36950	36979	37010	37040	37071	37101	37132	37163	37193	37224	37254	29
30	36920	-------	36980	37011	37041	37072	37102	37133	37164	37194	37225	37255	30
31	36921	-------	36981	-------	37042	-------	37103	37134	-------	37195	-------	37256	31

Day	Jan	Feb	Mar	Apr	May	Jun	Jul	Aug	Sep	Oct	Nov	Dec	Day
1	37257	37288	37316	37347	37377	37408	37438	37469	37500	37530	37561	37591	1
2	37258	37289	37317	37348	37378	37409	37439	37470	37501	37531	37562	37592	2
3	37259	37290	37318	37349	37379	37410	37440	37471	37502	37532	37563	37593	3
4	37260	37291	37319	37350	37380	37411	37441	37472	37503	37533	37564	37594	4
5	37261	37292	37320	37351	37381	37412	37442	37473	37504	37534	37565	37595	5
6	37262	37293	37321	37352	37382	37413	37443	37474	37505	37535	37566	37596	6
7	37263	37294	37322	37353	37383	37414	37444	37475	37506	37536	37567	37597	7
8	37264	37295	37323	37354	37384	37415	37445	37476	37507	37537	37568	37598	8
9	37265	37296	37324	37355	37385	37416	37446	37477	37508	37538	37569	37599	9
10	37266	37297	37325	37356	37386	37417	37447	37478	37509	37539	37570	37600	10
11	37267	37298	37326	37357	37387	37418	37448	37479	37510	37540	37571	37601	11
12	37268	37299	37327	37358	37388	37419	37449	37480	37511	37541	37572	37602	12
13	37269	37300	37328	37359	37389	37420	37450	37481	37512	37542	37573	37603	13
14	37270	37301	37329	37360	37390	37421	37451	37482	37513	37543	37574	37604	14
15	37271	37302	37330	37361	37391	37422	37452	37483	37514	37544	37575	37605	15
16	37272	37303	37331	37362	37392	37423	37453	37484	37515	37545	37576	37606	16
17	37273	37304	37332	37363	37393	37424	37454	37485	37516	37546	37577	37607	17
18	37274	37305	37333	37364	37394	37425	37455	37486	37517	37547	37578	37608	18
19	37275	37306	37334	37365	37395	37426	37456	37487	37518	37548	37579	37609	19
20	37276	37307	37335	37366	37396	37427	37457	37488	37519	37549	37580	37610	20
21	37277	37308	37336	37367	37397	37428	37458	37489	37520	37550	37581	37611	21
22	37278	37309	37337	37368	37398	37429	37459	37490	37521	37551	37582	37612	22
23	37279	37310	37338	37369	37399	37430	37460	37491	37522	37552	37583	37613	23
24	37280	37311	37339	37370	37400	37431	37461	37492	37523	37553	37584	37614	24
25	37281	37312	37340	37371	37401	37432	37462	37493	37524	37554	37585	37615	25
26	37282	37313	37341	37372	37402	37433	37463	37494	37525	37555	37586	37616	26
27	38283	37314	37342	37373	37403	37344	37464	37495	37526	37556	37587	37617	27
28	37284	37315	37343	37374	37404	37435	37465	37496	37527	37557	37588	37618	28
29	37285	-------	37344	37375	37405	37436	37466	37497	37528	37558	37589	37619	29
30	37286	-------	37345	37376	37406	37437	37467	37498	37529	37559	37590	37620	30
31	37287	-------	37346	-------	37407	-------	37468	37499	-------	37560	-------	37621	31

Figure T-96. 2045 Expiration Table

Day	Jan	Feb	Mar	Apr	May	Jun	Jul	Aug	Sep	Oct	Nov	Dec	Day
1	37622	37653	37681	37712	37742	37773	37803	37834	37865	37895	37926	37956	1
2	37623	37654	37682	37713	37743	37774	37804	37835	37866	37896	37927	37957	2
3	37624	37655	37683	37714	37744	37775	37805	37836	37867	37897	37928	37958	3
4	37625	37656	37684	37715	37745	37776	37806	37837	37868	37898	37929	37959	4
5	37626	37657	37685	37716	37746	37777	37807	37838	37869	37899	37930	37960	5
6	37627	37658	37686	37717	37747	37778	37808	37839	37870	37900	37931	37961	6
7	37628	37659	37687	37718	37748	37779	37809	37840	37871	37901	37932	37962	7
8	37629	37660	37688	37719	37749	37780	37810	37841	37872	37902	37933	37963	8
9	37630	37661	37689	37720	37750	37781	37811	37842	37873	37903	37934	37964	9
10	37631	37662	37690	37721	37751	37782	37812	37843	37874	37904	37935	37965	10
11	37632	37663	37691	37722	37752	37783	37813	37844	37875	37905	37936	37966	11
12	37633	37664	37692	37723	37753	37784	37814	37845	37876	37906	37937	37967	12
13	37634	37665	37693	37724	37754	37785	37815	37846	37877	37007	37938	37968	13
14	37635	37666	37694	37725	37755	37786	37816	37847	37878	37908	37939	37969	14
15	37636	37667	37695	37726	37756	37787	37817	37848	37879	37909	37940	37970	15
16	37637	37668	37696	37727	37757	37788	37818	37849	37880	37910	37941	37971	16
17	37638	37669	37697	37728	37758	37789	37819	37850	37881	37911	37942	37972	17
18	37639	37670	37698	37729	37759	37790	37820	37851	37882	37912	37943	37973	18
19	37640	37671	37699	37730	37760	37791	37821	37852	37883	37913	37944	37974	19
20	37641	37672	37700	37731	37761	37792	37822	37853	37884	37914	37945	37975	20
21	37642	37673	37701	37732	37762	37793	37823	37854	37885	37915	37946	37976	21
22	37643	37674	37702	37733	37763	37794	37824	37855	37886	37916	37947	37977	22
23	37644	37675	37703	37734	37764	37795	37825	37856	37887	37917	37948	37978	23
24	37645	37676	37704	37735	37765	37796	37826	37857	37889	37919	37949	37979	24
25	37646	37677	37705	37736	37766	37797	37827	37858	37889	37919	37950	37980	25
26	37647	37678	37706	37737	37767	37798	37828	37859	37890	37920	37951	37981	26
27	37648	37679	37707	37738	37768	37799	37829	37860	37891	37921	37952	37982	27
28	37649	37680	37708	37739	37769	37800	37830	37861	37892	37922	37953	37983	28
29	37650	-------	37709	37740	37770	37801	37831	37862	37893	37923	37954	37984	29
30	37651	-------	37710	37741	37771	37802	37832	37863	37894	37924	37955	37985	30
31	37652	-------	37711	-------	37772	-------	37833	37864	-------	37925	-------	37986	31

Figure T-97. 2046 Expiration Table

2047   Expiration Table   2047

Day	Jan	Feb	Mar	Apr	May	Jun	Jul	Aug	Sep	Oct	Nov	Dec	Day
1	37987	38018	38046	38077	38107	38138	38168	38199	38230	38260	38291	38321	1
2	37988	38019	38047	38078	38108	38139	38169	38200	38231	38261	38292	38322	2
3	37989	38020	28048	38079	38109	38140	38170	38201	38232	38262	38293	38323	3
4	37990	38021	38049	38080	38110	38141	38171	38202	38233	38263	38294	38324	4
5	37991	38022	38050	38081	38111	38142	38172	38203	38234	38264	38295	38325	5
6	37992	38023	38051	38082	38112	38143	38173	38204	38235	38265	38296	38326	6
7	37993	38024	38052	38083	38113	38144	38174	38205	38236	38266	38297	38327	7
8	37994	38025	38053	38084	38114	38145	38175	38206	38237	38267	38298	38328	8
9	37995	38026	38054	38085	38115	38146	38176	38207	38238	38268	38299	38329	9
10	37996	38027	38055	38086	38116	38147	38177	38208	28239	38269	38300	38330	10
11	37997	38028	38056	38087	38117	38148	38178	38209	38240	38270	38301	38331	11
12	37998	38029	38057	38088	38118	38149	38179	38210	38241	38271	38302	38332	12
13	37999	38030	38058	38089	38119	38150	38180	38211	38242	38272	38303	38333	13
14	38000	38031	38059	38090	38120	38151	38181	38212	38243	38273	38304	38334	14
15	38001	38032	38060	38091	38121	38152	38182	38213	38244	38274	38305	38335	15
16	38002	38033	38061	38092	38122	38153	38183	38214	38245	38275	38306	38336	16
17	38003	38034	38062	38093	38123	38154	38184	38215	38246	38276	38307	38337	17
18	38004	38035	38063	38094	38124	38155	38185	38216	38247	38277	38308	38338	18
19	38005	38036	38064	38095	38125	38156	38186	38217	38248	38278	37309	38339	19
20	38006	38037	38065	38096	38126	38157	38187	38218	38249	38279	38310	38340	20
21	38007	38038	38066	38097	38127	38158	38188	38219	38250	38280	38311	38341	21
22	38008	38039	38067	38098	38128	38159	38189	38220	38251	38281	38312	38342	22
23	38009	38040	38068	38099	38129	38160	38190	38221	38252	38282	38313	38343	23
24	38010	38041	38069	38100	38130	38161	38191	38222	38253	38283	38314	38244	24
25	38011	38042	38070	38101	38131	38162	38192	38223	38254	38284	38315	38345	25
26	38012	38043	38071	38102	38132	38163	38193	38224	38255	38285	38316	38346	26
27	38013	38044	38072	38103	38133	38164	38194	38225	38256	38286	38317	38347	27
28	38014	38045	38073	38104	38134	38165	38195	38226	38257	38287	38318	38348	28
29	38015	-------	38074	38105	38135	38166	38196	38227	38258	38288	38319	38349	29
30	38016	-------	38075	38106	38136	38167	38197	38228	38259	38289	38320	38350	30
31	38017	-------	38076	-------	38137	-------	38198	38229	-------	38290	-------	38351	31

Figure T-98. 2047 Expiration Table

Day	Jan	Feb	Mar	Apr	May	Jun	Jul	Aug	Sep	Oct	Nov	Dec	Day
1	38352	38383	38412	38443	38473	38504	38534	38565	38596	38626	38657	38687	1
2	38353	38384	38413	38444	38474	38505	38535	38566	38597	38627	38658	38688	2
3	38354	38385	38414	38445	38475	38506	38536	38567	38598	38628	38659	38689	3
4	38355	38386	38415	38446	38476	38507	38537	38568	38599	38629	38660	38690	4
5	38356	38387	38416	38447	38477	38508	38538	38569	38600	38630	38661	38691	5
6	38357	38388	38417	38448	38478	38509	38539	38570	38601	38631	38662	38692	6
7	38358	38389	38418	38449	38479	38510	38540	38571	38602	38632	38663	38693	7
8	38359	38390	38419	38450	38480	38511	38541	38572	38603	38633	38664	38694	8
9	38360	38391	38420	38451	38481	38512	38542	38573	38604	38634	38665	38695	9
10	38361	38392	38421	38452	38482	38513	38543	38574	38605	38635	38666	38696	10
11	38362	38393	38422	38453	38483	38514	38544	38575	38606	38636	38667	38697	11
12	38363	38394	38423	38454	38484	38515	38545	38576	38607	38637	38668	38698	12
13	38364	38395	38424	38455	38485	38516	38546	38577	38608	38638	38669	38699	13
14	38365	38396	38425	38456	38486	38517	38547	38578	38609	38639	38670	38700	14
15	38366	38397	38426	38457	38487	38518	38548	38579	38610	38640	38671	38701	15
16	38367	38398	38427	38458	38488	38519	38549	38580	38611	38641	38672	38702	16
17	38368	38399	38428	38459	38489	38520	38550	38581	38612	38642	38673	38703	17
18	38369	38400	38429	38460	38490	38521	38551	38582	38613	38643	38674	38704	18
19	38370	38401	38430	38461	38491	38522	38552	38583	38614	38644	38675	38705	19
20	38371	38402	38431	38462	38492	38523	38553	38584	38615	38645	38676	38706	20
21	38372	38403	38432	38463	38493	38524	38554	38585	38616	38646	38677	38707	21
22	38373	38404	38433	38464	38494	38525	38555	38586	38617	38647	38678	38708	22
23	38374	38405	38434	38465	38495	38526	38556	38587	38618	38648	38679	38709	23
24	38375	38406	38435	38466	38496	38527	38557	38588	38619	38649	38680	38710	24
25	38376	38407	38436	38467	38497	38528	38558	38589	38620	38650	38681	38711	25
26	38377	38408	38437	38468	38498	38529	38559	38590	38621	38651	38682	38712	26
27	38378	38409	38438	38469	38499	38530	38560	38591	38622	38652	38683	38713	27
28	38379	38410	38439	38470	38500	38531	38561	38592	38623	38653	38684	38714	28
29	38380	38411	38440	38471	38501	38532	38562	38593	38624	38654	38685	38715	29
30	38381	-------	38441	38472	38502	38533	38563	38594	38625	38655	38686	38716	30
31	38382	-------	38442	-------	38503	-------	38564	38595	-------	38656	-------	38717	31

Figure T-99. 2048 Expiration Table

Day	Jan	Feb	Mar	Apr	May	Jun	Jul	Aug	Sep	Oct	Nov	Dec	Day
1	38718	38749	38777	38808	38838	38869	38899	38930	38961	38991	39022	39052	1
2	38719	38750	38778	38809	38839	38870	38900	38931	38962	38992	39023	39053	2
3	38720	38751	38779	38810	38840	38871	38901	38932	38963	38993	39024	39054	3
4	38721	38752	38780	38811	38841	38872	38902	38933	38964	38994	39025	39055	4
5	38722	38753	38781	38812	38842	38873	38903	38934	38965	38995	39026	39056	5
6	38723	38754	38782	38813	38843	38874	38904	38935	38966	38996	39027	39057	6
7	38724	38755	38783	38814	38844	38875	38905	38936	38967	38997	39028	39058	7
8	38725	38756	38784	38815	38845	38876	38906	38937	38968	38998	39029	39059	8
9	38726	38757	38785	38816	38846	38877	38907	38938	38969	38999	39030	39060	9
10	38727	38758	38786	38817	38847	38878	38908	38939	38970	39000	39031	39061	10
11	38728	38759	38787	38818	38848	38879	38909	38940	38971	39001	39032	39062	11
12	38729	38760	38788	38819	38849	38880	38910	38941	38972	39002	39033	39063	12
13	38730	38761	38789	38820	38850	38881	38911	38942	38973	39003	39034	39064	13
14	38731	38762	38790	38821	38851	38882	38912	38943	38974	39004	39035	39065	14
15	38732	38763	38791	38822	38852	38883	38913	38944	38975	39005	39036	39066	15
16	38733	38764	38792	38823	38853	38884	38914	38945	38976	39006	39037	39067	16
17	38734	38765	38793	38824	38854	38885	38915	38946	38977	39007	39038	39068	17
18	38735	38766	38794	38825	38855	38886	38916	38947	38978	39008	39039	39069	18
19	38736	38767	38795	38826	38856	38887	38917	38948	38979	39009	39040	39070	19
20	38737	38768	38796	38827	38857	38888	38918	38949	38980	39010	39041	39071	20
21	38738	38769	38797	38828	38858	38889	38919	38950	38981	39011	39042	39072	21
22	38739	38770	38798	38829	38859	38890	38920	38951	38982	39012	39043	39073	22
23	38740	38771	38799	38830	38860	38891	38921	38952	38983	39013	39044	39074	23
24	38741	38772	38800	38831	38861	38892	38922	38953	38984	39014	39045	39075	24
25	38742	38773	38801	38832	38862	38893	38923	38954	38985	39015	39046	39076	25
26	38743	38774	38802	38833	38863	38894	38924	38955	38986	39016	39047	39077	26
27	38744	38775	38803	38834	38864	38895	38925	38956	38987	39017	39048	39078	27
28	38745	38776	38804	38835	38865	38896	38926	38957	38988	39018	39049	39079	28
29	38746	-------	38805	38836	38866	38897	38927	38958	38989	39019	39050	39080	29
30	38747	-------	38806	38837	38867	38898	38928	38959	38990	39020	39051	39081	30
31	38748	-------	38807	-------	38868	-------	38929	38960	-------	39021	-------	39082	31

Figure T-100. 2049 Expiration Table

Day	Jan	Feb	Mar	Apr	May	Jun	Jul	Aug	Sep	Oct	Nov	Dec	Day
1	39083	39114	39142	39173	39203	39234	39264	39295	39326	39356	39387	39417	1
2	39084	39115	39143	39174	39204	39235	39265	39296	39327	39357	39388	39418	2
3	39085	39116	39144	39175	39205	39236	39266	39297	39328	39358	39389	39419	3
4	39086	39117	39145	39176	39206	39237	39267	39298	39329	39359	39390	39420	4
5	39087	39118	39146	39177	39207	39238	39268	39299	39330	39360	39391	39421	5
6	39088	39119	39147	39178	39208	39239	39269	39300	39331	39361	39392	39422	6
7	39089	39120	39148	39179	39209	39240	39270	39301	39332	39362	39393	39423	7
8	39090	39121	39149	39180	39210	39241	39271	39302	39333	39363	39394	39424	8
9	39091	39122	39150	39181	39211	39242	39272	39303	39334	39364	39395	39425	9
10	39092	39123	39151	39182	39212	39243	39273	39304	39335	39365	39396	39426	10
11	39093	39124	39152	39183	39213	39244	39274	39305	39336	39366	39397	39427	11
12	39094	39125	39153	39184	39214	39245	39275	39306	39337	39367	39398	39428	12
13	30005	30126	39154	30185	30215	39246	39276	39307	39338	39368	39399	39429	13
14	39096	39127	39155	39186	39216	39247	39277	39308	39339	39370	39400	39430	14
15	39097	39128	39156	39187	39217	39248	39278	39309	39340	39371	39401	39431	15
16	39098	39129	39157	39188	39218	39249	39279	39310	39341	39371	39402	39432	16
17	39099	39130	39158	39189	39219	39250	39280	39311	39342	39372	39403	39433	17
18	39100	39131	39159	39190	39220	39251	39281	39312	39343	39373	39404	39434	18
19	39101	39132	39160	39191	39221	39252	39282	39313	39344	39374	39405	39435	19
20	39102	39133	39161	39192	39222	39253	39283	39314	39345	39375	39406	39436	20
21	39103	39134	39162	39193	39223	39254	39284	39315	39346	39376	39407	39437	21
22	39104	39135	39163	39194	39224	39255	39285	39316	39347	39377	39408	39438	22
23	39105	39136	39164	39195	39225	39256	39286	39317	39348	39378	39409	39439	23
24	39106	39137	39165	93196	39226	39257	39287	39318	39349	39379	39410	39440	24
25	39107	39138	39166	39197	39227	39258	39288	39319	39350	39380	39411	39441	25
26	39108	39139	39167	39198	39228	39259	39289	39320	39351	39381	39412	39442	26
27	39109	39140	39168	39199	39229	39260	39290	39321	39352	39382	39413	39443	27
28	39110	39141	39169	39200	39230	39261	39291	39322	39353	39383	39414	39444	28
29	39111	-------	39170	39201	39231	39262	39292	39323	39354	39384	39415	39445	29
30	39112	-------	39171	39202	39232	39263	39293	39324	39355	39385	39416	39446	30
31	39113	-------	39172	-------	39233	-------	39294	39325	-------	39386	-------	39447	31

Figure T-101. 2050 Expiration Table

2051 — Expiration Table — 2051

Day	Jan	Feb	Mar	Apr	May	Jun	Jul	Aug	Sep	Oct	Nov	Dec	Day
1	39448	39479	39507	39538	39568	39599	39629	39660	39691	39721	39752	39782	1
2	39449	39480	39508	39539	39569	39600	39630	39661	39692	39722	39753	39783	2
3	39450	39481	39509	39540	39570	39601	39631	39662	39693	39723	39754	39784	3
4	39451	39482	39510	39541	39571	39602	39632	39663	39694	39724	39755	39785	4
5	39452	39483	39511	39542	39572	39603	39633	39664	39695	39725	39756	39786	5
6	39453	39484	39512	39543	39573	39604	39634	39665	39696	39726	39757	39787	6
7	39454	39485	39513	39544	39574	39605	39635	39666	39697	39727	39758	39788	7
8	39455	39486	39514	39545	39575	39606	39636	39667	39698	39728	39759	39789	8
9	39456	39487	39515	39546	39576	39607	39637	39668	39699	39729	39760	39790	9
10	39457	39488	39516	39547	39577	39608	39638	39669	39700	39730	39761	39791	10
11	39458	39489	39517	39548	39578	39609	39639	39670	39701	39731	39762	39792	11
12	39459	39490	39518	39549	39579	39610	39640	39671	39702	39732	39763	39793	12
13	39460	39491	39519	39550	39580	39611	39641	39672	39703	39733	39764	39794	13
14	39461	39492	39520	39551	39581	39612	39642	39673	39704	39734	39765	39795	14
15	39462	39493	39521	39552	39582	39613	39643	39674	39705	39735	39766	39796	15
16	39463	39494	39522	39553	39583	39614	39644	39675	39706	39736	39767	39797	16
17	39464	39495	39523	39554	39584	39615	39645	39676	39707	39737	39768	39798	17
18	39465	39496	39524	39555	39585	39616	39646	39677	39708	39738	39769	39799	18
19	39466	39497	39525	39556	39586	39617	39647	39678	39709	39739	39770	39800	19
20	39467	39498	39526	39557	39587	39618	39648	39679	39710	39740	39771	39801	20
21	39468	39499	39527	39558	39588	39619	39649	39680	39711	39741	39772	39802	21
22	39469	39500	39528	39559	39589	39620	39650	39681	39712	39742	39773	39803	22
23	39470	39501	39529	39560	39590	39621	39651	39682	39713	39743	39774	39804	23
24	39471	39502	39530	39561	39591	39622	39652	39683	39714	39744	39775	39805	24
25	39472	39503	39531	39562	39592	39623	39653	39684	39715	39745	39776	39806	25
26	39473	39504	39532	39563	39593	39624	39654	39685	39716	39746	39777	39807	26
27	39474	39505	39533	39564	39594	39625	39655	39686	39717	39747	39778	39808	27
28	39475	39506	39534	39565	39595	39626	39656	39687	39718	39748	39779	39809	28
29	39476	-------	39535	39566	39596	39627	39657	39688	39719	39749	39780	39810	29
30	39477	-------	39536	39567	39597	39628	39658	39689	39720	39750	39781	39811	30
31	39478	-------	39537	-------	39598	-------	39659	39690	-------	39751	-------	39812	31

Figure T-102. 2051 Expiration Table

Day	Jan	Feb	Mar	Apr	May	Jun	Jul	Aug	Sep	Oct	Nov	Dec	Day
1	39813	39844	39873	39904	39934	39965	39995	40026	40057	44087	40118	40148	1
2	39814	39845	39874	39905	39935	39966	39996	40027	40058	40088	40119	40149	2
3	39815	39846	39875	39906	39936	39967	39997	40028	40059	40089	40120	40150	3
4	39816	39847	39876	39907	39937	39968	39998	40029	40060	40090	40121	40151	4
5	39817	39848	39877	39908	39938	39969	39999	40030	40061	40091	40122	40152	5
6	39818	39849	39878	39909	39939	39970	40000	40031	40062	40092	40123	40153	6
7	39819	39850	39879	39910	39940	39971	40001	40032	40063	40093	40124	40154	7
8	39820	39851	39880	39911	39941	39972	40002	40033	40064	40094	40125	40155	8
9	39821	39852	39881	39912	39942	39973	40003	40034	40065	40095	40126	40156	9
10	39822	39853	39882	39913	39943	39974	40004	40035	40066	40096	40127	40157	10
11	39823	39854	39883	39914	39944	39975	40005	40036	40067	40097	40128	40158	11
12	39824	39855	39884	39915	39945	49976	40006	40037	40068	40098	40129	40159	12
13	39825	39856	39885	39916	39946	39977	40007	40038	40069	40099	40130	40160	13
14	39826	39857	39886	39917	39947	39978	40008	40039	40070	40100	40131	40161	14
15	39827	39858	39887	39918	39948	39979	40009	40040	40071	40101	40132	40162	15
16	39828	39859	39888	39919	39949	39980	40010	40041	40072	40102	40133	40163	16
17	39829	39860	39889	39920	39950	39981	40011	40042	40073	40103	40134	40164	17
18	39830	39861	39890	39921	39951	39982	40012	40043	40074	40104	40135	40165	18
19	39831	39862	39891	39022	39952	39983	40013	40044	40075	40105	40136	40166	19
20	39832	39863	39892	39923	39953	39984	40014	40045	40076	40106	40137	40167	20
21	39833	39864	39893	39924	39954	39985	40015	40046	40077	40107	40138	40168	21
22	39834	39865	39894	39925	39955	39986	40016	40047	40078	40108	40139	40169	22
23	39835	39866	39895	39926	39956	39987	40017	40048	40079	40109	40140	40170	23
24	39836	39867	39896	39927	39957	39988	40018	40049	40080	40110	40141	40171	24
25	39837	39868	39897	39928	39958	39989	40019	40050	40081	40111	40142	40172	25
26	39838	39869	39898	39929	39959	39990	40020	40051	40082	40112	40143	40173	26
27	39839	39870	39899	39930	39960	39991	40021	40052	40083	40113	40144	40174	27
28	39840	39871	39900	39931	39961	39992	40022	40053	40084	40114	40145	40175	28
29	39841	39872	39901	39932	39962	39993	40023	40054	40085	40115	40146	40176	29
30	39842	-------	39902	39933	39963	39994	40024	40055	40086	40116	40147	40177	30
31	39843	-------	39903	-------	39964	-------	40025	40056	-------	40117	-------	40178	31

Figure T-103. 2052 Expiration Table

Day	Jan	Feb	Mar	Apr	May	Jun	Jul	Aug	Sep	Oct	Nov	Dec	Day
1	40179	40210	40238	40269	40299	40330	40360	40391	40422	40452	40483	40513	1
2	40180	40211	40239	40270	40300	40331	40361	40392	40423	40453	40484	40514	2
3	40181	40212	40240	40271	40301	40332	40362	40393	40424	40454	40485	40515	3
4	40182	40213	40241	40272	40302	40333	40363	40394	40425	40455	40486	40516	4
5	40183	40214	40242	40273	40303	40334	40364	40395	40426	40456	40487	40517	5
6	40184	40215	40243	40274	40304	40335	40365	40396	40427	40457	40488	40518	6
7	40185	40216	40244	40275	40305	40336	40366	40397	40428	40458	40489	40519	7
8	40186	40217	40245	40276	40306	40337	40367	40398	40429	40459	40490	40520	8
9	40187	40218	40246	40277	40307	40338	40368	40399	40430	40460	40491	40521	9
10	40188	40219	40247	40278	40308	40339	40369	40400	40431	40461	40492	40522	10
11	40189	40220	40248	40279	40309	40340	40370	40401	40432	40462	40493	40523	11
12	40190	40221	40249	40280	40310	40341	40371	40402	40433	40463	40494	40524	12
13	40191	40222	40250	40281	40311	40342	40372	40403	40434	40464	40495	40525	13
14	40192	40223	40251	40282	40312	40343	40373	40404	40435	40465	40496	40526	14
15	40193	40224	40252	40283	40313	40344	40374	40405	40436	40466	40497	40527	15
16	40194	40225	40253	40284	40314	40345	40375	40406	40437	40467	40498	40528	16
17	40195	40226	40254	40285	40315	40346	40376	40407	40438	40468	40499	40529	17
18	40196	40227	40255	40286	40316	40347	40377	40408	40439	40469	40500	40530	18
19	40197	40228	40256	40287	40317	40348	40378	40409	40440	40470	40501	40531	19
20	40198	40229	40257	40288	40318	40349	40379	40410	40441	40471	40502	40532	20
21	40199	40230	40258	40289	40319	40350	40380	40411	40442	40472	40503	40533	21
22	40200	40231	40259	40290	40320	40351	40381	40412	40443	40473	40504	40534	22
23	40201	40232	40260	40291	40321	40352	40382	40413	40444	40474	40505	40535	23
24	40202	40233	40261	40292	40322	40353	40383	40414	40445	40475	40506	40536	24
25	40203	40234	40262	40293	40323	40354	40384	40415	40446	40476	40507	40537	25
26	40204	40235	40263	40294	40324	40355	40385	40416	40447	40477	40508	40538	26
27	40205	40236	40264	40295	40325	40356	40386	40417	40448	40478	40509	40539	27
28	40206	40237	40265	40296	40326	40357	40387	40418	40449	40479	40510	40540	28
29	40207	-------	40266	40297	40327	40358	40388	40419	40450	40480	40511	40541	29
30	40208	-------	40267	40298	40328	40359	40389	40420	40451	40481	40512	40542	30
31	40209	-------	40268	-------	40329	-------	40390	40421	-------	40482	-------	40543	31

Figure T-104. 2053 Expiration Table

	2054				**Expiration Table**				**2054**				
Day	**Jan**	**Feb**	**Mar**	**Apr**	**May**	**Jun**	**Jul**	**Aug**	**Sep**	**Oct**	**Nov**	**Dec**	**Day**
1	40544	40575	40603	40634	40664	40695	40725	40756	40787	40817	40848	40878	1
2	40545	40576	40604	40635	40665	40696	40726	40757	40788	40818	40849	40879	2
3	40546	40577	40605	40636	40666	40697	40727	40758	40789	40819	40850	40880	3
4	40547	40578	40606	40637	40667	40698	40728	40759	40790	40820	40851	40881	4
5	40548	40579	40607	40638	40668	40699	40729	40760	40791	40821	40852	40882	5
6	40549	40580	40608	40639	40669	40700	40730	40761	40792	40822	40853	40883	6
7	40550	40581	40609	40640	40670	40701	40731	40762	40793	40823	40854	40884	7
8	40551	40582	40610	40641	40671	40702	40732	40763	40794	40824	40855	40885	8
9	40552	40583	40611	40642	40672	40703	40733	40764	40795	40825	40856	40886	9
10	40553	40584	40612	40643	40673	40704	40734	40765	40796	40826	40857	40887	10
11	40554	40585	40613	40644	40674	40705	40735	40766	10707	10827	40858	40888	11
12	40555	40586	40614	40645	40675	40706	40736	40767	40798	40829	40859	40889	12
13	40556	40587	40615	40646	40676	40707	40737	40768	40799	40829	40860	40890	13
14	40557	40588	40616	40647	40677	40708	40738	40769	40800	40830	40861	40891	14
15	40558	40589	40617	40648	40678	40709	40739	40770	40801	40831	40862	40892	15
16	40559	40590	40618	40649	40679	40710	40740	40771	40802	40832	40863	40893	16
17	40560	40591	40619	40650	40680	40711	40741	40772	40803	40833	40864	40894	17
18	40561	40592	40620	40651	40681	40712	40742	40773	40804	40834	40865	40895	18
19	40562	40593	40621	40652	40682	40713	40743	40774	40805	40835	40866	40896	19
20	40563	40594	40622	40653	40683	40714	40744	40775	40806	40836	40867	40897	20
21	40564	40595	40623	40654	40684	40715	40745	40776	40807	40837	40868	40898	21
22	40565	40596	40624	40655	40685	40716	40746	40777	40808	40838	40869	40899	22
23	40566	40597	40625	40656	40686	40717	40747	40778	40809	40839	40870	40900	23
24	40567	40598	40626	40657	40687	40718	40748	40779	40810	40840	40871	40901	24
25	40568	40599	40627	40658	40688	40719	40749	40780	40811	40841	40872	49002	25
26	40569	40600	40628	40659	40689	40720	40750	40781	40812	40842	40873	40903	26
27	40570	40601	40629	40660	40690	40721	40751	40782	40813	40843	40874	40904	27
28	40571	40602	40630	40661	40691	40722	40752	40783	40814	40844	40875	40905	28
29	40572	-------	40631	40662	40692	40723	40753	40784	40815	40845	40876	40906	29
30	40573	-------	40632	40663	40693	40724	40754	40785	40816	40846	40877	40907	30
31	40574	-------	40633	-------	40694	-------	40755	40786	-------	40847	-------	40908	31

Figure T-105. 2054 Expiration Table

Day	Jan	Feb	Mar	Apr	May	Jun	Jul	Aug	Sep	Oct	Nov	Dec	Day
1	40909	40940	40968	40999	41029	41060	41090	41121	41152	41182	41213	41243	1
2	40910	40941	40969	41000	41030	41061	41091	41122	41153	41183	41214	41244	2
3	40911	40942	40970	41001	41031	41062	41092	41123	41154	41184	41215	41245	3
4	40912	40943	40971	41002	41032	41063	41093	41124	41155	41185	41216	41246	4
5	40913	40944	40972	41003	41033	41064	41094	41125	41156	41186	41217	41247	5
6	40914	40945	40973	41004	41034	41065	41095	41126	41157	41187	41218	41248	6
7	40915	40946	40974	41005	41035	41066	41096	41127	41158	41188	41219	41249	7
8	40916	40947	40975	41006	41036	41067	41097	41128	41159	41189	41220	41250	8
9	40917	40948	40976	41007	41037	41068	41098	41129	41160	41190	41221	41251	9
10	40918	40949	40977	41008	41038	41069	41099	41130	41161	41191	41222	41252	10
11	40919	40950	40978	41009	41039	41070	41100	41131	41162	41192	41223	41253	11
12	40920	40951	40979	41010	41040	41071	41101	41132	41163	41193	41224	41254	12
13	40921	40952	40980	41011	41041	41072	41102	41133	41164	41194	41225	41255	13
14	40922	40953	40981	41012	41042	41073	41103	41134	41165	41195	41226	41256	14
15	40923	40954	40982	41013	41043	41074	41104	41135	41166	41196	41227	41257	15
16	40924	40955	40983	41014	41044	41075	41105	41136	41167	41197	41228	41258	16
17	40925	40956	40984	41015	41045	41076	41106	41137	41168	41198	41229	41259	17
18	40926	40957	40985	41016	41046	41077	41107	41138	41169	41199	41230	41260	18
19	40927	40958	40986	41017	41047	41078	41108	41139	41170	41200	41231	41261	19
20	40928	40959	40987	41018	41048	41079	41109	41140	41171	41201	41232	41262	20
21	40929	40960	40988	41019	41049	41080	41110	41141	41172	41202	41233	41263	21
22	40930	40961	40989	41020	41050	41081	41111	41142	41173	41203	41234	41264	22
23	40931	40962	40990	41021	41051	41082	41112	41143	41174	41204	41235	41265	23
24	40932	40963	40991	41022	41052	41083	41113	41144	41175	41205	41236	41266	24
25	40933	40964	40992	41023	41053	41084	41114	41145	41176	41206	41237	41267	25
26	40934	40965	40993	41024	41054	41085	41115	41146	41177	41207	41238	41268	26
27	40935	40966	40994	41025	41055	41086	41116	41147	41178	41208	41239	41269	27
28	40936	40967	40995	41026	41056	41087	41117	41148	41179	41209	41240	41270	28
29	40937	-------	40996	41027	41057	41088	41118	41149	41180	41210	41241	41271	29
30	40938	-------	40997	41028	41058	41089	41119	41150	41181	41211	41242	41272	30
31	40939	-------	40998	-------	41059	-------	41120	41151	-------	41212	-------	41273	31

Figure T-106. 2055 Expiration Table

Day	Jan	Feb	Mar	Apr	May	Jun	Jul	Aug	Sep	Oct	Nov	Dec	Day
1	41274	41305	41334	41365	41395	41426	41456	41487	41518	41548	41579	41609	1
2	41275	41306	41335	41366	41396	41427	41457	41488	41519	41549	41580	41610	2
3	41276	41307	41336	41367	41397	41428	41458	41489	41520	41550	41581	41611	3
4	41277	41308	41337	41368	41398	41429	41459	41490	41521	41551	41582	41612	4
5	41278	41309	41338	41369	41399	41430	41460	41491	41522	41552	41583	41613	5
6	41279	41310	41339	41370	41400	41431	41461	41492	41523	41553	41584	41614	6
7	41280	41311	41340	41371	41401	41432	41462	41493	41524	41554	41585	41615	7
8	41281	41312	41341	41372	41402	41433	41463	41494	41525	41555	41586	41616	8
9	41282	41313	41342	41373	41403	41434	41464	41495	41526	41556	41587	41617	9
10	41283	41314	41343	41374	41404	41435	41465	41496	41527	41557	41588	41618	10
11	41284	41315	41344	41375	41405	41436	41466	41497	41528	41558	41589	41619	11
12	41285	41316	41345	41376	41406	41437	41467	41498	41529	41559	41590	41620	12
13	41286	41317	41346	41377	41407	41438	41468	41499	41530	41560	41591	41621	13
14	41287	41318	41347	41378	41408	41439	41469	41500	41531	41561	41592	41622	14
15	41288	41319	41348	41379	41409	41440	41470	41501	41532	41562	41593	41623	15
16	41289	41320	41349	41380	41410	41441	41471	41502	41533	41563	41594	41624	16
17	41290	41321	41350	41381	41411	41442	41472	41503	41534	41564	41595	41625	17
18	41291	41322	41351	41382	41412	41443	41473	41504	41535	41565	41596	41626	18
19	41292	41323	41352	41383	41413	41444	41474	41505	41536	41566	41597	41627	19
20	41293	41324	41353	41384	41414	41445	41475	41506	41537	41567	41598	41628	20
21	41294	41325	41354	41385	41415	41446	41476	41507	41538	41568	41599	41629	21
22	41295	41326	41355	41386	41416	41447	41477	41508	41539	41569	41600	41630	22
23	41296	41327	41356	41387	41417	41448	41478	41509	41540	41570	41601	41631	23
24	41297	41328	41357	41388	41418	41449	41479	41510	41541	41571	41602	41632	24
25	41298	41329	41358	41389	41419	41450	41480	41511	41542	41572	41603	41633	25
26	41299	41330	41359	41390	41420	41451	41481	41512	41543	41573	41604	41634	26
27	41300	41331	41360	41391	41421	41452	41482	41513	41544	41574	41605	41635	27
28	41301	41332	41361	41392	41422	41453	41483	41514	41545	41575	41606	41636	28
29	41302	41333	41362	41393	41423	41454	41484	41515	41546	41576	41607	41637	29
30	41303	....	41363	41394	41424	41455	41485	41516	41547	41577	41608	41638	30
31	41304	....	41364	....	41425	....	41486	41517	....	41578	....	41639	31

Figure T-107. 2056 Expiration Table

Expiration Table

Day	Jan	Feb	Mar	Apr	May	Jun	Jul	Aug	Sep	Oct	Nov	Dec	Day
1	41640	41671	41699	41730	41760	41791	41821	41852	41883	41913	41944	41974	1
2	41641	41672	41700	41731	41761	41792	41822	41853	41884	41914	41945	41975	2
3	41642	41673	41701	41732	41762	41793	41823	41854	41885	41915	41946	41976	3
4	41643	41674	41702	41733	41763	41794	41824	41855	41886	41916	41947	41977	4
5	41644	41675	41703	41734	41764	41795	41825	41856	41887	41917	41948	41978	5
6	41645	41676	41704	41735	41765	41796	41826	41857	41888	41918	41949	41979	6
7	41646	41677	41705	41736	41766	41797	41827	41858	41889	41919	41950	41980	7
8	41647	41678	41706	41737	41767	41798	41828	41859	41890	41920	41951	41981	8
9	41648	41679	41707	41738	41768	41799	41829	41860	41891	41921	41952	31982	9
10	41649	41680	41708	41739	41769	41800	41830	41861	41892	41922	41953	41983	10
11	41650	41681	41709	41740	41770	41801	41831	41862	41893	41923	41954	41984	11
12	41651	41682	41710	41741	41771	41802	41832	41863	41894	41924	41955	41985	12
13	41652	41683	41711	41742	41772	41803	41833	41864	41895	41925	41956	41986	13
14	41653	41684	41712	41743	41773	41804	41834	41865	41896	41926	41957	41987	14
15	41654	41685	41713	41744	41774	41805	41835	41866	41897	41927	41958	41988	15
16	41655	41686	41714	41745	41775	41806	41836	41867	41898	41928	41959	41989	16
17	41656	41687	41715	41746	41776	41807	41837	41868	41899	41929	41960	41990	17
18	41657	41688	41716	41747	41777	41808	41838	41869	41900	41930	41961	41991	18
19	41658	41689	41717	41748	41778	41809	41839	41870	41901	41931	41962	41992	19
20	41659	41690	41718	41749	41779	41810	41840	41871	41902	41932	41963	41993	20
21	41660	41691	41719	41750	41780	41811	41841	41872	41903	41933	41964	41994	21
22	41661	41692	41720	41751	41781	41812	41842	41873	41904	41934	41965	41995	22
23	41662	41693	41721	41752	41782	41813	41843	41874	41905	41935	41966	41996	23
24	41663	41694	41722	41753	41783	41814	41844	41875	41906	41936	41967	41997	24
25	41664	41695	41723	41754	41784	41815	41845	41876	41907	41937	41968	41998	25
26	41665	41696	41724	41755	41785	41816	41846	41877	41908	41938	41969	41999	26
27	41666	41697	41725	41756	41786	41817	41847	41878	41909	41939	41970	42000	27
28	41667	41698	41726	41757	41787	41818	41848	41879	41910	41940	41971	42001	28
29	41668	-------	41727	41758	41788	41819	41849	41880	41911	41941	41972	42002	29
30	41669	-------	41728	41759	41789	41820	41850	41881	41912	41942	41973	42003	30
31	41670	-------	41729	-------	41790	-------	41851	41882	-------	41943	-------	42004	31

Figure T-108. 2057 Expiration Table

| | | | | | **2060** | | **Expiration Table** | | | | **2060** | | | |
Day	Jan	Feb	Mar	Apr	May	Jun	Jul	Aug	Sep	Oct	Nov	Dec	Day
1	42735	42766	42795	42826	42856	42887	42917	42948	42979	43009	43040	43070	1
2	42736	42767	42796	42827	42857	42888	42918	42949	42980	43010	43041	43071	2
3	42737	42768	42797	42828	42858	42889	42919	42950	42981	43011	43042	43072	3
4	42738	42769	42798	42829	42859	42890	42920	42951	42982	43012	43043	43073	4
5	42739	42770	42799	42830	42860	42891	42921	42952	42983	43013	43044	43074	5
6	42740	42771	42800	42831	42861	42892	42922	42953	42984	43014	43045	43075	6
7	42741	42772	42801	42832	42862	42893	42923	42954	42985	43015	43046	43076	7
8	42742	42773	42802	42833	42863	42894	42924	42955	42986	43016	43047	43077	8
9	42743	42774	42803	42834	42864	42895	42925	42956	42987	43017	43048	43078	9
10	42744	42775	42804	42835	42865	42896	42926	42957	42988	43018	43049	43079	10
11	42745	42776	42805	42836	42866	42897	42927	42958	42989	43019	43050	43080	11
12	42746	42777	42806	42837	42867	42898	42928	42959	42990	43020	43051	43081	12
13	42747	42778	42807	42838	42868	42899	42929	42960	42991	43021	43052	43082	13
14	42748	42779	42808	42839	42869	42900	42930	42961	42992	43022	43053	43083	14
15	42749	42780	42809	42840	42870	42901	42931	42962	42993	43023	43054	43084	15
16	42750	42781	42810	42841	42871	42902	42932	42963	42994	43024	43055	43085	16
17	42751	42782	42811	42842	42872	42903	42933	42964	42995	43025	43056	43086	17
18	42752	42783	42812	42843	42873	42904	42934	42965	42996	43026	43057	43087	18
19	42753	42784	42813	42844	42874	42905	42935	42966	42997	43027	43058	43088	19
20	42754	42785	42814	42845	42875	42906	42936	42967	42998	43028	43059	43089	20
21	42755	42786	42815	42846	42876	42907	42937	42968	42999	43029	43060	43090	21
22	42756	42787	42816	42847	42877	42908	42938	42969	43000	43030	43061	43091	22
23	42757	42788	42817	42848	42878	42909	42939	42970	43001	43031	43062	43092	23
24	42758	42789	42818	42849	42879	42910	42940	42971	43002	43032	43063	43093	24
25	42759	42790	42819	42850	42880	42911	42941	42972	43003	43033	43064	43094	25
26	42760	42791	42820	42851	42881	42912	42942	42973	43004	43034	43065	43095	26
27	42761	42792	42821	42852	42882	42913	42943	42974	43005	43035	43066	43096	27
28	42762	42793	42822	42853	42883	42914	42944	42975	43006	43036	43067	43097	28
29	42763	42794	42823	42854	42884	42915	42945	42976	43007	43037	43068	43098	29
30	42764	....	42824	42855	42885	42916	42946	42977	43008	43038	43069	43099	30
31	42765	....	42825	....	42886	....	42947	42978	....	43039	....	43100	31

Figure T-109. 2058 Expiration Table

Day	Jan	Feb	Mar	Apr	May	Jun	Jul	Aug	Sep	Oct	Nov	Dec	Day
1	42370	42401	42429	42460	42490	42521	42551	42582	42613	42643	42674	42704	1
2	42371	42402	42430	42461	42491	42522	42552	42583	42614	42644	42675	42705	2
3	42372	42403	42431	42462	42492	42523	42553	42584	42615	42645	42676	42706	3
4	42373	42404	42432	42463	42493	42524	42554	42585	42616	42646	42677	42707	4
5	42374	42405	42433	42464	42494	42525	42555	42586	42617	42647	42678	42708	5
6	42375	42406	42434	42465	42495	42526	42556	42587	42618	42648	42679	42709	6
7	42376	42407	42435	42466	42496	42527	42557	42588	42619	42649	42680	42710	7
8	42377	42408	42436	42467	42497	42528	42558	42589	42620	42650	42681	42711	8
9	43278	42409	42437	42468	42498	42529	42559	42590	42621	42651	42682	42712	9
10	42379	42410	42438	42469	42499	42530	42560	42591	42622	42652	42683	42713	10
11	42380	42411	42439	42470	42500	42531	42561	42592	42623	42653	42684	42714	11
12	42381	42412	42440	42471	42501	42532	42562	42593	42624	42654	42685	42715	12
13	42382	42413	42441	42472	42502	42533	42563	42594	42625	42655	42686	42716	13
14	42383	42414	42442	42473	42503	42534	42564	42595	42626	42656	42687	42717	14
15	42384	42415	42443	42474	42504	42535	42565	42596	42627	42657	42688	42718	15
16	42385	42416	42444	42475	42505	42536	42566	42597	42628	42658	42689	42719	16
17	42386	42417	42445	42476	42506	42537	42567	42598	42629	42659	42690	42720	17
18	42387	42418	42446	42477	42507	42538	42568	42599	42630	42660	42691	42721	18
19	42388	42419	42447	42478	42508	42539	42569	42600	42631	42661	42692	42722	19
20	42389	42420	42448	42479	42509	42540	42570	42601	42632	42662	42693	42723	20
21	42390	42421	42449	42480	42510	42541	42571	42602	42633	42663	42694	42724	21
22	42391	42422	42450	42481	42511	42542	42572	42603	42634	42664	42695	42725	22
23	42392	42423	42451	42482	42512	42543	42573	42604	42635	42665	42696	42726	23
24	42393	42424	42452	42483	42513	42544	42574	42605	42636	42666	42697	42727	24
25	42394	42425	42453	42484	42514	42545	42575	42606	42637	42667	42698	42728	25
26	42395	42426	42454	42485	42515	42546	42576	42607	42638	42668	42699	42729	26
27	42396	42427	42455	42486	42516	42547	42577	42608	42639	42669	42700	42730	27
28	42397	42428	42456	42487	42517	42548	42578	42609	42640	42670	42701	42731	28
29	42398	-------	42457	42488	42518	42549	42579	42610	42641	42671	42702	42732	29
30	42399	-------	42458	42489	42519	42550	42580	42611	42642	42672	42703	42733	30
31	42400	-------	42459	-------	42520	-------	42581	42612	-------	42673	-------	42734	31

Figure T-110. 2059 Expiration Table

2060
Expiration Table

2060

Day	Jan	Feb	Mar	Apr	May	Jun	Jul	Aug	Sep	Oct	Nov	Dec	Day
1	42735	42766	42795	42826	42856	42887	42917	42948	42979	43009	43040	43070	1
2	42736	42767	42796	42827	42857	42888	42918	42949	42980	43010	43041	43071	2
3	42737	42768	42797	42828	42858	42889	42919	42950	42981	43011	43042	43072	3
4	42738	42769	42798	42829	42859	42890	42920	42951	42982	43012	43043	43073	4
5	42739	42770	42799	42830	42860	42891	42921	42952	42983	43013	43044	43074	5
6	42740	42771	42800	42831	42861	42892	42922	42953	42984	43014	43045	43075	6
7	42741	42772	42801	42832	42862	42893	42923	42954	42985	43015	43046	43076	7
8	42742	42773	42802	42833	42863	42894	42924	42955	42986	43016	43047	43077	8
9	42743	42774	42803	42834	42864	42895	42925	42956	42987	43017	43048	43078	9
10	42744	42775	42804	42835	42865	42896	42926	42957	42988	43018	43049	43079	10
11	42745	42776	42805	42836	42866	42897	42927	42958	42989	43019	43050	43080	11
12	42746	42777	42806	42837	42867	42898	42928	42959	42990	43020	43051	43081	12
13	42747	42778	42807	42838	42868	42899	42929	42960	42991	43021	43052	43082	13
14	42748	42779	42808	42839	42869	42900	42930	42961	42992	43022	43053	43083	14
15	42749	42780	42809	42840	42870	42901	42931	42962	42993	43023	43054	43084	15
16	42750	42781	42810	42841	42871	42902	42932	42963	42994	43024	43055	43085	16
17	42751	42782	42811	42842	42872	42903	42933	42964	42995	43025	43056	43086	17
18	42752	42783	42812	42843	42873	42904	42934	42965	42996	43026	43057	43087	18
19	42753	42784	42813	42844	42874	42905	42935	42966	42997	43027	43058	43088	19
20	42754	42785	42814	42845	42875	42906	42936	42967	42998	43028	43059	43089	20
21	42755	42786	42815	42846	42876	42907	42937	42968	42999	43029	43060	43090	21
22	42756	42787	42816	42847	42877	42908	42938	42969	43000	43030	43061	43091	22
23	42757	42788	42817	42848	42878	42909	42939	42970	43001	43031	43062	43092	23
24	42758	42789	42818	42849	42879	42910	42940	42971	43002	43032	43063	43093	24
25	42759	42790	42819	42850	42880	42911	42941	42972	43003	43033	43064	43094	25
26	42760	42791	42820	42851	42881	42912	42942	42973	43004	43034	43065	43095	26
27	42761	42792	42821	42852	42882	42913	42943	42974	43005	43035	43066	43096	27
28	42762	42793	42822	42853	42883	42914	42944	42975	43006	43036	43067	43097	28
29	42763	42794	42823	42854	42884	42915	42945	42976	43007	43037	43068	43098	29
30	42764	-------	42824	42855	42885	42916	42946	42977	43008	43038	43069	43099	30
31	42765	-------	42825	-------	42886	-------	42947	42978	-------	43039	-------	43100	31

Figure T-111. 2060 Expiration Table

Day	Jan	Feb	Mar	Apr	May	Jun	Jul	Aug	Sep	Oct	Nov	Dec	Day
1	43101	43132	43160	43191	43221	43252	43282	43313	43344	43374	43405	43435	1
2	43102	43133	43161	43192	43222	43253	43283	43314	43345	43375	43406	43436	2
3	43103	43134	43162	43193	43223	43254	43284	43315	43346	43376	43407	43437	3
4	43104	43135	43163	43194	43224	43255	43285	43316	43347	43377	43408	43438	4
5	43105	43136	43164	43195	43225	43256	43286	43317	43348	43378	43409	43439	5
6	43106	43137	43165	43196	43226	43257	43287	43318	43349	43379	43410	43440	6
7	43107	43138	43166	43197	43227	43258	43288	43319	43350	43380	43411	43441	7
8	43108	43139	43167	43198	43228	43259	43289	43320	43351	43381	43412	43442	8
9	43109	43140	43168	43199	43229	43260	43290	43321	43352	43382	43413	43443	9
10	43110	43141	43169	43200	43230	43261	43291	43322	43353	43383	43414	43444	10
11	43111	43142	43170	43201	43231	43262	43292	43323	43354	43384	43415	43445	11
12	43112	43143	43171	43202	43232	43263	43293	43324	43355	43385	43416	43446	12
13	43113	43144	43172	43203	43233	43264	43294	43325	43356	43386	43417	43447	13
14	43114	43145	43173	43204	43234	43265	43295	43326	43357	43387	43418	43448	14
15	43115	43146	43174	43205	43235	43266	43296	43327	43358	43388	43419	43449	15
16	43116	43147	43175	43206	43236	43267	43297	43328	43359	43389	43420	43450	16
17	43117	43148	43176	43207	43237	43268	43298	43329	43360	43390	43421	43451	17
18	43118	43149	43177	43208	43238	43269	43299	43330	43361	43391	43422	43452	18
19	43119	43150	43178	43209	43239	43270	43300	43331	43362	43392	43423	43453	19
20	43120	43151	43179	43210	43240	43271	43301	43332	43363	43393	43424	43454	20
21	43121	43152	43180	43211	43241	43272	43302	43333	43364	43394	43425	43455	21
22	43122	43153	43181	43212	43242	43273	43303	43334	43365	43395	43426	43456	22
23	43123	43154	43182	43213	43243	43274	43304	43335	43366	43396	43427	43457	23
24	43124	43155	43183	43214	43244	43275	43305	43336	43367	43397	43428	43458	24
25	43125	43156	43184	43215	43245	43276	43306	43337	43368	43398	43429	43459	25
26	43126	43157	43185	43216	43246	43277	43307	43338	43369	43399	43430	43460	26
27	43127	43158	43186	43217	43247	43278	43308	43339	43370	43400	43431	43461	27
28	43128	43159	43187	43218	43248	43279	43309	43340	43371	43401	43432	43462	28
29	43129	-------	43188	43219	43249	43280	43310	43341	43372	43402	43433	43463	29
30	43130	-------	43189	43220	43250	43281	43311	43342	43373	43403	43434	43464	30
31	43131	-------	43190	-------	43251	-------	43312	43343	-------	43404	-------	43465	31

Figure T-112. 2061 Expiration Table

	2062				**Expiration Table**				**2062**				
Day	Jan	Feb	Mar	Apr	May	Jun	Jul	Aug	Sep	Oct	Nov	Dec	Day
1	43466	43497	43525	43556	43586	43617	43647	43678	43709	43739	43770	43800	1
2	43467	43498	43526	43557	43587	43618	43648	43679	43710	43740	43771	43801	2
3	43468	43499	43527	43558	43588	43619	43649	43680	43711	43741	43772	43802	3
4	43469	43500	43528	43559	43589	43620	43650	43681	43712	43742	43773	43803	4
5	43470	43501	43529	43560	43590	43621	43651	43682	43713	43743	43774	43804	5
6	43471	43502	43530	43561	43591	43622	43652	43683	43714	43744	43775	43805	6
7	43472	43503	43531	43562	43592	43623	43653	43684	43715	43745	43776	43806	7
8	43473	43504	43532	43563	43593	43624	43654	43685	43716	43746	43777	43807	8
9	43474	43505	43533	43564	43594	43625	43655	43686	43717	43747	43778	43808	9
10	43475	43506	43534	43565	43595	43626	43656	43687	43718	43748	43779	43809	10
11	43476	43507	43535	43566	43596	43627	43657	43688	43719	43749	43780	43810	11
12	43477	43508	43536	43567	43597	43628	43658	43689	43720	43750	43781	43811	12
13	43478	43509	43537	43568	43598	43629	43659	43690	43721	43751	43782	43812	13
14	43479	43510	43538	43569	43599	43630	43660	43691	43722	43752	43783	43813	14
15	43480	43511	43539	43570	43600	43631	43661	43692	43723	43753	43784	43814	15
16	43481	43512	43540	43571	43601	43632	43662	43693	43724	43754	43785	43815	16
17	43482	43513	43541	43572	43602	43633	43663	43694	43725	43755	43786	43816	17
18	43483	43514	43542	43573	43603	43634	43664	43695	43726	43756	43787	43817	18
19	43484	43515	43543	43574	43604	43635	43665	43696	43727	43757	43788	43818	19
20	43485	43516	43544	43575	43605	43636	43666	43697	43728	43758	43789	43819	20
21	43486	43517	43545	43576	43606	43637	43667	43698	43729	43759	43730	43820	21
22	43487	43518	43546	43577	43607	43638	43668	43699	43730	43760	43791	43821	22
23	43488	43519	43547	43578	43608	43639	43669	43700	43731	43761	43792	43822	23
24	43489	43520	43548	43579	43609	43640	43670	43701	43732	43762	43793	43823	24
25	43490	43521	43549	43580	43610	43641	43671	43702	43733	43763	43794	43824	25
26	43491	43522	43550	43581	43611	43642	43672	43703	43734	43764	43795	43825	26
27	43492	43523	43551	43582	43612	43643	43673	43704	43735	43765	43796	43826	27
28	43493	43524	43552	43583	43613	43644	43674	43705	43736	43766	43797	43827	28
29	43494	-------	43553	43584	43614	43645	43675	43706	43737	43767	43798	43828	29
30	43495	-------	43554	43585	43615	43646	43676	43707	43738	43768	43799	43829	30
31	43496	-------	43555	-------	43616	-------	43677	43708	-------	43769	-------	43830	31

Figure T-113. 2062 Expiration Table

Day	Jan	Feb	Mar	Apr	May	Jun	Jul	Aug	Sep	Oct	Nov	Dec	Day
	2063				Expiration Table				**2063**				
1	43831	43862	43890	43921	43951	43982	44012	44043	44074	44104	44135	44165	1
2	43832	43863	43891	43922	43952	43983	44013	44044	44075	44105	44136	44166	2
3	43833	43864	43892	43923	43953	43984	44014	44045	44076	44106	44137	44167	3
4	43834	43865	43893	43924	43954	43985	44015	44046	44077	44107	44138	44168	4
5	43835	43866	43894	43925	43955	43986	44016	44047	44078	44108	44139	44169	5
6	43836	43867	43895	43926	43956	43987	44017	44048	44079	44109	44140	44170	6
7	43837	43868	43896	43927	43957	43988	44018	44049	44080	44110	44141	44171	7
8	43838	43869	43897	43928	43958	43989	44019	44050	44081	44111	44142	44172	8
9	48339	43870	43898	43929	43959	43990	44020	44051	44082	44112	44143	44173	9
10	43840	43871	43899	43930	43960	43991	44021	44052	44083	44113	44144	44174	10
11	43841	43872	43900	43931	43961	43992	44022	44053	44084	44114	44145	44175	11
12	43842	43873	43901	43932	43962	43993	44023	44054	44085	44115	44146	44176	12
13	43843	43874	43902	43933	43963	43994	44024	44055	44086	44116	44147	44177	13
14	43844	43875	43903	43934	43964	43995	44025	44056	44087	44117	44148	44178	14
15	43845	43876	43904	43935	43965	43996	44026	44057	44088	44118	44149	44179	15
16	43846	43877	43905	43936	43966	43997	44027	44058	44089	44119	44150	44180	16
17	43847	43878	43906	43937	43967	43998	44028	44059	44090	44120	44151	44181	17
18	43848	43879	43907	43938	43968	43999	44029	44060	44091	44121	44152	44182	18
19	43849	43880	43908	43939	43969	44000	44030	44061	44092	44122	44153	44183	19
20	43850	43881	43909	43940	43970	44001	44031	44062	44093	44123	44154	44184	20
21	43851	43882	43910	43941	43971	44002	44032	44063	44094	44124	44155	44185	21
22	43852	43883	43911	43942	43972	44003	44033	44064	44095	44125	44156	44186	22
23	43853	43884	43912	43943	43973	44004	44034	44065	44096	44126	44157	44187	23
24	43854	43885	43913	43944	43974	44005	44035	44066	44097	44127	44158	44188	24
25	43855	43886	43914	43945	43975	44006	44036	44067	44098	44128	44159	44189	25
26	43856	43887	43915	43946	43976	44007	44037	44068	44099	44129	44160	44190	26
27	43857	43888	43916	43947	43977	44008	44038	44069	44100	44130	44161	44191	27
28	43858	43889	43917	43948	43978	44009	44039	44070	44101	44131	44162	44192	28
29	43859	-------	43918	43949	43979	44010	44040	44071	44102	44132	44163	44193	29
30	43860	-------	43919	43950	43980	44011	44041	44072	44103	44133	44164	44194	30
31	43861	-------	43920	-------	43981	-------	44042	44073	-------	44134	-------	44195	31

Figure T-114. 2063 Expiration Table

Day	Jan	Feb	Mar	Apr	May	Jun	Jul	Aug	Sep	Oct	Nov	Dec	Day
1	44196	44227	44256	44287	44317	44348	44378	44409	44440	44470	44501	44531	1
2	44197	44228	44257	44288	44318	44349	44379	44410	44441	44471	44502	44532	2
3	44198	44229	44258	44289	44319	44350	44380	44411	44442	44472	44503	44533	3
4	44199	44230	44259	44290	44320	44351	44381	44412	44443	44473	44504	44534	4
5	44200	44231	44260	44291	44321	44352	44382	44413	44444	44474	44505	44535	5
6	44201	44232	44261	44292	44322	44353	44383	44414	44445	44475	44506	44536	6
7	44202	44233	44262	44293	44323	44354	44384	44415	44446	44476	44507	44537	7
8	44203	44234	44263	44294	44324	44355	44385	44416	44447	44477	44508	44538	8
9	44204	44235	44264	44295	44325	44356	44386	44417	44448	44478	44509	44539	9
10	44205	44236	44265	44296	44326	44357	44387	44418	44449	44479	44510	44540	10
11	44206	44237	44266	44297	44327	44358	44388	44419	44450	44480	44511	44541	11
12	44207	44238	44267	44298	44328	44359	44389	44420	44451	44481	44512	44542	12
13	44208	44239	44268	44299	44329	44360	44390	44421	44452	44482	44513	44543	13
14	44209	44240	44269	44300	44330	44361	44391	44422	44453	44483	44514	44544	14
15	44210	44241	44270	44301	44331	44362	44392	44423	44454	44484	44515	44545	15
16	44211	44242	44271	44302	44332	44363	44393	44424	44455	44485	44516	44546	16
17	44212	44243	44272	44303	44333	44364	44394	44425	44456	44486	44517	44547	17
18	44213	44244	44273	44304	44334	44365	44395	44426	44457	44487	44518	44548	18
19	44214	44245	44274	44305	44335	44366	44396	44427	44458	44488	44519	44549	19
20	44215	44246	44275	44306	44336	44367	44397	44428	44459	44489	44520	44550	20
21	44216	44247	44276	44307	44337	44368	44398	44429	44460	44490	44521	44551	21
22	44217	44248	44277	44308	44338	44369	44399	44430	44461	44491	44522	44552	22
23	44218	44249	44278	44309	44339	44370	44400	44431	44462	44492	44523	44553	23
24	44219	44250	44279	44310	44340	44371	44401	44432	44463	44493	44524	44554	24
25	44220	44251	44280	44311	44341	44372	44402	44433	44464	44494	44525	44555	25
26	44221	44252	44281	44312	44342	44373	44403	44434	44465	44495	44526	44556	26
27	44222	44253	44282	44313	44343	44374	44404	44435	44466	44496	44527	44557	27
28	44223	44254	44283	44314	44344	44375	44405	44436	44467	44497	44528	44558	28
29	44224	44255	44284	44315	44345	44376	44406	44437	44468	44498	44529	44559	29
30	44225	-------	44285	44316	44346	44377	44407	44438	44469	44499	44530	44560	30
31	44226	-------	44286	-------	44347	-------	44408	44439	-------	44500	-------	44561	31

Figure T-115. 2064 Expiration Table

PIN 006455–006

USAPA

ELECTRONIC PUBLISHING SYSTEM
OneCol FORMATTER .WIN32 Version 141

PIN: 006455–006
DATE: 03- 2-01
TIME: 11:36:45
PAGES SET: 141

DATA FILE: C:\wincomp\yonatan.fil
DOCUMENT: AR 633–30
DOC STATUS: NEW PUBLICATION

www.ingramcontent.com/pod-product-compliance
Lightning Source LLC
Chambersburg PA
CBHW081150180526

45170CB00006B/2015